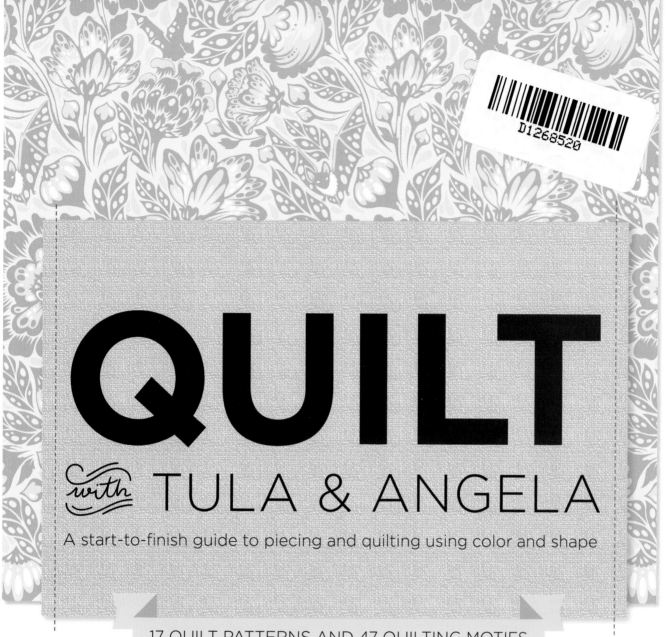

QUILT

with TULA & ANGELA

A start-to-finish guide to piecing and quilting using color and shape

17 QUILT PATTERNS AND 47 QUILTING MOTIFS

TULA PINK *and* ANGELA WALTERS

PHOTOGRAPHY BY ELIZABETH MAXSON

Fons&Porter

fw

a content + ecommerce company

www.fwcommunity.com

22 21 20 19 18   9 8 7 6 5

DISTRIBUTED IN THE U.K. AND EUROPE BY F&W MEDIA INTERNATIONAL
Brunel House, Newton Abbot, Devon, TQ12 4PU, England
Tel: (+44) 1626 323200, Fax: (+44) 1626 323319
E-mail: enquiries@fwmedia.com
SRN: S3159
ISBN-13: 978-1-4402-4545-9

EDITOR • Leslie T. O'Neill

TECHNICAL EDITOR • Lisa Silverman

COVER DESIGNER • Tula Pink

DESIGNER • Charlene Tiedemann

ILLUSTRATOR • Tula Pink

BEAUTY PHOTOGRAPHY • Elizabeth Maxon

FABRIC SWATCH PHOTOGRAPHY • George Boe

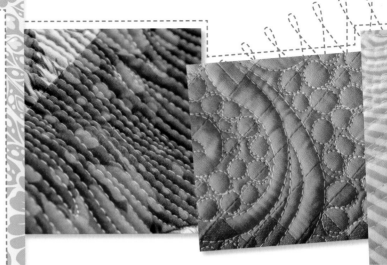

table of

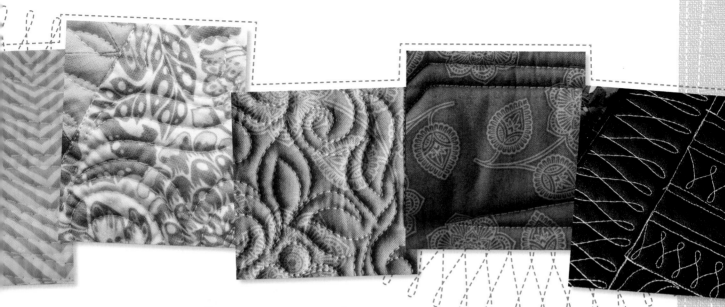

contents

Guardians of the Past,
GUIDES TO THE FUTURE

When I tell people what I do, I am usually greeted with a blank look of confusion, followed almost inevitably by, "Oh, I think my grandma used to make quilts!" For anyone outside of our little sub-culture, this statement pretty much sums up everything that there is to know about the subject of quilting.

My grandma did not make quilts, but I do. I have come to embrace that blank stare with a sort of secret pride. They don't know what we know. They don't know that we are immersed in a cultural revolution. They can't make the things that we can make with only a bit of cotton, a threaded needle, and our bare hands. We quilters hold the power to warm a person in both body and spirit. We have created an international community of knowledge and inspired and shown love to family and strangers alike. We document history while relentlessly pursuing the future. We are passion personified.

We are the guardians of a treasure trove of print and pattern, with a complexity and beauty so vast that were it painted on a chapel ceiling it wouldbe called art. We seek new prints, collecting them like rare gems or sacred scrolls, only to cut them up and piece them back together in intricate chains of shapes and forms, which are so deceptively simple it is often difficult to tell where one ends and another one begins. We explore pattern and color in a way that can't possibly be contained on a canvas or replicated with a tube of colored goop.

Our desire to make quilts defines us. We make to celebrate miracles and accomplishments, to soothe our battered souls, and to satisfy our creative hunger. We are desperate to make, stealing time away from our busy lives, dedicating closets, coveted spaces, and whole rooms to the tools of our trade. We travel great distances, literally and virtually, to be with our kind, to share our stories, our lives, and our talents over the gentle hum of a sewing machine.

If these are the things grandmothers do, then that is what I aspire to be. Who says I can't do all of this in a leather jacket with tattooed knuckles and a bit of a potty mouth? I can and I will because I am a maker, a quilter. There is not a single person in the world I would rather be and not another community on earth I would rather be a part of.

CATCH A RAINBOW

In every part of the world, people stop to look at rainbows. That perfect moment when the rain has cleared and the sun explodes from behind the clouds to drench us in the full power of its light is a magical, fleeting moment. No matter how close we get , a rainbow remains at an unreachable distance, never to be captured.

This is the raw power of color. We can spend a lot of time talking about color theory and arranging colors into wheels, charts, and graphs, but the true test of color is the emotional response. Color theory is important—it is a scientific approach to color, and if you have the desire and the time to understand it, it can be enlightening and informative. Often when we really like something, we can go back and analyze why based on what we know about color theory. But when we stop everything we're doing to admire the elusive rainbow, it is not because we understand the concepts of color and light. It is an emotional reaction to something beautiful and elusive. When it comes to choosing colors for a quilt, I am always trying to catch that rainbow.

The simplest quilt can become a masterpiece with dynamic fabric selection and thoughtful quilting. Choosing fabrics can often be the biggest hurdle in the quiltmaking process. As a passionate fabric enthusiast, I have approached the subject of fabric selection by breaking down the quilts in this book by color, each with its own personality.

I begin every chapter with a single color, and then I elaborate on that color by exploring a narrative of print and hue, shade, and texture. It is more of a conversation about color than a manifesto. It would have been much easier to make each quilt a monochromatic statement, but, just as with people, fabrics are rarely that straight forward. A red can rise from the dark depth of burgundy to the lightest of pinks, while blue can run the gamut from navy to teal to the controversial aqua/turquoise (is it blue or is it green?).

Selecting fabrics for a quilt is subjective. Each person sees something uniquely personal in a design or a color. What I have described is my approach to making those selections and how I arrived at my choices. I hope that each of you will take what you need from these pages and fold that knowledge into your own personal approach to fabric selection and quilt making.

IT'S NOT A QUILT UNTIL IT'S QUILTED

Have you ever finished a quilt top and looked upon it with pride? "It's done, and it's just want I wanted it to look like," you think. Seconds later you realize, "Oh no! Now I have to Figure out how to quilt it!"

It's not a quilt until it's quilted. I remember that feeling well! When I started machine quilting more than a decade ago, I was so frustrated when my quilting didn't turn out as beautiful as I imagined it. But, with a little practice and a go-for-it attitude, the machine-quilting process got easier and easier—as it will for you, too. Soon you will love it as much as I do!

No matter how much you enjoy quilting, deciding on a design can be harder than actually quilting it. It depends on your preferences, your skill level, and what the quilt is going to be used for. When it comes to picking out quilting designs, a good place to start is your quilt top. Decide what is the most important aspect of your quilt top, then pick a design to enhance that area.

Working with Tula has taught me just how important and effective this can be. We have been working together a long time, and from the very beginning she has conveyed what she wants the quilting to accomplish. It is this collaborative relationship that has resulted in the stunning quilts in this book.

For most of the quilts in this book, I incorporated several different quilting designs into each one, choosing each one of them based on the piecing of the quilt top. On Sugar Skulls (page 104) and The Hood (page 164), I used quilting to add pictorial details, extending the design to suggest eyebrows and teeth in one quilt and architectural elements in the other quilt. On others, such as Ikat Moth (page 32) and Patina (page 118) I used traditional all over quilting designs, including swirls and pebbles, to quilt these very modern quilt tops. And on The Big Hex (page 76) and Total Eclipse (page 14), I used the piecing as my guide for the quilting, highlighting specific sections with different designs.

Each chapter shows up-close pictures of the quilting as well as instructions on how to quilt the primary designs I used. I want this book to be as visually inspiring as it is informational, so that no matter your skill level or what type of quilting machine you have, you will feel inspired, not intimidated. I hope that these instructions will help you take the next step in mastering the process of machine quilting, either by teaching you new designs or inspiring you to invent your own variations.

So, as you make your own quilts, I challenge you to use the quilting as another layer of art. You can enhance your favorite areas with contrasting designs or add details that hint at the inspiration of the quilt. You can add movement or create secondary designs with allover patterns. But no matter what you choose to do, remember, a finished quilt is better that a perfect quilt top. Don't focus on perfection—instead, enjoy the quilting process!

BUILDING a QUILT

Sewing a well-made quilt top has more to do with being prepared than it does with talent. The two most important skills for great piecing are accurately cut fabrics and consistently sewn seams. Throw in some good pressing habits, and you are well on your way down the road of near perfection.

PIECING 101

Accurate cutting depends on the preparation of your fabric, the sharpness of your blade, and the quality of your quilter's ruler. Taking a little extra time here will make all the difference in the world.

Before beginning any quilt project, treat and press all of the fabrics that you will be using. Change the blade on your rotary cutter before every project. A dull blade will push the fabric around rather than cut it. A good quilter's ruler is also key. For general purposes, I prefer an 8½" × 24" (21.5 × 61 cm) clear quilter's ruler. These rulers typically come with both light and dark printed lines so that they work across both light and dark fabrics.

You may note that most of the patterns in this book ask you to press your seams open. Although this is not a requirement, the technique does lead to flatter, more flexible seams, which will become very important during the quilting process.

TOOLS OF THE TRADE: PIECING THE TOP

These aren't all of the tools available for quilters, but they're the only ones you really need.

Rotary Cutter and Replacement Blades
Your rotary cutter is your main cutting tool. It should feel like an extension of your hand. A 45 mm cutter is ideal for most quilting projects. Keep a small stash of extra blades on hand.

Self-Healing Cutting Mat
A good self-healing cutting mat will keep your rotary blade sharp for a longer period of time and won't leave visible signs of cutting or grooves that can affect future cuts. A 24" × 36" (61 × 91.5 cm) mat provides enough room to cut fabric straight off of the bolt. Store the mat flat whenever possible and protect it from heat because it will warp.

Scissors
Second only to the rotary cutter, quality fabric scissors are like the Holy Grail of quilting tools. Good solid steel scissors should be protected from all non-fabric items such as paper and cardboard, which will dull its edges in the blink of an eye. Guard your good fabric scissors with your life!

Thread Snippers
Small scissors, such as an EZ-Snip, are a great tool to keep near your sewing machine. They are light and easy on the hands and great for clipping threads between pieces when chain piecing.

Quilter's Rulers
A clear quilter's ruler with crisp measurement lines is worth its weight in gold. An 8½" × 24" (21.5 × 61 cm) ruler is perfect for cutting most quilt pieces. A large square ruler is also quite handy to keep around for squaring up blocks and cutting smaller bits. The ruler should have obvious 1", ¼", and ⅛" (2.5 cm, 6 mm, and 3 mm) markings for most of your quilting needs. Some slide-resistant pads on the back of the ruler are also extremely helpful when you need to cut a lot of pieces.

Iron and Ironing Board
A good iron is essential. It doesn't even need to be expensive—it just needs to get hot. A steam component can also be really helpful in prepping and pressing wrinkled fabric. Any ironing board will do, as long as it has a flat, even surface that is heat resistant and clean.

Sewing Machine and Needles
Although all of the quilts in this book could be hand sewn, the instructions are written with machine sewing in mind. To piece any of these quilts, you need a machine that produces a good, solid straight stitch. Like the rotary blade, it is important to change your sewing machine needle often, before each project. A sharp needle will glide effortlessly through fabrics and produce more accurate seams. I prefer a supersharp Microtex 80/12 needle for piecing with cotton fabrics.

Sewing Machine Foot with a Guide
Almost every sewing machine manufacturer offers a ¼" (6 mm) foot with a small guide on the right side. The guide keeps your fabric from sliding past the edge of the foot, nearly ensuring accurate ¼" (6 mm) seams throughout the construction of the quilt top.

Straight Pins
The difference between quilts with near perfectly lined-up seams and ones that are not usually comes down to pinning. It can seem like a pain to constantly pin at each seam intersection, but a little extra effort can go a long way. I prefer a fine silk pin for most of my pinning needs, but pins with a long glass head or even standard quilting pins also work quite well.

ESSENTIAL TOOLS FOR PIECING

cutting mat

seam rippers

rotary cutters

sewing machine foot

straight pins

steel scissors

machine needles

Seam Ripper

Let's face it, things don't always go according to your plans. Occasionally, some stitching just needs to be removed. Keep a seam ripper on hand for these rare moments.

Marking Tools

There are a number of removable marking tools out there, so choosing one largely comes down to personal preference. Whether you choose chalk pencils, water-soluble ink pens, or heat-removing ink pens, make sure to test the implement on a scrap piece of fabric before using it to make sure that it is actually removable.

Template Plastic

Template plastic is a sheet of thin, strong, clear plastic that can be cut with regular scissors. This is an ideal material for tracing and cutting a template. It can also be written on, so mark it with any information that might be necessary to identify it should you wish to use it again later.

Starch Alternative

I am a firm believer in fabric prep before cutting, especially when working with angles or curves. Spraying the raw fabric with a starch alternative, such as Best Press or Flatter, will completely smooth out the fabric, stiffen it slightly, prevent movement while cutting, and take some of the stretch out of the fabric to reduce bias issues.

GET READY TO QUILT!

Now that you have the quilt top finished and have gathered all the supplies needed for machine quilting, it's time to get started. If just the thought of machine quilting makes you more than a little nervous, you aren't alone. A lot of quilters dread the machine-quilting process, mostly because they are worried that they will ruin their quilt top. Great quilting will enhance a quilt top, and it doesn't have to be a scary process. Let me walk you through it!

Prepare your quilt top for quilting.

Before you start, be sure that the quilt top is ready for quilting. A well-prepared quilt top will make the whole process easier. Check it over to make sure there are no holes in the tops and no loose threads. This will ensure that your quilt doesn't get caught up while machine quilting.

Also make sure that the seams are pressed flat. While this isn't mandatory for machine quilting, a flat, well-pressed quilt top is a lot easier to manage. I know this from experience! I used to hate pressing my seams, but realized quickly that avoiding this step makes it harder to quilt.

Prepare your quilt sandwich.

Choose your batting. There are many different kinds of battings available, so it can be overwhelming to know what to pick.

I like to use Quilter's Dream Poly batting. It's thin, has a nice drape, and is made for machine quilting. Because it is made from polyester fibers, it resists creasing more than natural fibers.

If you love a crinkly, just-washed-looking quilt, then a high-quality cotton batting would be great for you. This is also a great selection if you like a lot of quilting but don't want the quilt to be stiff. Also, battings such as Quilter's Dream Wool or Quilter's Dream Puff are great options for quilts that you want to be thicker or more like a comforter.

Ultimately, it doesn't matter what kind of batting you use as long as it's a high-quality batting. Cheaper batting will beard, or poke through the quilt top, after time and won't hold up to repeated washings. I used cheap batting in some of my first quilts and they are already starting to fall apart!

Next, select your quilt-backing fabric. When preparing the quilt backing, be sure that any seams are ironed and any selevedges are removed. I like to use ½" (1.3 cm) seams for the quilt back, and I press them open.

Also, think about the color of the backing fabric. If you like to see the quilting on the back, use a light, solid fabric that contrasts with the bobbin thread. On the other hand, if you don't want to see the quilting, using a busy multicolored print or coordinating solid will hide it.

If using a longarm quilting machine, make the backing about 4" (10 cm) bigger than the quilt top all around. If quilting on a home sewing machine, I like 1" (2.5 cm) or so of extra backing.

Finally, baste the quilt sandwich, but only if you are quilting on a sewing machine. There are various ways to baste a quilt, including fusible batting (this is my preference), pins, or a fusible spray. Use whatever works best for you, but be sure to baste the quilt with care. Paying attention in this step will help ensure that you don't get tucks on the back.

Get Quilting!

Pick a spot and start. If you aren't sure what to quilt on your quilt top, just start somewhere. Even if you are just stitching in the ditch, chances are that something will come to mind.

"What about stitch length?" is a common question. Don't worry about your stitch length. Consistent stitch size will come with practice. Honestly, I don't worry about it when I am quilting. I Figure that if my little toe doesn't catch in a stitch when I pull the quilt over me, it's okay.

Finished is better than perfect. When quilting, instead of focusing on perfection, focus on the purpose of the quilt. Doing so will help keep you motivated during the quilting process. Above all, remember that a finished quilt is better than a perfect quilt top.

TOOLS OF THE TRADE: QUILTING

You only need a couple of tools to get started quilting your beautiful quilt top. Once you get into machine quilting, you can see if any other optional supplies might make the process easier for you.

Sewing Machine

ESSENTIAL TOOLS FOR QUILTING

quilting thread

ruler

free motion stitching sewing machine foot

As a professional machine quilter, I do most of my quilting on a longarm quilting machine. But that doesn't mean that you have to have one to accomplish the quilting designs in this book. All the designs can be done any machine, including a home sewing machine.

If you are quilting on a home sewing machine, make sure that you have the correct foot. There are many different types for free-motion stitching, but as long as it allow the fabric move freely in between stitches without the feed dogs, it should work.

Quilting Thread

If quilting is my therapy, then threads are my meds! Of course, quilting thread is a given for any project—but not just any thread will do. Be sure to choose high-quality thread especially made for machine quilting. Trust me, it makes a huge difference.

So many different thread options are available, so find one that fits your quilting preferences. I personally like to use a 50 wt thread. It's a little bit thinner than 40 wt thread, which means it blends in nicely with the quilt. If you want your quilting to show up a little more, then a thicker thread will be perfect for you.

OPTIONAL SUPPLIES

Many notions and products are available that will make machine quilting a little easier. Here are just a few that I find are helpful for me:

Rulers

A lot of the quilting designs in this book incorporate straight lines. When quilting on my longarm, I like to use a ruler for diagonal lines. It's just too hard to

get a consistent line without one. You could also use a ruler while quilting on your sewing machine, but be sure that you use the foot your sewing machine manufacturer recommends. Also, be sure to use a ruler made especially for machine quilting. It must be thick enough that it doesn't slide under the foot while quilting.

A ruler is handy for more than just quilting diagonal lines. It can be used for stitching in the ditch, quilting horizontal or vertical lines, and even smoothing out the quilt top as you work. There are many different types of templates and rulers on the market, but the size that works the best for me is 2" × 10" (5 × 25.5 cm).

Marking Tools

I don't usually mark out my designs before quilting, but sometimes it is nice to have a guideline marked out. If you are newer to quilting, or are learning a new quilting design, go ahead and mark it out. It will give you one less thing to worry about!

There are a lot of marking pens on the market, but I like a trusty water-soluble pen (Dritz is my favorite) or a basic chalk pencil.

Supreme Slider and Quilting Gloves

Even though I have a longarm, I will quilt smaller projects or class samples on my sit-down machine. When that is the case, I always use a Supreme Slider-Teflon quilting mat, which reduces friction between my quilt top and sewing machine, and quilting gloves. I figure I can use all the help I can get when moving the quilt through the machine. If you are new to quilting, I would definitely suggest getting these tools!

red

Red is a fiery little vixen. She is bold and assertive. She knows exactly what she wants, and she is not afraid to go after it. Red will pull the fire alarm between classes to get out of taking a test. She will key your car if you talk behind her back. Red always throws the best parties, the kind that never seem to end, and no matter how bad you feel the next day, they are always worth it. Red insists on being first. In any rainbow worth its colors, every hue knows that it's best to queue up behind Red.

The only one who can tame Red, even a little, is White. White has the unique ability to soften Red's overbearing demeanor to a softer shade of pink. The irony is that Pink, most often looked upon by the other colors as a sweet, innocent little thing, is basically just red in disguise.

RED QUILT TECHNIQUES

Sewing Circles

There are so many tricks for sewing circles out there. There are special sewing machine feet, clever rulers, origami-like methods, as well as appliqué techniques. These are all valid ways to sew a curve, and many of them work quite well. But I am an old-fashioned kind of girl, and a few well-placed pins have never let me down.

Knowing how to sew a proper curve is a great tool to have in a piecer's arsenal. Along with squares and triangles, curves are the essential building blocks to every pieced quilt. Master these and you can master just about anything!

The red Total Eclipse quilt is broken up into ⅛ circles. These small slivers of a circle are barely considered curves. By sewing only ⅛ of a circle at a time, you avoid the bulk of the curve altogether.

Foundation Piecing

I have provided an alternate block for the Total Eclipse quilt that includes foundation piecing. Much like curved piecing, people either love it or hate it. But foundation piecing is simply the most accurate way to piece complicated or awkward angles with total precision.

It only takes a little extra time. At the end, you come out looking like the ultimate champion of sewing. Who doesn't want that? If you just can't get past it, that's okay. You don't have to do it. Options are fun!

13

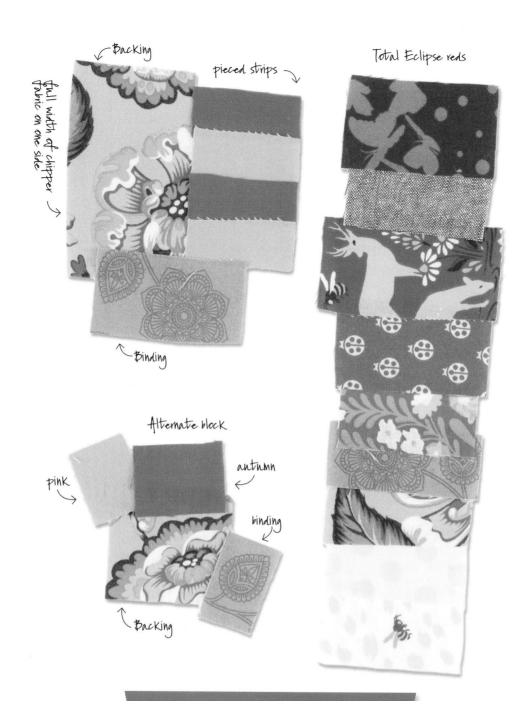

Backing

full width of chipper fabric on one side

pieced strips

Total Eclipse reds

Binding

Alternate block

pink

autumn

binding

Backing

CHOOSING FABRICS

Red is such a strong color that it ultimately takes over any print or quilt that it inhabits. Designing the Total Eclipse quilt, I began with a bright, true red (the ladybug print). From there I chose fabrics that inched their way toward their darker cousin, burgundy, and in the other direction toward red's lightest incarnation, pink. I selected a blend of different shades of red, a variety of print density—from almost solid to tonal prints to all-out edge-to-edge multi-colored prints—and a very wide range of contrast, from cream to a dark burgundy.

When working in a single color, the fabrics can really push the boundaries of print and texture without becoming a crazy mess. I wanted to balance out the sheer hotness of the red with some cooler tones, so I threw in the mint with the red floral as well as the light aqua and pink polka dot for good measure.

All of this variety allows some of the blocks on the blended backgrounds to fall into their surroundings, while other blocks jump right off of the quilt. This achieves a sort of scrappy look with only nine fabrics.

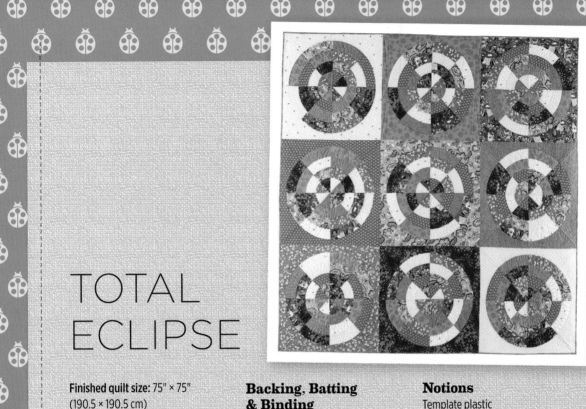

TOTAL ECLIPSE

Finished quilt size: 75" × 75" (190.5 × 190.5 cm)

Finished block size: 25" × 25" (63.5 × 63.5 cm)

Templates: Eclipse A, B, C, D, E

Fabrics

1½ yd (137 cm) each of 9 different red print fabrics

Backing, Batting & Binding

4¾ yd (4.3 m) of 40"/42" (102/107 cm) wide fabric or 2⅓ yd (2 m) of 108" (274 cm) wide backing fabric

⅝ yd (57 cm) of fabric to make 310" (7.9 m) of 2½" (6.5 cm) bias binding

83" × 83" (211 × 211 cm) of batting

Notions

Template plastic

Erasable fabric_marking tool

TIP!

Pinning and sewing curves is all about pin placement. Place one pin in the center of the two curved pieces, as in **Figure 1** (page 16). Place a pin at either end of the two pieces. Place the final pins along the side edges of the two pieces 1" (2.5 cm) down from the corner pins.

Sew slowly, gently turning the seam edge as it moves through the sewing machine. Watch the edge of the seam at the ¼" (6 mm) guide and not the needle of the sewing machine.

CUT FABRICS

1. Trace Eclipse Templates A, B, C, D, and E (pages 184–186) once each onto the template plastic, label each template, and cut them out on the drawn line. Use a ruler and rotary cutter to cut the straight edges and scissors to cut the curved edges.

2. Following the cutting diagrams on page 18, cut four 12" (30.5 cm) × WOF (width of fabric) strips from each of the 9 red fabrics.

Then from the WOF strips, cut:
- » 8 Template A pieces
- » 8 Template B pieces
- » 8 Template C pieces
- » 8 Template D pieces
- » 8 Template E pieces: Cut 4 pieces with the template right side up, then flip the template over and cut 4 more pieces with the template wrong side up.

MAKE ONE BLOCK

3. Select 8 matching Template E pieces and set them aside for the block background. Do not use that fabric anywhere else in the block.

4. Select 8 pieces, 2 each from the Templates A, B, C, and D pieces. Each set should include every print except the background print of Template E.

   Sew the top curved edge of 1 Template A piece to the bottom curved edge of 1 Template B piece **(Figure 1)**. Press curved seams toward the wide end of the wedge.

5. Sew the Template C piece to the top of the Template B piece. Press seams toward the wide end of the wedge **(Figure 2)**.

6. Sew the Template D piece to the top of the Template C piece **(Figure 2)**.

7. Repeat Steps 3 and 4 to create a total of 8 wedges, changing the sequence of colors in each wedge.

8. Sew the wedges together in pairs, pinning at each seam intersection, to create four ¼ circles **(Figure 3)**.

9. Sew 2 mirror-image Template E pieces along the diagonal edge to create a ¼-circle background **(Figure 4)**.
   Repeat to create 3 more ¼-circle background units.

10. Sew one ¼-circle background to one ¼ wedge. Use the center seam of each piece as a marker and pin at the intersection. Repeat to create 3 more ¼-circle blocks **(Figure 5)**.

11. Sew 2 pairs of ¼ circle blocks along the pieced edge to create 2 half-circle blocks **(Figure 6)**. Join the half-circle blocks along the pieced edge to complete the block **(Figure 7)**.

ASSEMBLE THE QUILT

12. Repeat Steps 1–9 to create 8 more Total Eclipse blocks.

13. Square up each block to 25½ " (65 cm) square, then follow the Total Eclipse Assembly Diagram on page 19 to complete the quilt top.

TIP!

Use the straight grain edge of the strip to line up each of the templates. This way you get at least one edge that won't stretch on the bias. In the case of the Template E pieces, all of the outside edges will be on the straight grain and reduce the stretch around the entire finished block.

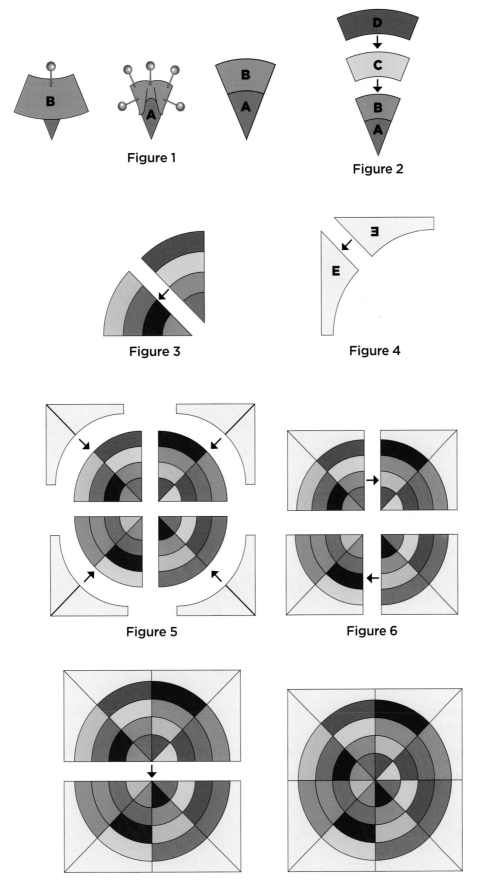

Figure 1

Figure 2

Figure 3

Figure 4

Figure 5

Figure 6

Figure 7

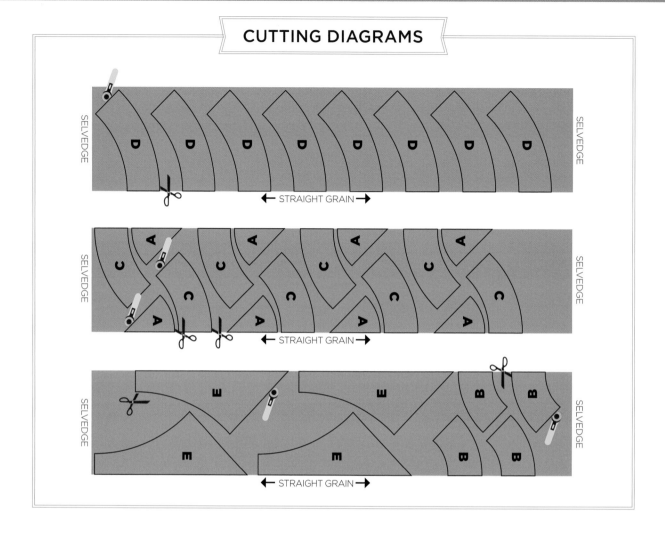

CUTTING DIAGRAMS

PIECE THE BACKING

14. To make the backing from 40"/42" (102/107 cm) backing fabric, trim the selvedge. Cut the trimmed backing yardage in half to create two 85" (216 cm) WOF pieces (**Figure 8**, page 17).

15. Place the 2 backing pieces right sides together and sew along the long edge **(Figure 9)**.

Backing should measure about 85" × 84" (216 × 213 cm).

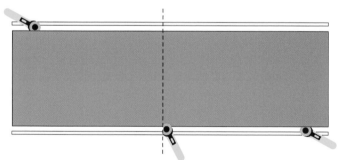

Figure 8

FINISH THE QUILT

16. Follow the instructions for preparing the quilt top for quilting on page 10.

17. Follow the quilting instructions on page 20.

18. To complete the quilt, follow the bias binding instructions on page 183.

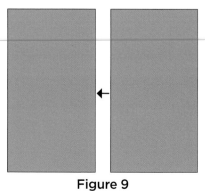

Figure 9

TOTAL ECLIPSE ASSEMBLY DIAGRAM

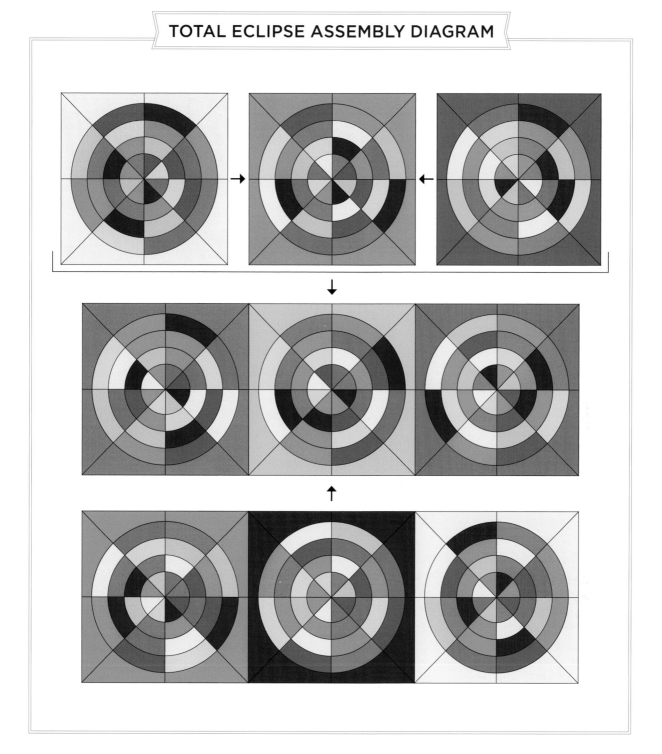

QUILTING WITH THE PIECING AS A GUIDE

Sometimes picking out quilting designs can be harder than actually quilting them! When trying to decide what designs to use for a particular quilt, try breaking it down into smaller parts. Looking at the pieces of a block, instead of the whole quilt, can make it easier to come up with ideas. This is especially the case when working with larger blocks with several pieces, like the Total Eclipse quilt. These big and beautiful blocks can be broken up into different shapes, including wedges and rings.

WEDGES: CONNECT THE DOTS

Because the Total Eclipse block is pieced in wedges, making intricate-looking designs is as easy as

connecting the dots. You'll soon see that even basic quilting designs can create amazing secondary patterns when repeated in each of the wedges. All you have to do is use the outer seams of the block as a guide.

This particular design combines straight lines and curves, which really make the blocks shine. As an added bonus, the whole block can be quilted without starting and stopping. Always a favorite of mine!

1. Quilt a diagonal line from the outer point of a wedge toward the center, about 1" (2.5 cm) away from the center. Quilt a diagonal line back up to the opposite outer point of **(Figure 1)** the wedge.

   Echo three more times, landing on the same points on the outside of the circle. End on the starting point **(Figure 2)**.

2. Starting at the same point of the wedge, quilt a line that curves to the bottom point of the last echo, curving out toward the outer edge of the block and back to form a leaf, then onto the next wedge **(Figure 3)**.

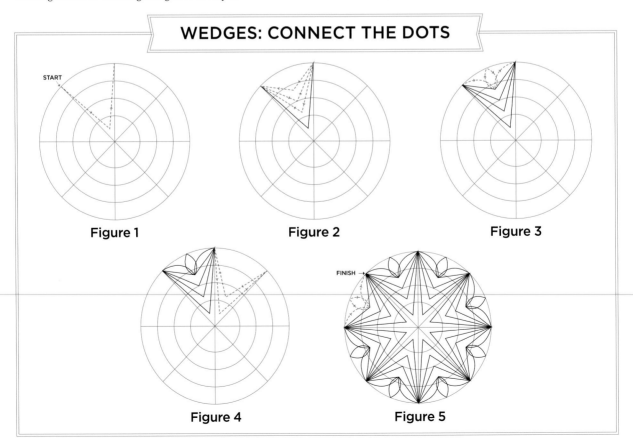

WEDGES: CONNECT THE DOTS

Figure 1

Figure 2

Figure 3

Figure 4

Figure 5

3. Repeat Steps 1 and 2 in the next wedge **(Figure 4)**.

4. Continue quilting all of the wedges in the same way until the block is quilted **(Figure 5)**.

This design might look complex when finished, but it's just the same design quilted in each wedge. I love a quilting design that looks harder than it actually is!

RINGS: WISHBONE AND RIBBON CANDY

Perhaps you want a softer look or prefer to enhance the curvy shape of the block. Instead of dividing the block into wedges, break it up into rings. Quilt the individual pieces of the block. To give the quilt even more texture, you could also alternate between two different quilting designs. For this quilt, I chose wishbone and ribbon candy, two of my go-to quilting designs.

I used these designs because they are so easy and versatile, and they're quick to stitch. They also work well in narrow borders and sashings as well as inside blocks.

1. Starting in the outermost ring and at the seam between 2 wedges, quilt a diagonal line toward the bottom seam, curving in a loop before reaching the edge. In a continuous motion, quilt another diagonal line toward the top seam, looping around before reaching the edge. Because the block is curved, quilt the loops toward the center of the block slightly closer together than the outer loops **(Figure 6)**.

2. Continue quilting the wishbone designs, until you reach the bottom corner of the next portion of the ring **(Figure 7)**.

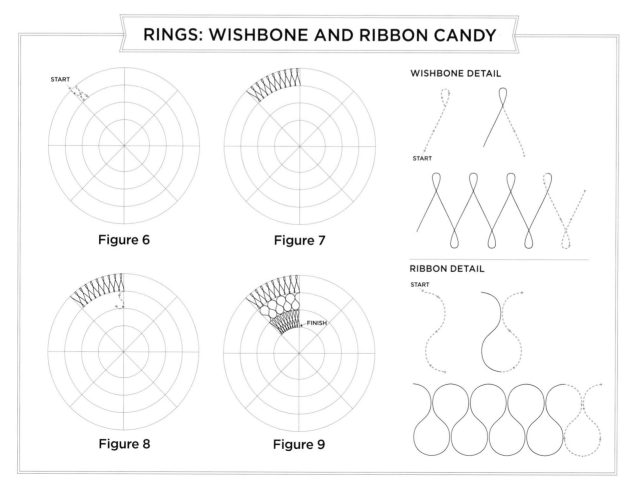

RINGS: WISHBONE AND RIBBON CANDY

START

Figure 6

Figure 7

Figure 8

Figure 9

FINISH

WISHBONE DETAIL

START

RIBBON DETAIL

START

3. Starting at the right seam in the second ring, quilt the ribbon candy design. Start by stitching a line that curves away from and then back toward the edge of the ring. It should resemble an "S" shape (**Figure 8**, page 21).

4. Continue quilting the ribbon candy design until you reach the next seam. End so that your quilting is touching the edge of the next wedge.

5. Continue alternating between the wishbone and ribbon candy designs using the piecing as your guide. As the wedge gets narrower, stitch the designs to best fit each section (**Figure 9**, page 21).

CENTER FLOWER

To switch it up a bit, you can use a different design in the center of the block. I chose to quilt a continuous curve flower.

1. Starting at the left edge of the center wedge piece, quilt a line that curves from the outer point to the center of the block and out to the next point.

Continue into the next wedge by repeating the same shape (**Figure 10**).

2. Continue quilting curved line around the center wedges until you reach the starting point (**Figure 11**).

3. If you want to add more detail, echo lines are just the thing. Stitch a line that echoes around the outside of the flower, curving from the top of one petal to the space between petals and back up to the top of the next petal. You can make the echo line as close, or as far from, the flower as you like (**Figures 12 and 13**).

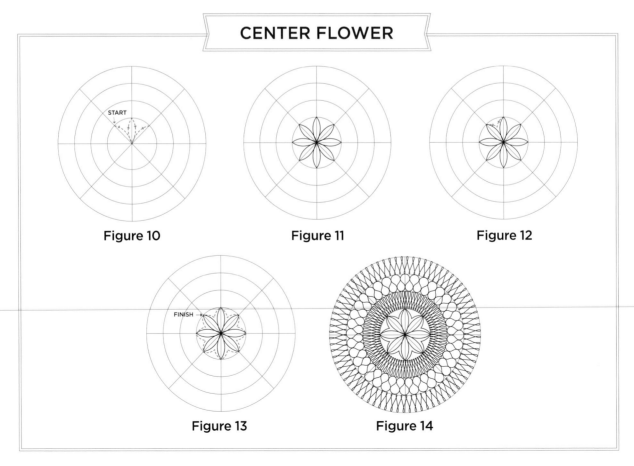

CENTER FLOWER

Figure 10

Figure 11

Figure 12

Figure 13

Figure 14

A LITTLE OF BOTH

But who says that you have to choose between quilting the wedges or rings? If you can't decide which one to go with, try incorporating both techniques in the same block. That's what I did in the center ring of the center block of the Total Eclipse quilt.

It's not difficult at all! Quilt the two outer rings of the block with the wishbone and ribbon candy designs, then switch to the flower design in the center **(Figure 14)**. It's the perfect compromise!

OUTSIDE THE BLOCK: ECHO STITCH

This quilt is simply amazing in more ways than one! The piecing not only makes the block a breeze to quilt, it also makes quilting the background a snap. Echoing the diagonal seams can make a fun secondary design in the background.

1. Starting from the edge of the outer ring and working toward the corner of the block, quilt a about a ¼" (6 mm) away from the seam. Travel along the edge of the block to ¼" (6 mm) on the other side of the seam, and echo stitch **(Figure 15)** the seam.

2. Continue echo stitching all four sides of the seam until you have reached the starting point **(Figure 16)**.

Fill in the rest of the background space with your favorite quilting design. To keep it interesting, I alternated between two different designs. In some of the background spaces, I quilted a design used often in this book, swirls. I could give an artistic reason, but honestly, I just love quilting them! I'll show you how to quilt them a little later in the book. But if you can't wait, the instructions are on page 41.

In the rest of the background spaces, I quilted wavy lines page 54.) The texture is similar to the swirls, but is a little quicker to quilt. Adding them helped me to get the quilt done a little quicker without taking away from the swirls.

Simple background quilting can still make a big impact.

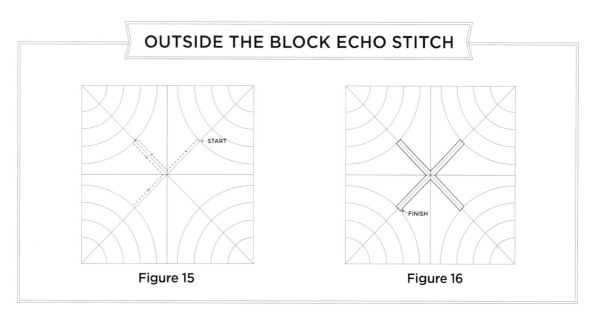

OUTSIDE THE BLOCK ECHO STITCH

Figure 15

Figure 16

PARTIAL ECLIPSE

The Partial Eclipse block can stand alone as a small wall-hanging quilt, or, if you feel like turning up the volume on the Total Eclipse quilt, switch out one or more of the Total Eclipse blocks for an alternate Partial Eclipse block. It's always fun to throw a visual curveball into a quilt that has a repeating block, just to keep everyone on their toes!

Finished block size: 25" × 25" (63.5 × 63.5 cm)

Templates: Eclipse A, B, C, D

Fabrics

⅞ yd (80 cm) of red solid

⅞ yd (80 cm) of pink solid

Backing, Batting & Binding

1 yd of 40"/42" (102/107 cm) wide fabric

⅓ yd (30 cm) of fabric to make 110" (280 cm) of 2½" (6.5 cm) bias binding

33" × 33" (84 × 84 cm) of batting

Notions

Template plastic

Erasable fabric-marking tool

Permanent pen

Foundation paper

TIP!

Reduce the stitch length on your sewing machine to 1.5 mm to 1.8 mm. A tiny stitch is very important for foundation piecing. It creates more holes in the paper, which perforate the paper, and makes the paper much easier to tear away when the block is complete.

CUT THE FABRICS

1. Trace Eclipse Templates A, B, C, and D (pages 184-186) once each onto the template plastic, label each template, and cut them out on the drawn line. Use a ruler and rotary cutter to cut the straight edges and scissors to cut the curved edges.

2. To make 4 foundation templates, trace all of the lines on Template C onto foundation paper. Number the sections to match the template **(Figure 1)**.

3. Cut one 4" (10 cm) × WOF (width of fabric) strip from each of the 2 fabrics. Then, from each strip, cut ten 4" × 4" (10 × 10 cm) squares.

4. Following the cutting diagram on page 28, cut two 12" (30.5 cm) × WOF strips.

Then from the WOF strips, cut:

» 4 Template A pieces
» 4 Template B pieces
» 2 Template C pieces
» 4 Template D pieces
» 4 Template E pieces: Cut 4 pieces from one fabric by placing the template right side up, then flip the template over and cut 4 more pieces by placing the template wrong side up on the second fabric.

SEW THE BLOCK

5. On the wrong side of the foundationTemplate C, place two 4" × 4" (10 10 cm) squares, one of each fabric, right sides together, with the fabric face up covering section 1 first. Align one edge with the line between sections 1 and 2, then slide them ¼"

(6 mm) past the line into section 2. Pin in place **(Figure 2)**.

6. Flip the template and fabric squares right side up and sew on the line between sections 1 and 2 **(Figure 3)**.

7. From the wrong side of the template, trim the seam allowance to ¼" (6 mm) and fold the top fabric back over the seam and press **(Figure 4)**. Do this after each seam.

8. From the right side of the template, push a straight pin through the intersecting points between sections 2 and 3 to mark where to line up the next piece of fabric **(Figure 5)**.

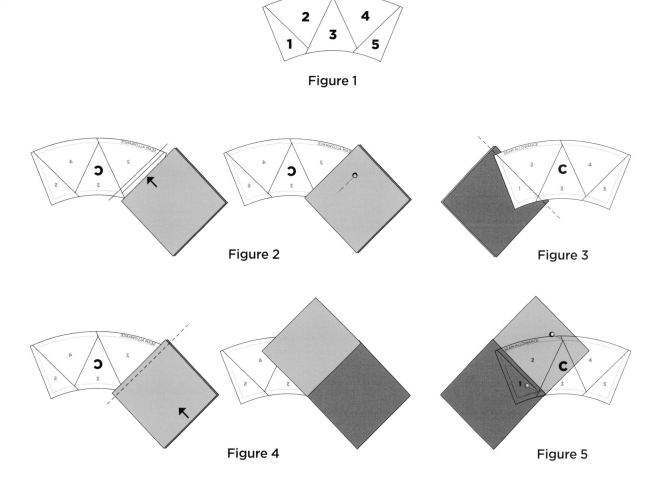

Figure 1

Figure 2

Figure 3

Figure 4

Figure 5

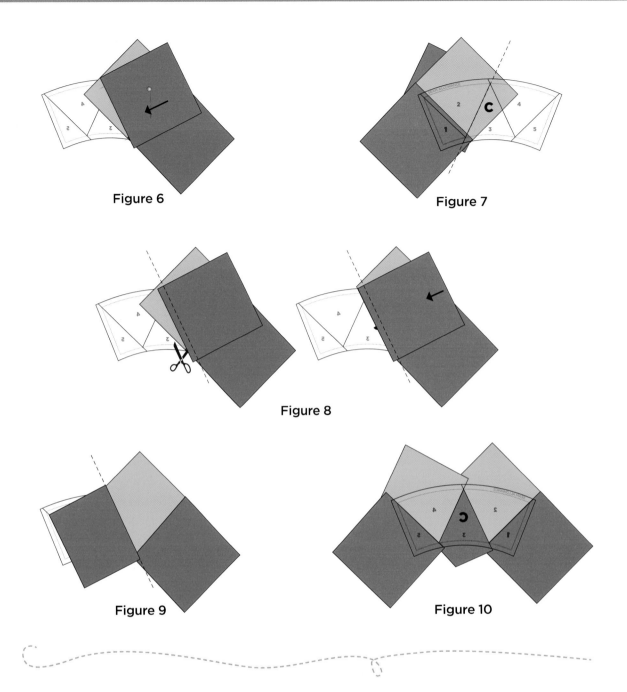

Figure 6

Figure 7

Figure 8

Figure 9

Figure 10

9. From the wrong side of the template, line up the straight edge of the next piece of fabric with the point where the pin pushes through the fabric. Slide the fabric ¼" (6 mm) past the marker, then pin in place **(Figure 6)**. Remove the marker pin.

10. From the right side of the template, sew on the line between sections 2 and 3 **(Figure 7)**.

11. From the wrong side of the template, trim away the excess fabric, leaving a ¼" (6 mm) seam allowance **(Figure8)**.

12. Fold the fabric back over the seam and press **(Figure 9)**.

13. Continue marking, sewing, trimming, and pressing across the template until all 5 sections are covered in fabric and every line has been sewn in place **(Figure 10)**.

14. Sew around the edge of the template between the seam allowance and the outside edge of the template.

15. Trim away the excess fabric on the template's outside line **(Figure 11)**.

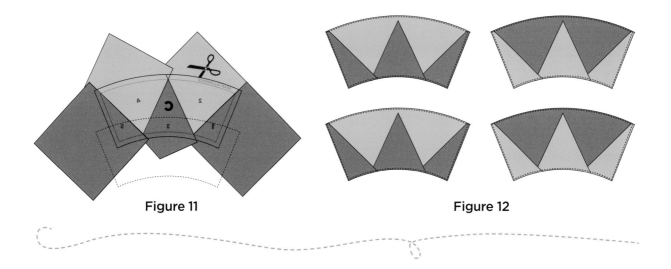

Figure 11

Figure 12

Remove the foundation paper by carefully tearing it away along the perforated seam lines.

16. Repeat Steps 1–12 to make one more foundation-pieced Template C unit.

17. Repeat Steps 1–12 to make 2 more foundation-pieced Template C units, but this time reverse the fabric placement **(Figure 12)**.

ASSEMBLE THE BLOCK

18. Follow the Partial Eclipse Assembly Diagram (page 27) to complete the block.

19. Square the block to 25½" (65 cm) square. Finish the single quilt block as a small wall hanging or make more blocks and use them as alternate blocks in the Total Eclipse quilt.

PARTIAL ECLIPSE BLOCK ASSEMBLY DIAGRAM

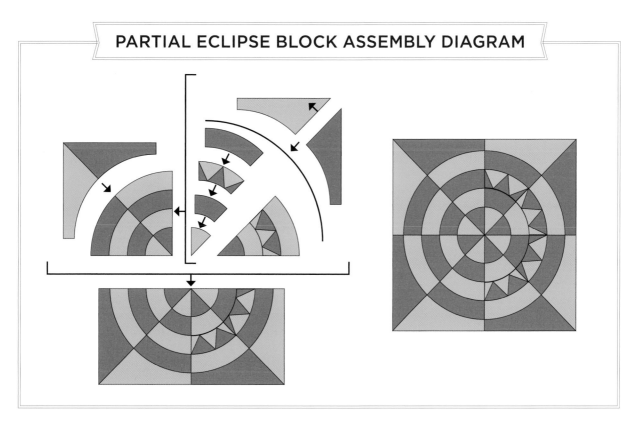

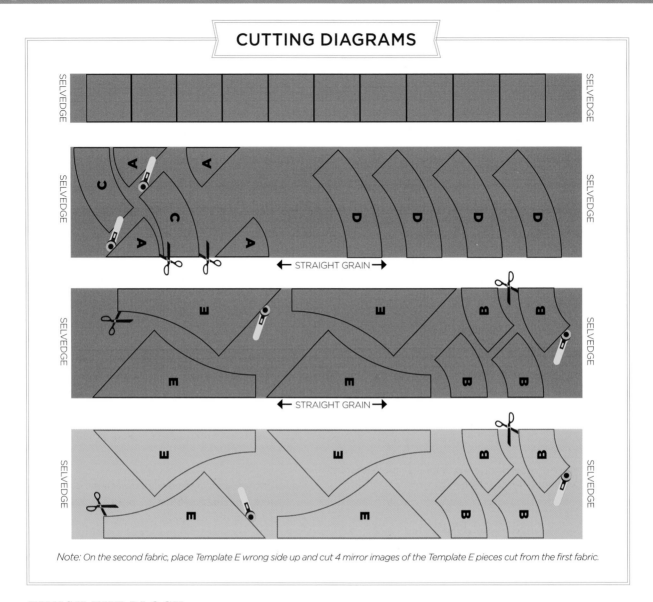

CUTTING DIAGRAMS

Note: On the second fabric, place Template E wrong side up and cut 4 mirror images of the Template E pieces cut from the first fabric.

FINISH THE BLOCK

20. Follow the instructions for preparing the quilt top for quilting on page 10.

21. Follow the quilting instructions on page 28.

22. To complete the wall hanging, follow the bias binding instructions on page 183.

QUILTING WITH CONTRAST

The contrast, or difference, among the quilting designs used on a quilt can highlight or hide certain parts. Because I like to use a matching thread color on my quilts, contrast between the designs can help show that they are, in fact, different.

Because the solid red and pink fabrics are so distinct, alternating between geometric and curvy lines is a fun way to go. I decided to quilt curvier designs in the pink and angular designs in the red.

In the pink pieces, I quilted feathers, serpentine lines, and swirls that help soften the hard edges of the pattern. In the red pieces, I quilted simple diagonal lines, radiating lines, and complex geometric motifs that fill in irregular blocks.

SERPENTINE LINES

I use this design often. Because it extends between the edges of the block, it can fill a variety of shapes. It's easy

TIP!

One common mistake when quilting this design is overthinking. Once you have the first line quilted, all you have to do is echo it. Don't feel as though you have to re-create the shape each time.

to execute, but it can be a little tricky the first couple of times you try it. If you find quilting it to be a struggle, try drawing it a few times to get the hang of it.

1. Starting from one edge of the block, quilt a line resembling a gentle "S" shape to the next side of the block (**Figure 1**). It should curve out and back so that it looks as though it will merge into the other edge of the block (**Figure 1**).

2. Travel up the edge a bit, then echo the "S" shape quilted in Step 1 until you reach the first side of the block (**Figure 2**).

3. Repeat Step 2 and echo to the opposite side of the block (**Figure 3**).

4. Continue working your way between the sides of the block, echoing the "S" shape, until you reach the end of the block (**Figure 4**).

I also quilted swirls (see page 41 for instructions) and feathers (page 45) on this mini-quilt.

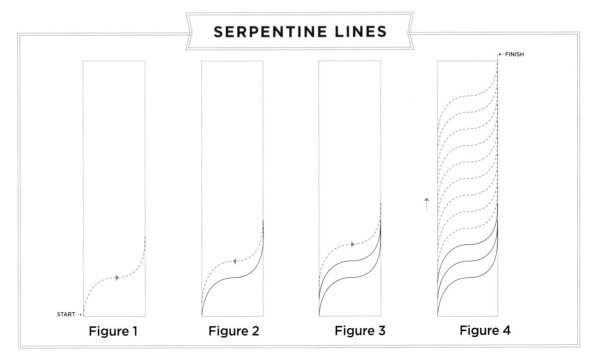

SERPENTINE LINES

Figure 1   Figure 2   Figure 3   Figure 4

orange

Orange has always been a little insecure about being neither red nor yellow, so naturally she overcompensates. Caught between fiery assertiveness and cheerful optimism can't be an easy place to exist, but Orange manages with warmth and charisma.

No one is ambivalent about Orange. From butterflies to her signature fruit, there is no mistaking her acidic hue. She leaves her mark on all things. Orange turns a sweet pink to a punchy peach and has been known to put Red in her place with a well-tossed tomato. Orange is the burning warmth of a flame and the unmistakable sign that fall is coming and Halloween is on the horizon.

ORANGE QUILT TECHNIQUES

Sewing Small

When creating an image with many small pieces of fabric, such as this pixelated moth, the process can easily become overwhelming. Although the sewing is simple—all rectangles and straight seams—organization and patience are the keys to keeping this small quilt top headache-free.

Every piece is cut to measure and plays a specific part in the overall design. With so many different lengths of rectangles, taking this pattern one row at a time will greatly reduce the opportunity for errors. This means there are almost no seams to line up!

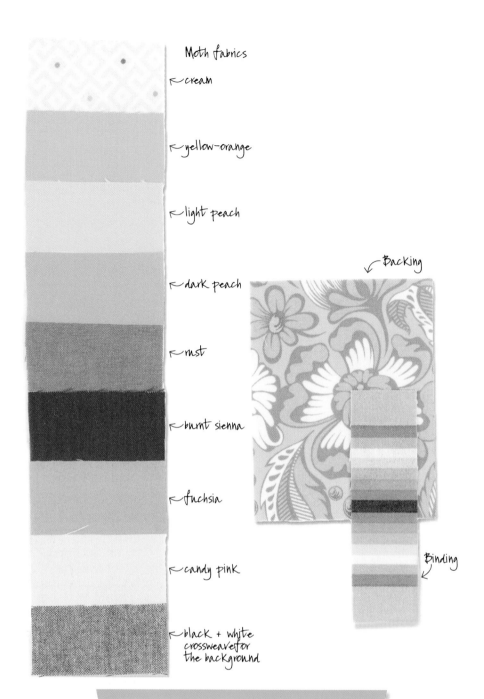

Moth fabrics

← cream

← yellow-orange

← light peach

← dark peach

← rust

← burnt sienna

← fuchsia

← candy pink

← black + white
crossweave for
the background

↙ Backing

Binding ↙

CHOOSING FABRICS

Sometimes a quilt top is more than the sum of its parts. This is exactly the case in the Ikat Moth quilt. The fabrics are a mix of simple solids and a small print for added visual texture. It is the subtle variation in color that gives this combination of fabrics its depth.

Even though I was exploring the color orange, I didn't want to fall back on the obvious true orange. I focused on orange adjacent colors rather than going straight to the source—yellow-orange, peachy

oranges, rust, and a dark sienna with touches of hot pink and light pink to break up the monotony of a single color inspiration. By dancing around a color and using many of its subtle variations, the palette becomes richer and more interesting.

The crucial piece of this palette comes in the background color. A high-contrast charcoal gray falls back, allowing the oranges to really stand out while

containing the colors in a definitive frame. An equally contrasting choice would be a bright aqua or a deep plum.

For the backing and binding, I searched for prints that incorporated all of the colors from the quilt top. I often use the backing and the binding fabrics to tie a palette together. After all, a quilt is a three-dimensional object, and every angle serves as another opportunity for color, design, and continuity.

IKAT MOTH

Finished quilt size: 42" × 42" (106.5 × 106.5 cm)

Fabrics

¼ yd (23 cm) of cream print

¼ yd (23 cm) of yellow-orange solid

¼ yd (23 cm) of light peach solid

⅜ yd (38.5 cm) of dark peach solid

¼ yd (23 cm) of rust solid

¼ yd (23 cm) of burnt sienna solid

⅛ yd (11.5 cm) of hot pink solid

⅛ yd (11.5 cm) of pink solid

2 yd (183 cm) of charcoal gray crossweave

Backing, Batting & Binding

3 yd (2.75 m) of 40"/42" (102/107 cm) wide fabric or 1½ yd (137 cm) of 108" (274 cm) wide backing fabric

⅜ yd (34.5 cm) of fabric to make 190" (483 cm) of 2½" (6.5 cm) bias binding

50" × 50" (127 × 127 cm) of batting

TIP!

When sewing multiple long strips together, alternate the direction of sewing. For example, sew the pair of Column 1 strips to the Center Column from top to bottom. Then sew the pair of Column 2 strips to Column 1 from bottom to top. This will keep the fabrics from shifting too far in one direction and maintain a straight line across the top and bottom edges of your quilt top.

CUT THE FABRICS

1. From the cream fabric, cut four 1" (2.5 cm) × WOF (width of fabric) strips. Mark them as Fabric A.

2. From the light peach fabric, cut six 1" (2.5 cm) × WOF strips. Mark them as Fabric B.

3. From the yellow-orange fabric, cut seven 1" (2.5 cm) × WOF strips. Mark them as Fabric C.

4. From the dark peach fabric, cut eleven 1" (2.5 cm) × WOF strips. Mark them as Fabric D.

5. From the rust fabric, cut seven 1" (2.5 cm) × WOF strips. Mark them as Fabric E.

6. From the burnt sienna fabric, cut six 1" (2.5 cm) × WOF strips. Mark them as Fabric F.

7. From the hot pink fabric, cut two 1" (2.5 cm) × WOF strips. Mark them as Fabric G.

8. From the light pink fabric, cut three 1" (2.5 cm) × WOF strips. Mark them as Fabric H.

9. From the charcoal gray fabric, cut fifty 1" (2.5 cm) × WOF strips and five 3½" (9 cm) × WOF strips for the borders. Mark them as Fabric BG.

PIECE THE CENTER COLUMN

10. Make 1 Center Column according to the column diagram. Use the measurements indicated to cut each piece of fabric.

11. Mark the top of the Center Column unit with a pin and set aside.

PIECE THE SIDE COLUMNS

12. Make Side Columns 1–38 in pairs to create symmetrical Ikat Moth wings, following the column ciagrams on pages 35–40. Use the indicated measurements in the charts to cut each piece of fabric.

13. Fold the 1" (2.5 cm) rectangles in half and cut 2 pieces at a time to make two identical columns.

14. When each set of columns is complete, join it to the center column before moving on to the next column. Following the Ikat Moth Center Assembly Diagram (page 40).

    The Ikat Moth center should measure approximately 39" × 36" (99 × 91.5 cm).

15. Continue adding the columns to both sides of the moth center unit until all of them have been joined.

ASSEMBLE THE QUILT TOP

16. Sew the 3½" (9 cm) × WOF gray background strips together end to end to create one long 3½" (9 cm) wide strip.

    From the strip, sub cut two 3½" × 36" (9 × 91.5 cm) rectangles for the side borders and two 3½" × 45½" (9 × 115.5 cm) rectangles for the top and bottom borders.

17. Sew one 3½" × 36" (9 × 91.5 cm) rectangle to the right side and one to the left side of the Ikat Moth Center. Press seams toward the background strip.

    Sew one 3½" × 45½" (9 × 115.5 cm) rectangle to the bottom and one to the top of the Ikat Moth Center, following the assembly diagram. Press seams toward the background strip.

18. Using a clear quilter's ruler and a rotary cutter, trim the completed quilt top to 42" × 42" (106.5 × 106.5 cm).

PIECE THE BACKING

19. To make the backing from 40"/42" (102/107 cm) backing fabric, trim the selvedge. Cut the trimmed backing yardage in half to create two 54" WOF pieces **(Figure 1)**.

20. Place the 2 backing pieces right sides together and sew along the long edge **(Figure 2)**.

    Backing should measure about 82" × 54" (216 × 213 cm).

FINISH THE QUILT

21. Follow the instructions for preparing the quilt top for quilting on page 10.

22. Follow the quilting instructions on page 41.

23. To complete the quilt, follow the bias binding instructions on page 183.

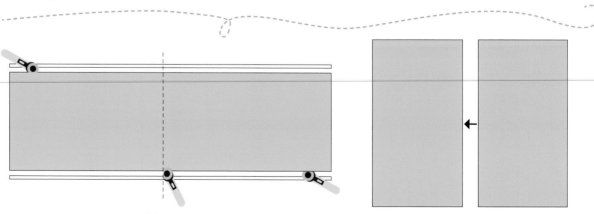

Figure 1   Figure 2

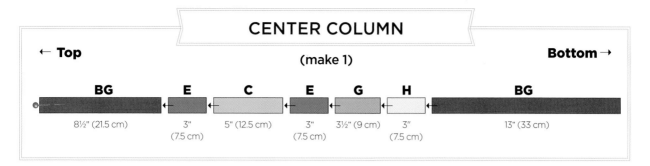

CENTER COLUMN

← **Top**   **Bottom** →

(make 1)

BG	E	C	E	G	H	BG
8½" (21.5 cm)	3" (7.5 cm)	5" (12.5 cm)	3" (7.5 cm)	3½" (9 cm)	3" (7.5 cm)	13" (33 cm)

SIDE COLUMNS 1–7

← **Top**   **Bottom** →

(make 2 each)

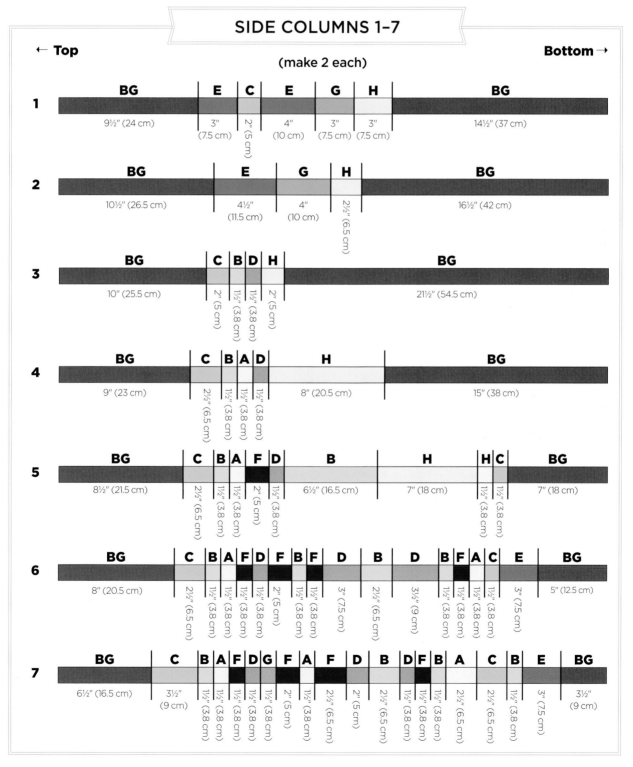

1 BG 9½" (24 cm) | E 3" (7.5 cm) | C 2" (5 cm) | E 4" (10 cm) | G 3" (7.5 cm) | H 3" (7.5 cm) | BG 14½" (37 cm)

2 BG 10½" (26.5 cm) | E 4½" (11.5 cm) | G 4" (10 cm) | H 2½" (6.5 cm) | BG 16½" (42 cm)

3 BG 10" (25.5 cm) | C 2" (5 cm) | B 1½" (3.8 cm) | D 1½" (3.8 cm) | H 2" (5 cm) | BG 21½" (54.5 cm)

4 BG 9" (23 cm) | C 2½" (6.5 cm) | B 1½" (3.8 cm) | A 1½" (3.8 cm) | D 1½" (3.8 cm) | H 8" (20.5 cm) | BG 15" (38 cm)

5 BG 8½" (21.5 cm) | C 2½" (6.5 cm) | B 1½" (3.8 cm) | A 1½" (3.8 cm) | F 2" (5 cm) | D 1½" (3.8 cm) | B 6½" (16.5 cm) | H 7" (18 cm) | H 1½" (3.8 cm) | C 1½" (3.8 cm) | BG 7" (18 cm)

6 BG 8" (20.5 cm) | C 2½" (6.5 cm) | B 1½" (3.8 cm) | A 1½" (3.8 cm) | F 1½" (3.8 cm) | D 1½" (3.8 cm) | F 2" (5 cm) | B 1½" (3.8 cm) | F 1½" (3.8 cm) | D 3" (7.5 cm) | B 2½" (6.5 cm) | D 3½" (9 cm) | B 1½" (3.8 cm) | F 1½" (3.8 cm) | A 1½" (3.8 cm) | C 1½" (3.8 cm) | E 3" (7.5 cm) | BG 5" (12.5 cm)

7 BG 6½" (16.5 cm) | C 3½" (9 cm) | B 1½" (3.8 cm) | A 1½" (3.8 cm) | F 1½" (3.8 cm) | D 1½" (3.8 cm) | G 1½" (3.8 cm) | F 2" (5 cm) | A 1½" (3.8 cm) | F 2½" (6.5 cm) | D 2" (5 cm) | B 2½" (6.5 cm) | D 1½" (3.8 cm) | F 1½" (3.8 cm) | B 1½" (3.8 cm) | A 2½" (6.5 cm) | C 2½" (6.5 cm) | B 1½" (3.8 cm) | E 3" (7.5 cm) | BG 3½" (9 cm)

← **Top**

(make 2 each)

Bottom →

8

| BG | C | B | A | F | D | G | F | A | F | D | F | B | A | C | E | BG |

8½" (21.5 cm) · 2" (5 cm) · 1½" (3.8 cm) · 1½" (3.8 cm) · 1½" (3.8 cm) · 1½" (3.8 cm) · 2" (5 cm) · 2½" (6.5 cm) · 1½" (3.8 cm) · 3" (7.5 cm) · 2½" (6.5 cm) · 1½" (3.8 cm) · 1½" (3.8 cm) · 4" (10 cm) · 2½" (6.5 cm) · 5" (12.5 cm)

9

| BG | C | B | A | F | D | G | A | F | D | F | B | C | B | C | E | BG |

7½" (19 cm) · 2½" (6.5 cm) · 1½" (3.8 cm) · 1½" (3.8 cm) · 1½" (3.8 cm) · 2½" (6.5 cm) · 1½" (3.8 cm) · 4" (10 cm) · 1½" (3.8 cm) · 1½" (3.8 cm) · 2" (5 cm) · 3½" (9 cm) · 1½" (3.8 cm) · 1½" (3.8 cm) · 1½" (3.8 cm) · 4½" (11.5 cm) · 4" (10 cm)

10

| BG | C | D | B | F | D | G | A | F | B | C | B | D | E | BG |

7" (18 cm) · 1½" (3.8 cm) · 1½" (3.8 cm) · 1½" (3.8 cm) · 1½" (3.8 cm) · 4½" (11.5 cm) · 1½" (3.8 cm) · 4" (10 cm) · 3" (7.5 cm) · 2" (5 cm) · 2½" (6.5 cm) · 2" (5 cm) · 1½" (3.8 cm) · 3½" (9 cm) · 5½" (14 cm)

11

| BG | C | D | F | D | G | F | A | F | B | C | D | B | D | E | BG |

7½" (19 cm) · 1½" (3.8 cm) · 1½" (3.8 cm) · 2½" (6.5 cm) · 4½" (11.5 cm) · 1½" (3.8 cm) · 1½" (3.8 cm) · 3" (7.5 cm) · 2" (5 cm) · 1½" (3.8 cm) · 3" (7.5 cm) · 1½" (3.8 cm) · 3½" (9 cm) · 1½" (3.8 cm) · 3" (7.5 cm) · 4" (10 cm)

12

| BG | C | D | F | A | F | D | F | B | C | D | B | D | B | D | E | BG |

7" (18 cm) · 1½" (3.8 cm) · 1½" (3.8 cm) · 1½" (3.8 cm) · 1½" (3.8 cm) · 1½" (3.8 cm) · 4½" (11.5 cm) · 4" (10 cm) · 2" (5 cm) · 2½" (6.5 cm) · 2" (5 cm) · 1½" (3.8 cm) · 2" (5 cm) · 2" (5 cm) · 1½" (3.8 cm) · 5" (12.5 cm) · 2½" (6.5 cm)

13

| BG | C | D | F | A | F | D | F | B | D | B | D | E | BG |

6½" (16.5 cm) · 1½" (3.8 cm) · 1½" (3.8 cm) · 1½" (3.8 cm) · 2½" (6.5 cm) · 1½" (3.8 cm) · 4½" (11.5 cm) · 3" (7.5 cm) · 2" (5 cm) · 3½" (9 cm) · 3½" (9 cm) · 2" (5 cm) · 3" (7.5 cm) · 6" (15 cm)

14

| BG | C | D | F | A | F | D | F | B | C | D | B | D | E | BG |

5" (12.5 cm) · 2½" (6.5 cm) · 1½" (3.8 cm) · 1½" (3.8 cm) · 3½" (9 cm) · 1½" (3.8 cm) · 4½" (11.5 cm) · 1½" (3.8 cm) · 2" (5 cm) · 2½" (6.5 cm) · 3½" (9 cm) · 2" (5 cm) · 3" (7.5 cm) · 3" (7.5 cm) · 5½" (14 cm)

← **Top**

(make 2 each)

Bottom →

15

BG | C | D | F | A | F | D | F | A | G | C | D | B | D | E | BG

6" (15 cm) · 2" (5 cm) · 1½" (3.8 cm) · 1½" (3.8 cm) · 2½" (6.5 cm) · 1½" (3.8 cm) · 2½" (6.5 cm) · 1½" (3.8 cm) · 2½" (6.5 cm) · 1½" (3.8 cm) · 2" (5 cm) · 2" (5 cm) · 3" (7.5 cm) · 2½" (6.5 cm) · 3½" (9 cm) · 7½" (19 cm)

16

BG | C | D | F | A | F | A | D | G | C | D | B | D | B | D | E | BG

5½" (14 cm) · 1½" (3.8 cm) · 2" (5 cm) · 1½" (3.8 cm) · 3½" (9 cm) · 2½" (6.5 cm) · 2½" (6.5 cm) · 2½" (6.5 cm) · 1½" (3.8 cm) · 1½" (3.8 cm) · 2½" (6.5 cm) · 1½" (3.8 cm) · 2" (5 cm) · 2" (5 cm) · 3½" (9 cm) · 6½" (16.5 cm)

17

BG | C | D | F | A | F | A | D | C | D | G | D | B | D | E | BG

5" (12.5 cm) · 2½" (6.5 cm) · 2" (5 cm) · 1½" (3.8 cm) · 2½" (6.5 cm) · 2" (5 cm) · 2" (5 cm) · 2" (5 cm) · 1½" (3.8 cm) · 2" (5 cm) · 1½" (3.8 cm) · 2½" (6.5 cm) · 1½" (3.8 cm) · 3" (7.5 cm) · 3½" (9 cm) · 8½" (21.5 cm)

18

BG | C | D | F | A | F | A | D | C | D | G | D | E | BG

5½" (14 cm) · 2½" (6.5 cm) · 2½" (6.5 cm) · 1½" (3.8 cm) · 1½" (3.8 cm) · 1½" (3.8 cm) · 1½" (3.8 cm) · 2" (5 cm) · 2" (5 cm) · 3" (7.5 cm) · 2" (5 cm) · 4½" (11.5 cm) · 3½" (9 cm) · 9" (23.5 cm)

19

BG | C | D | F | A | F | D | C | D | E | G | D | E | BG

4½" (11.5 cm) · 1½" (3.8 cm) · 3" (7.5 cm) · 2½" (6.5 cm) · 1½" (3.8 cm) · 1½" (3.8 cm) · 2" (5 cm) · 2" (5 cm) · 4½" (11.5 cm) · 1½" (3.8 cm) · 1½" (3.8 cm) · 2½" (6.5 cm) · 3½" (9 cm) · 10½" (26.5 cm)

20

BG | C | D | F | A | F | A | D | C | D | E | G | E | BG

3" (7.5 cm) · 1½" (3.8 cm) · 2½" (6.5 cm) · 2" (5 cm) · 2" (5 cm) · 2" (5 cm) · 1½" (3.8 cm) · 2" (5 cm) · 1½" (3.8 cm) · 3½" (9 cm) · 3" (7.5 cm) · 1½" (3.8 cm) · 3½" (9 cm) · 13" (33 cm)

21

BG | C | D | F | A | F | A | D | C | D | E | G | E | BG

2½" (6.5 cm) · 1½" (3.8 cm) · 2½" (6.5 cm) · 2" (5 cm) · 1½" (3.8 cm) · 1½" (3.8 cm) · 1½" (3.8 cm) · 1½" (3.8 cm) · 2½" (6.5 cm) · 5" (12.5 cm) · 2" (5 cm) · 2½" (6.5 cm) · 2" (5 cm) · 14" (35.5 cm)

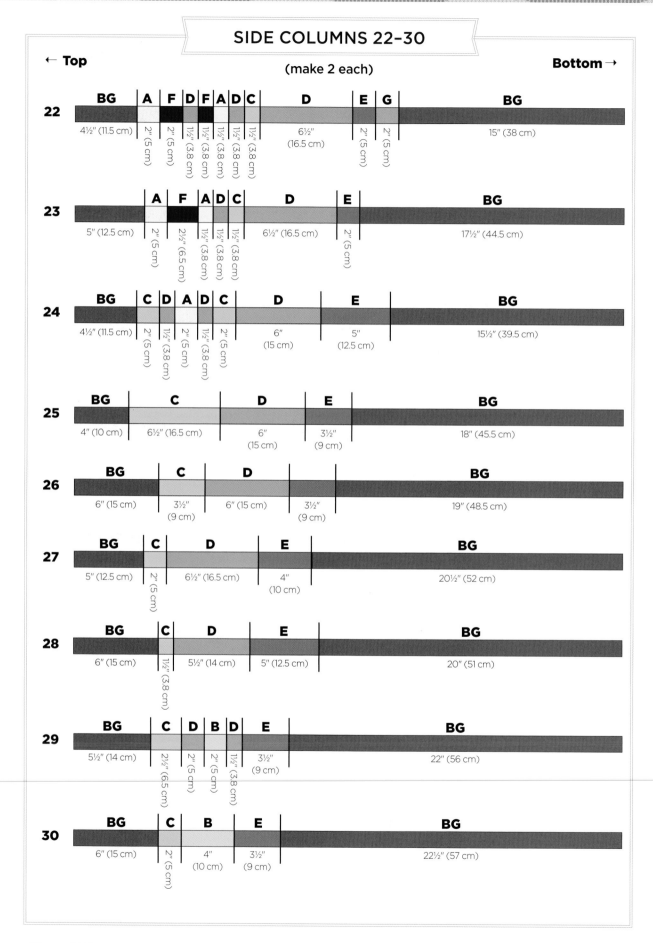

← **Top**

(make 2 each)

Bottom →

22

BG	A	F	D	F	A	D	C	D		E	G	BG

4½" (11.5 cm) | 2" (5 cm) | 2" (5 cm) | 1½" (3.8 cm) | 1½" (3.8 cm) | 1½" (3.8 cm) | 1½" (3.8 cm) | 1½" (3.8 cm) | 6½" (16.5 cm) | 2" (5 cm) | 2" (5 cm) | 15" (38 cm)

23

A	F	A	D	C	D		E	BG

5" (12.5 cm) | 2" (5 cm) | 2½" (6.5 cm) | 1½" (3.8 cm) | 1½" (3.8 cm) | 1½" (3.8 cm) | 6½" (16.5 cm) | 2" (5 cm) | 17½" (44.5 cm)

24

BG	C	D	A	D	C	D		E		BG

4½" (11.5 cm) | 2" (5 cm) | 1½" (3.8 cm) | 2" (5 cm) | 1½" (3.8 cm) | 2" (5 cm) | 6" (15 cm) | 5" (12.5 cm) | 15½" (39.5 cm)

25

BG	C	D	E		BG

4" (10 cm) | 6½" (16.5 cm) | 6" (15 cm) | 3½" (9 cm) | 18" (45.5 cm)

26

BG	C	D		BG

6" (15 cm) | 3½" (9 cm) | 6" (15 cm) | 3½" (9 cm) | 19" (48.5 cm)

27

BG	C	D	E		BG

5" (12.5 cm) | 2" (5 cm) | 6½" (16.5 cm) | 4" (10 cm) | 20½" (52 cm)

28

BG	C	D	E		BG

6" (15 cm) | 1½" (3.8 cm) | 5½" (14 cm) | 5" (12.5 cm) | 20" (51 cm)

29

BG	C	D	B	D	E		BG

5½" (14 cm) | 2½" (6.5 cm) | 2" (5 cm) | 2" (5 cm) | 1½" (3.8 cm) | 3½" (9 cm) | 22" (56 cm)

30

BG	C	B	E		BG

6" (15 cm) | 2" (5 cm) | 4" (10 cm) | 3½" (9 cm) | 22½" (57 cm)

← **Top**

(make 2 each)

Bottom →

31

| BG | C | B | H | B | E | BG |

6½" (16.5 cm) — 2" (5 cm) — 2½" (6.5 cm) — 1½" (3.8 cm) — 2" (5 cm) — 1½" (3.8 cm) — 23" (58.5 cm)

32

| BG | C | B | H | B | E | BG |

6" (15 cm) — 3" (7.5 cm) — 1½" (3.8 cm) — 3" (7.5 cm) — 1½" (3.8 cm) — 2" (5 cm) — 22" (56 cm)

33

| BG | C | B | H | B | E | BG |

7" (18 cm) — 1½" (3.8 cm) — 1½" (3.8 cm) — 3" (7.5 cm) — 1½" (3.8 cm) — 1½" (3.8 cm) — 23" (58.5 cm)

34

| BG | C | B | H | B | E | BG |

7½" (19.5 cm) — 1½" (3.8 cm) — 2" (5 cm) — 1½" (3.8 cm) — 2½" (6.5 cm) — 1½" (3.8 cm) — 22½" (57 cm)

35

| BG | C | B | H | B | E | BG |

8" (20.5 cm) — 1½" (3.8 cm) — 2" (5 cm) — 1½" (3.8 cm) — 1½" (3.8 cm) — 2½" (6.5 cm) — 22" (56 cm)

36

| BG | C | B | E | BG |

9" (23 cm) — 1½" (3.8 cm) — 3½" (9 cm) — 5" (12.5 cm) — 19" (48.5 cm)

37

| BG | B | E | BG |

10½" (26.5 cm) — 2½" (6.5 cm) — 2½" (6.5 cm) — 22" (56 cm)

38

| BG | B | E | BG |

11½" (29 cm) — 2" (5 cm) — 1½" (3.8 cm) — 22½" (57 cm)

IKAT MOTH CENTER ASSEMBLY DIAGRAM

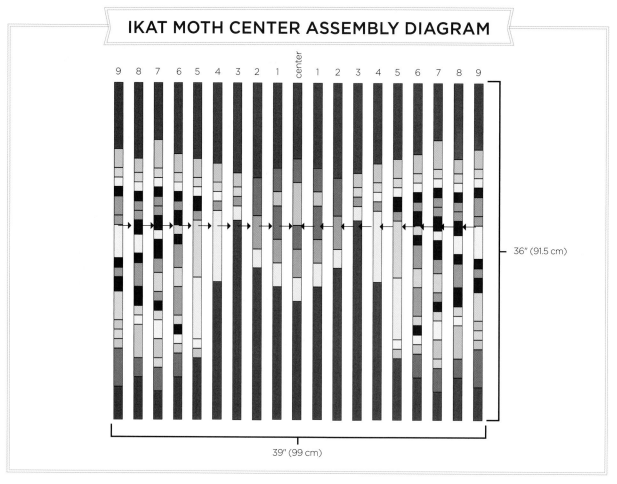

9 8 7 6 5 4 3 2 1 center 1 2 3 4 5 6 7 8 9

36" (91.5 cm)

39" (99 cm)

IKAT MOTH ASSEMBLY DIAGRAM

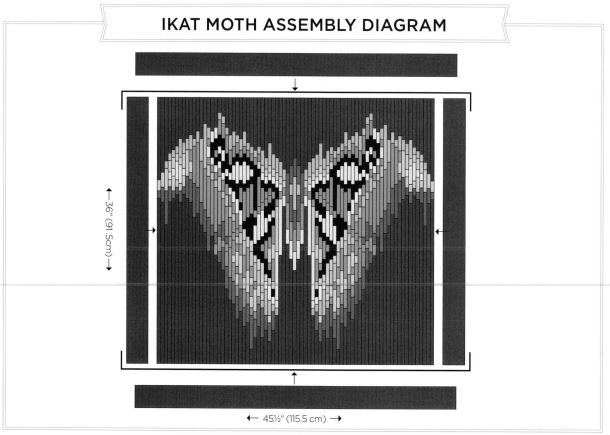

36" (91.5cm)

45½" (115.5 cm)

QUILTING ORGANIC SHAPES

When Tula showed this quilt to me, I was instantly wowed and scared at the same time. It's a stunning quilt, so I wanted the quilting to really show off the beauty and intricacy of this pattern.

I envisioned swirly flowers gently moving down the quilt, behind the moth. Then, I decided to add leaves to either side of the flowers as well as the swirl scroll filler with pebbles. When planning your quilting layout, try drawing a few lines, then quilt in the spaces. Try several different fillers or maybe just use your two favorite designs. Remember, it doesn't have to be perfect!

Before tackling any quilt, take a moment and think about how you want the quilting to flow across the quilt. You don't need a hardcore plan, just a general idea. It's always good to have an idea where you are going before you get started. Before quilting the background, instead of just winging it (pun intended), I took a moment and marked a guideline. This line helped ensure that the designs ended up about where I wanted them to without having to overplay the quilting.

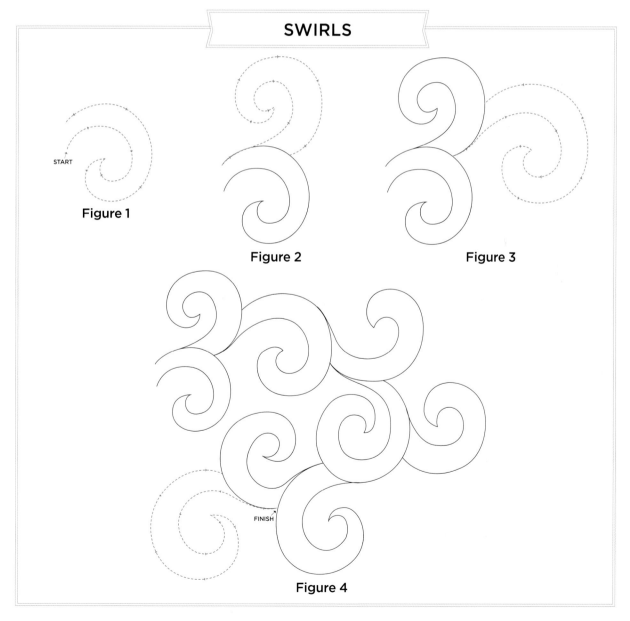

SWIRLS

START

Figure 1

Figure 2

Figure 3

FINISH

Figure 4

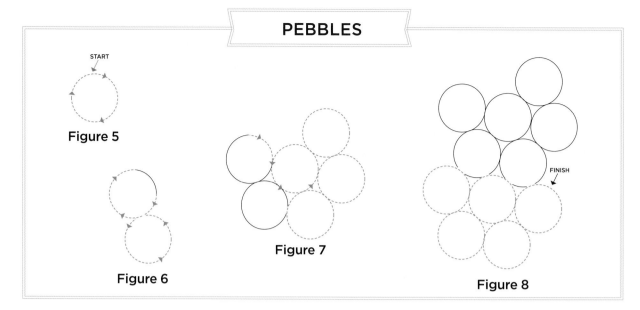

PEBBLES

Figure 5

Figure 6

Figure 7

Figure 8

SWIRLS

The best thing about swirls is they can be quilted in so many different ways, all equally beautiful. For this quilt, however, I opted for a swirl that resembles scrolls. The result is an elegant design that highlights and frames the moth, really making it shine.

1. Starting at any point on the background of the quilt, stitch a swirl and echo back, leaving ½" (1.3 cm) between the lines (**Figure 1**, page 41).

Note: Leaving at least ½" (1.3 cm) between lines will make the scrolls pop out from the rest of the quilting when you start quilting the pebbles. If you want less dense quilting, you can make the spacing between the lines larger. The more swirls you stitch, the fewer pebbles you will quilt in between.

2. Travel along the line you just quilted 1" (2.5 cm), then quilt the next swirl so that it faces the opposite direction of the first one. Echo around the outside until you run into the first swirl (**Figure 2**, page 41).

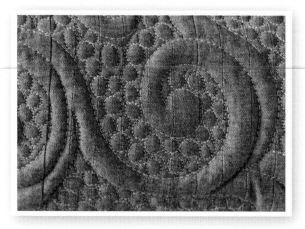

3. Repeat to quilt another swirl, facing away from the second swirl you quilted (**Figure 3**, page 41).

4. Continue quilting swirls so that they all appear connected and that they meander around the moth (**Figure 4**, page 41).

PEBBLES

I have a love/hate relationship with pebbles. I love how they look on a quilt, but I hate how tedious they can be to quilt. I love using them around other designs because I don't have to quilt as many of them. Even though I squeezed them between the swirl scrolls, they look amazing all by themselves.

1. Start by quilting a ½" (1.3 cm) or larger circle (**Figure 5**).

2. Quilt the next circle so that it goes in the opposite direction, almost like a figure eight, so that the pebbles touch each other (**Figure 6**).

3. If needed, travel along the circle until you have room to quilt the next pebble. Change direction as you quilt the circles (clockwise or counter clockwise) to make them fill in the space consistently (**Figure 7**).

4. Continue stitching, adding pebbles and filling in the area as consistently as possible (**Figure 8**).

FLOWERS

This flower design is beginner-friendly, making it perfect for your quilt, no matter your skill level. It's great as an allover design or as a motif inside blocks.

1. Start by quilting a small swirl, leaving a ½" (1.3 cm) space between the lines **(Figure 9)**.

2. Quilt a line that arcs away from and back to the swirl, creating a petal shape. Make it as small or as large as you like, depending on how dense you want the quilting **(Figure 10)**.

3. Continue quilting petals around the outside of the swirl **(Figure 11)**.

4. Begin quilting the next row, stitching a line that extends past the first row of petals. Quilt the arc shapes around the previously quilted row, keeping the arc shapes consistent in size so that they don't always touch a petal in the row below **(Figure 12)**.

5. Start the next flower, quilting a partial row of petals. Quilt another small swirl, then stitch rows of petals around the swirl **(Figure 13)**.

6. Continue quilting flowers until you have filled in the area completely **(Figure 14)**.

A combination of organic and geometric designs give life to the Ikat Moth quilt.

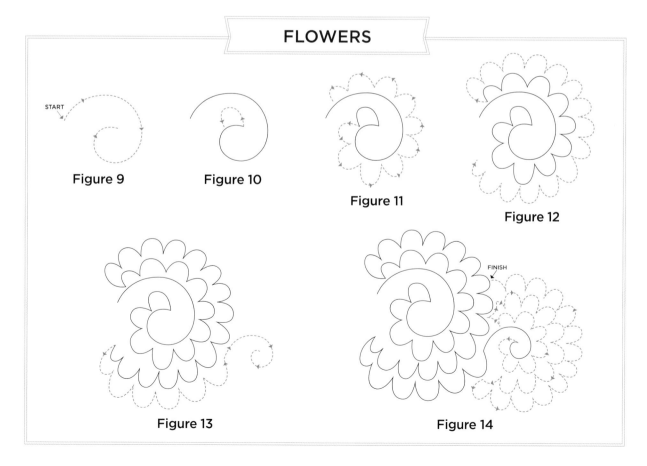

FLOWERS

Figure 9

Figure 10

Figure 11

Figure 12

Figure 13

Figure 14

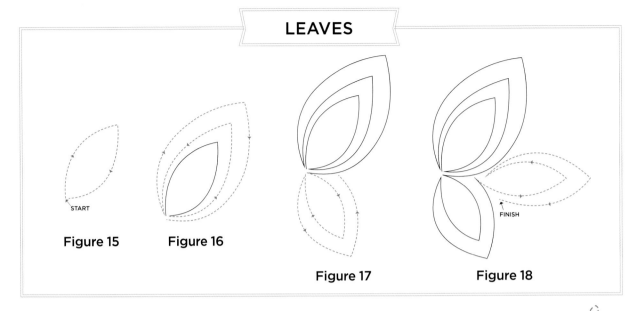

LEAVES

START

Figure 15   Figure 16   Figure 17   Figure 18

FINISH

LEAVES

What are flowers without leaves? A leafy meander is the perfect complement to the flower quilting design.

1. Quilt a line that arcs out to a point and back **(Figure 15)**.

2. Echo stitch around the outside of the leaf twice, returning to the starting point **(Figure 16)**.

3. To start the next leaf, repeat Step 1, quilting the shape so that it points away from the first leaf **(Figure 17)**.

4. Continue quilting the leaf shapes and echo stitching around them to fill in the area completely **(Figure 18)**.

QUILTING INSIDE THE MOTH

The piecing is so tiny and intricate, I wanted to make sure that the quilting wouldn't overwhelm or distract from the quilt. So instead of quilting all of the pieces separately, I quilted each part of the wing as one solid piece, including a few curvy echo lines that rounded out the outer edge of the moth and helped it stand out from the filler.

For the upper wings, I used a smaller version of the swirl scroll background filler. I love how it adds so much texture to the quilt. Follow the directions above, simply scaling it down a little.

I switched things up a bit in the bottom part of the moth. In contrast to the dense quilting of the upper wings, I used wavy lines to mimic the look of an actual moth. It was a quick change of pace from the swirls

TIP!

• Don't worry about making each of the left-to-right arcs the same size. In fact, I think it looks better if they are a little asymmetrical.

• Make the arcs closer together or farther apart depending on how dense you want the quilting to be.

• Move in a fluid motion. Even if the arcs aren't perfect, they will look better if the curve is smooth. So aim for curvy, not perfect, arcs.

When quilting these drippy feathers, it's important to not overthink the quilting too much. Just relax and go for it!

You could also use this design over the whole moth as well, especially if you don't have the time or patience for all the pebbles.

DRIPPY FEATHERS

1. Start with the left wing. From the center of the moth, quilt a wavy line 1" (2.5 cm) from the edge of the wing toward the bottom side. Curve around before you reach the bottom of the wing, then quilt another wavy line back to the starting point **(Figure 19)**.

Note: The lines should be farther apart toward the edge of the wing and closer together toward the center of the moth.

2. Repeat quilting wavy lines that are 1" (2.5 cm) apart until you run out of space. Maintain similar spacing

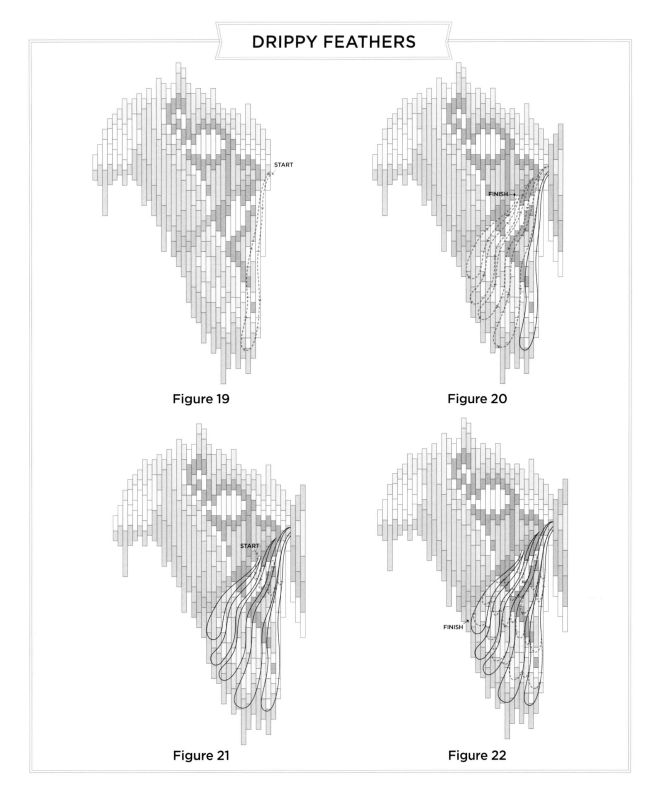

DRIPPY FEATHERS

Figure 19

Figure 20

Figure 21

Figure 22

in each elongated oval shape at the top and at the bottom **(Figure 20)**.

3. Once the lower wing is filled, travel down the last wavy line 1" (2.5 cm) or so and quilt arcs from left to right between each of the wavy lines. Quilt the arcs as shallow or as deep as you like. Continue until you get to the first wavy line **(Figure 21)**.

4. Travel down the edge of your last wavy line another 1" (2.5 cm) or so and repeat, quilting arcs from right to left between the wavy lines **(Figure 22)**.

5. Continue until the lower wing is completely quilted.

6. Repeat to quilt the right lower wing of the moth.

YELLOW

Lovely, laid back, luminous Yellow. Yellow is bright and happy, and she absolutely never has a bad thing to say about anyone. Yellow loves babies and animals, so baby animals just send her right over the edge, overflowing with pure delight. She really does fill a room with sunshine. Yellow will happily sit between Orange and Green, letting her mellow shine make them feel better about being neither first nor last. She would never, ever bring up the fact that it is she, our dear yellow, that makes both of them possible.

--------- YELLOW QUILT TECHNIQUES ---------

Sewing Strips

Strip sewing is one of the easiest ways of piecing there is. The strength of a simple stripe is one that has endured for centuries. By making a series of strip sets the same width and then cutting across the strips to create blocks, you can achieve a variety of different combinations of color and pattern without hardly thinking at all. This is a quilt top that is truly about the combination of fabric and color converging into a field of texture.

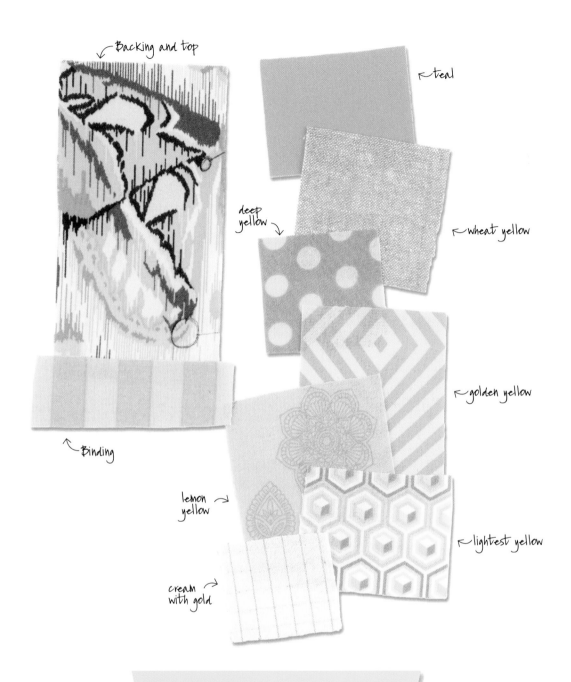

Backing and top

teal

deep yellow

wheat yellow

golden yellow

lemon yellow

lightest yellow

cream with gold

Binding

CHOOSING FABRICS

The first fabric that I pulled for this chapter is hardly yellow at all. This may seem like a strange choice, but allow me to explain. The yellow in the mostly teal "Atlas Moth" print fabric energizes the design. The yellow may be minimal, but it makes this fabric vibrant and gives it movement. This fabric is the star, but only because the supporting cast—tonals and solids—highlights its best qualities.

I knew that an entirely yellow quilt could feel washed out really quickly. Using the "Atlas Moth" print and a solid teal fabric for contrast, I was free to pull from a variety of yellows without concern because I had a little something to break them up.

I began with a dark wheat yellow and chose a yarn-dyed fabric that looks like linen for texture. I worked my way through true yellow, golden yellow, orange-yellow, and lemon yellow all the way to a creamy white with a touch of metallic gold woven in. The subtle supporting prints, the woven texture, the pop of teal, and the metallic woven gold each add a layer of depth and a little luxe to an otherwise easygoing quilt.

WOVEN SUNSHINE

Finished quilt size: 72"×72"
(183 × 183 cm)

Finished block size: 6"×12"
(50 × 30.5 cm)

Fabrics
¾ yd (68.5 cm) each of 8 yellow
and teal print and solid fabrics

**Backing, Batting
& Binding**
4½ yd (4 m) of 40"/42" (102/107 cm)
wide fabric or 2¼ yd (2 m) of 108"
(274 cm) wide backing fabric

⅝ yd (57 cm) of fabric to make 298"
(757 cm) of bias binding

80" × 80" (203 × 203 cm) of batting

CUT THE FABRICS

1. From each of the 8 yellow fabrics, cut:
    » One 4½" (11.5 cm) × WOF (width of fabric) strip
    » One 3½" (9 cm) × WOF strip
    » One 5½" (14 cm) × WOF strip
    » Two 2½" (6.5 cm) × WOF strips
    » Two 1½" (3.8 cm) × WOF strips

ASSEMBLE THE STRIP SETS

Notes: Sew all strips right sides together. Add each new strp to the strip set in the order stated below. Each strip sets measures 12½" (31.5 cm) × WOF.

When sewing multiple long strips together, remember to alternate the direction of sewing. Sew the first two strips together from the left to the right, then add the third strip by sewing from the right to the left. When fabric is run through a sewing machine, the fabrics will shift slightly,

TIP!

Because you are using one of each strip block in each row, it is very unlikely that two of the same fabrics, cut the same exact size, will end up next to each other. Don't bother laying out the entire quilt before sewing. You can lay out each row one at a time and still get a varied effect of color and texture without a lot of overlap.

so alternating the sewing direction will keep the fabrics from shifting too far in one direction.

2. Make a total of 12 strip sets in these combinations:

STRIP SET A

Select 3 WOF strips in these widths:

» $5\frac{1}{2}$" + $2\frac{1}{2}$" + $5\frac{1}{2}$" (14 cm + 6.5 cm + 14 cm)

STRIP SET B

Select 6 WOF strips in these widths:

» $2\frac{1}{2}$" + $2\frac{1}{2}$" + $2\frac{1}{2}$" + $2\frac{1}{2}$" + $2\frac{1}{2}$" + $2\frac{1}{2}$" (6.5 cm + 6.5 cm + 6.5 cm + 6.5 cm + 6.5 cm + 6.5 cm)

STRIP SET C

Select 5 WOF strips in these widths:

» $2\frac{1}{2}$" + $2\frac{1}{2}$" + $2\frac{1}{2}$" + $2\frac{1}{2}$" + $4\frac{1}{2}$" (6.5 cm + 6.5 cm + 6.5 cm + 6.5 cm + 11.5 cm)

STRIP SET D

Select 7 WOF strips in these widths:

» $2\frac{1}{2}$" + $4\frac{1}{2}$" + $1\frac{1}{2}$" + $1\frac{1}{2}$" + $2\frac{1}{2}$" + $1\frac{1}{2}$" + $1\frac{1}{2}$" (6.5 cm + 11.5 cm + 3.8 cm + 3.8 cm + 6.5 cm + 3.8 cm + 3.8 cm)

STRIP SET E

Select 4 WOF strips in these widths:

» $4\frac{1}{2}$" + $2\frac{1}{2}$" + $2\frac{1}{2}$" + $4\frac{1}{2}$" (11.5 cm + 6.5 cm + 6.5 cm + 11.5 cm)

STRIP SET F

Select 3 WOF strips in these widths:

» $3\frac{1}{2}$" + $4\frac{1}{2}$" + $5\frac{1}{2}$" (9 cm + 11.5 cm + 14 cm)

STRIP SET G

Select 5 WOF strips in these widths:

» $1\frac{1}{2}$" + $1\frac{1}{2}$" + $1\frac{1}{2}$" + $5\frac{1}{2}$" + $4\frac{1}{2}$" (3.8 cm + 3.8 cm + 3.8 cm + 14 cm + 11.5 cm)

STRIP SET H

Select 5 WOF strips in these widths:

» $3\frac{1}{2}$" + $1\frac{1}{2}$" + $1\frac{1}{2}$" + $3\frac{1}{2}$" + $4\frac{1}{2}$" (9 cm + 3.8 cm + 3.8 cm + 9 cm + 11.5 cm)

STRIP SET I

Select 3 WOF strips in these widths:

» $3\frac{1}{2}$" + $4\frac{1}{2}$" + $5\frac{1}{2}$" (9 cm + 11.5 cm + 14 cm)

STRIP SET J

Select 3 WOF strips in these widths:

» $2\frac{1}{2}$" + $5\frac{1}{2}$" + $5\frac{1}{2}$" (6.5 cm + 14 cm + 14 cm)

STRIP SET K

Select 6 WOF strips in these widths:

» $1\frac{1}{2}$" + $3\frac{1}{2}$" + $1\frac{1}{2}$" + $1\frac{1}{2}$" + $1\frac{1}{2}$" + $5\frac{1}{2}$" (3.8 cm + 9 cm + 3.8 cm + 3.8 cm + 3.8 cm + 14 cm)

STRIP SET L

Select 6 WOF strips in these widths:

» $1\frac{1}{2}$" + $1\frac{1}{2}$" + $1\frac{1}{2}$" + $3\frac{1}{2}$" + $3\frac{1}{2}$" + $3\frac{1}{2}$" (3.8 cm + 3.8 cm + 9 cm + 9 cm + 9 cm)

3. Using a clear quilter's ruler and a rotary cutter, trim away any selvedge and uneven edges to create a clean edge to measure from along one $12\frac{1}{2}$" (31.5 cm) side of Strip Set A **(Figure 1)**.

4. Sub cut Strip Set A, cutting across the seams, at $6\frac{1}{2}$" (16.5 cm) intervals to create six $6\frac{1}{2}$" × $12\frac{1}{2}$" (16.5 × 31.5 cm) strip blocks. Discard the remaining uneven edge **(Figure 2)**.

5. Repeat Steps 2 and 3 to sub cut the remaining strip sets, B–L, for a combined total of 72 strip blocks. Each strip block should measure $6\frac{1}{2}$" × $12\frac{1}{2}$" (16.5 × 31.5 cm).

6. Choose 1 strip block from each set, A–L. Sew the 12 strip blocks together to form a row. Each row should measure $12\frac{1}{2}$" × $72\frac{1}{2}$" (31.5 × 184 cm).

ASSEMBLE THE QUILT

7. Repeat Step 5 to make 6 rows of 12 blocks each, mixing up the arrangements for each row and turning some of them upside down.

8. Sew Rows 1–6 together along the $72\frac{1}{2}$" (184 cm) edge according to the Woven Sunshine Assembly Diagram on page 52.

PIECE THE BACKING

9. To make the backing from 40"/42" (102/107 cm) backing fabric, trim the selvedge. Cut the trimmed backing yardage in half to create two 80" (203 cm) × WOF pieces **(Figure 3)**.

10. Place the 2 backing pieces right sides together and sew along the 80" (203 cm) edge **(Figure 4)**. Backing should measure about 80" × 80" (203 × 203 cm).

FINISH THE QUILT

11. Follow the instructions for preparing the quilt top for quilting on page 10.

12. Follow the quilting instructions on page 53.

13. To complete the quilt, follow the bias binding instructions on page 183.

STRIP SETS A–L

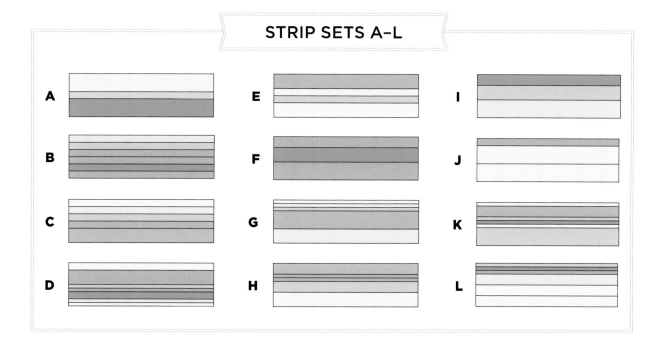

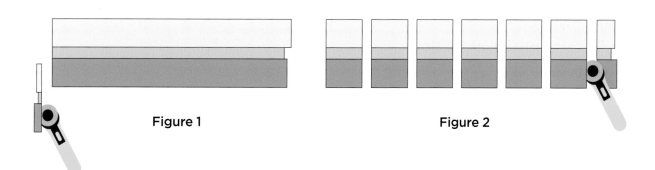

Figure 1

Figure 2

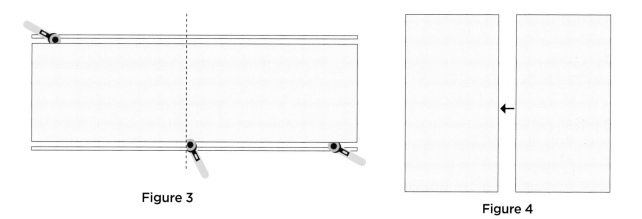

Figure 3

Figure 4

WOVEN SUNSHINE ASSEMBLY DIAGRAM

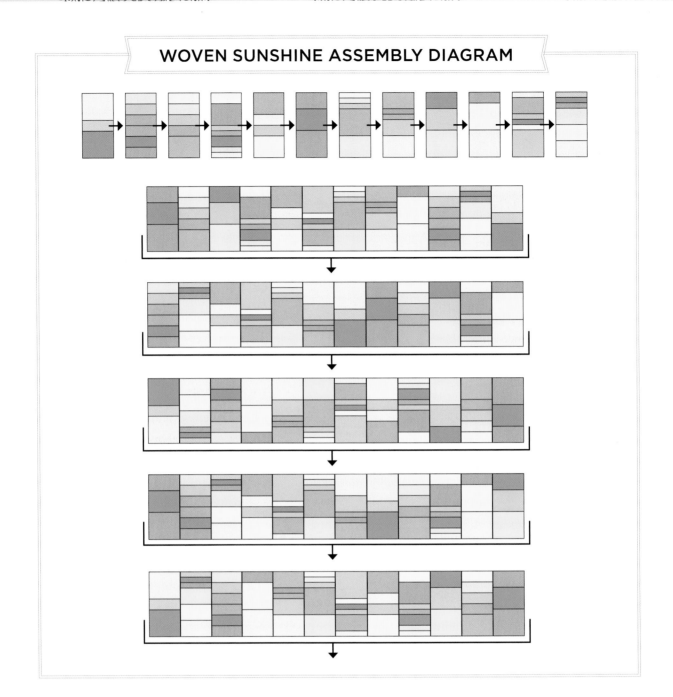

QUILTING WAVES

This quilt is all about the fabrics. The way the colors interact with each other gives this easy quilt pattern a stunning look. With so many beautiful colors and prints, quilting each block separately could take away from the overall effect of Woven Sunshine. So, instead, I opted for a wavy quilting design that adds texture to the quilt and highlights some of my favorite blocks. When quilting your Woven Sunshine quilt, try not to overthink the placement of your waves. This design is meant to be random, not overly structured.

Before we jump into the design, I want to mention a few things. First, this design goes from one edge of the quilt to the other. If you are quilting on a longarm quilting machine, it's easy enough to work from side to side in a horizontal motion. However, if you are quilting on a sewing machine, quilting this design in a vertical motion might be easier.

First, single out the blocks that you want to show off, then decide what to quilt inside. You could use a contrasting quilting design, such as boxy squares, use a contrasting thread color that draws the eye to that favorite block, or use minimal quilting in a few blocks, especially the small ones. To make some really stand out, you could skip quilting them altogether! Make sure you leave several blocks unquilted so that it looks intentional.

TIP!

You may notice that my stitches aren't all the same size. When quilting, I don't use a stitch regulator. I feel that I can get a more fluid line and quilt more quickly without using the regulator. I always encourage quilters to not worry too much about stitch length. Consistent stitches come with practice.

WAVY LINES

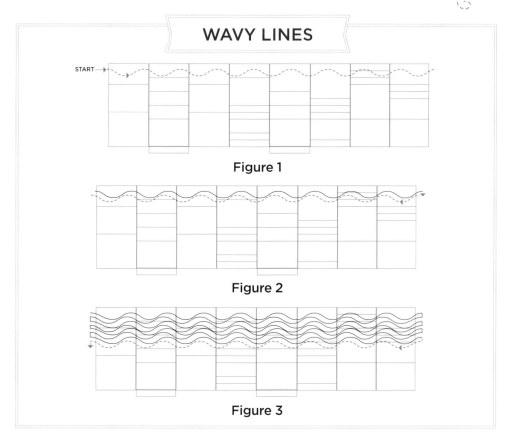

Figure 1

Figure 2

Figure 3

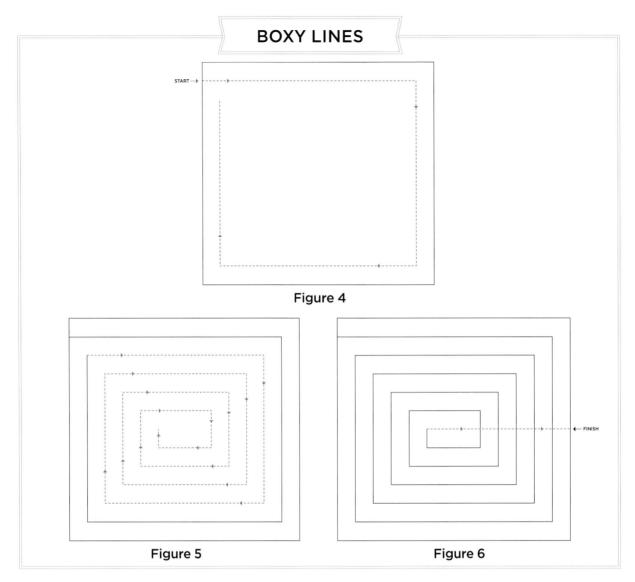

Figure 4

Figure 5

Figure 6

WAVY LINES

The wavy lines can actually pull double duty! This design adds great texture to the quilt and can be used to highlight random blocks. Simply quilt the wavy lines so that they run into the block, then travel along the edge and quilt the next wavy line This will give the illusion that the wavy lines are going behind the block.

1. Starting on the left edge of the quilt, stitch a wavy line from one side of the quilt to the other, staying within the width of the smallest rectangle piece. If you quilt a gently wavy line, the next step will be a little easier (**Figure 1**, page 53).

2. Travel down along the right edge of the quilt ½" (1.3 cm) and stitch another wavy line that runs into and then away from the first line. The waves will be slightly offset, giving this quilting design so much beautiful texture (**Figure 2**, page 53).

3. Continue quilting gently wavy lines until the entire quilt top is filled, traveling ½" (1.3 cm) along the sides of the quilt to start the next line (**Figure 3**, page 53).

BOXY LINES

1. Starting ¼" (6 mm) away from any point of the square, quilt a line that echoes the sides of the square. Stop ¼" (6 mm) away from the starting point (**Figure 4**).

2. Continue echoing inside the lines previously quilted until you reach the center of the block. Try to keep the spacing as consistent as possible (**Figure 5**).

3. Getting out of the block is as easy as crossing the lines. Quilt a line directly across the lines until you reach the edge. Continue quilting the wavy lines (**Figure 6**).

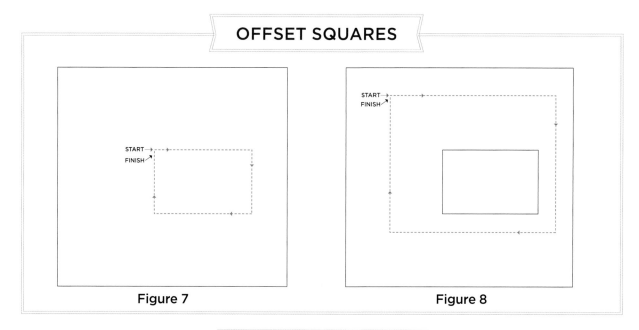

OFFSET SQUARES

Figure 7

Figure 8

PARALLEL LINES

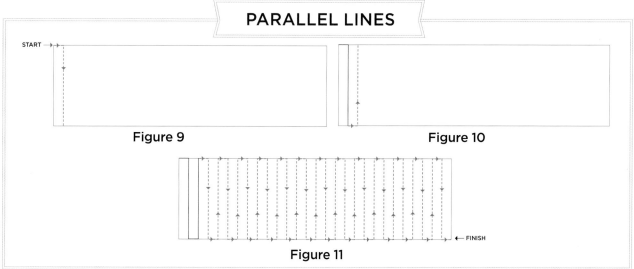

Figure 9

Figure 10

Figure 11

OFFSET SQUARES

These lines take a little longer to quilt because you start a new line of quilting for each one. The extra effort is well worth the fun offset look they give the block. Using a contrasting thread is especially effective for this basic design.

1. Quilt a square in the center of the block, taking care to not make it too centered. The more random the quilted squares look, the better **(Figure 7)**.

2. Tie off the line of quilting and quilt other box outside of the center one. Again, quilt it so that the center block isn't perfectly centered **(Figure 8)**.

PARALLEL LINES

Another easy option is to quilt vertical parallel lines in some of the blocks. Because they are going in the opposite direction of the wavy lines, they really help the blocks stand out.

1. Starting from the upper left corner of a block, travel along the top edge ½" (1.3 cm), then quilt a line vertically down to the bottom edge **(Figure 9)**.

2. Travel along the bottom edge of the block ½" (1.3 cm), then quilt a straight line to the top edge **(Figure 10)**.

3. Continue alternating between travelling lines and straight lines until you reach the right edge of the block **(Figure 11)**. Don't worry if the lines aren't perfectly spaced out—close enough is good enough!

warm

When Red, Orange, and Yellow get together, it's like a major volcanic explosion. They can, quite literally, set the place on fire. They stay out all night, rarely leaving the dance floor. Red typically ends up on stage at some point. Yellow mostly twirls until she gets dizzy, which takes a lot longer than you might think. Orange just gets lost in the music, eyes closed, hands in the air without a care in the world. Together they vibrate on a whole other frequency. Occasionally they invite Green, but usually just to pay the bill and make sure they all get home before curfew.

---------- WARM QUILT TECHNIQUES ----------

Sewing Tumbling Blocks

A tumbling block is a classic quilt block that uses light, medium, and dark values to create the three-dimensional look of a cube. Typically, this block is made with three diamonds and involves a somewhat complicated Y seam. Y seams are not particularly difficult to sew, but they do require a few extra steps to prepare and more careful stitching.

Instead, this pattern uses a different method of composing the block from two 60-degree diamonds and two 60-degree triangles to create the same effect. Without that tricky little Y seam, the tumbling blocks are assembled in columns.

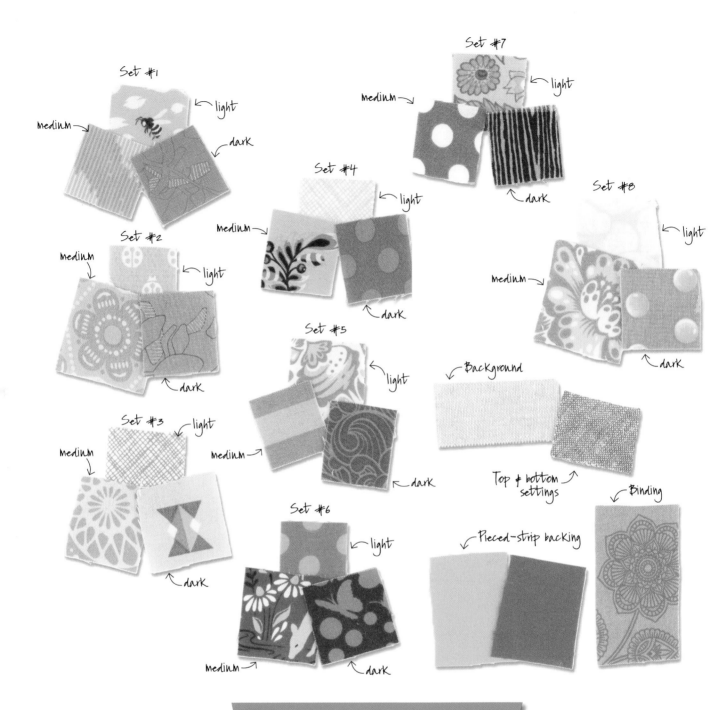

Set #1 — medium, light, dark
Set #2 — medium, light, dark
Set #3 — light, medium, dark
Set #4 — medium, light, dark
Set #5 — light, medium, dark
Set #6 — light, medium, dark
Set #7 — medium, light, dark
Set #8 — medium, light, dark
Background
Top & bottom settings
Binding
Pieced-strip backing

CHOOSING FABRICS

When choosing fabrics for a tumbling block pattern, always choose fabrics in sets of three: a light, a medium, and a dark. Select the medium-value fabric first; this will be the foundation of that block's color. The medium value bridges the dark and light values in the block. Then select a darker value and a lighter value of that color. When working with prints, try squinting your eyes to blur the details of the print, visually blending the colors to determine its value.

Choosing a background color that will play nicely with so many prints and colors is every quilter's dilemma. White or cream is an obvious choice—it's crisp and it creates an intense contrast to warm colors. Because red, orange, and yellow are already so strong, I chose to go with a pale blue chambray, or woven fabric, instead. It is a soft color with less contrast than the traditional white and also lends a bit of coolness to a warm color palette. It also adds an unexpected subtle texture in the background in place of a pure solid.

FUTURE FLOWER GARDEN

Finished quilt size: 85" × 95"
(216 × 241 cm)

Templates: Flower A, B, C

Fabrics

½ yd (45.5 cm) each of 8 light-value prints*

½ yd (45.5 cm) each of 8 medium-value prints*

½ yd (45.5 cm) each of 8 dark-value prints*

Choose a total of 24 prints divided into 8 different colored sets of three values.

2 yd (1.8 m) of light blue chambray

½ yd (45.5 cm) of medium blue chambray

Backing, Batting & Binding

8 yd (7.3 m) of 40"/42" (102/107 cm) wide backing fabric or 2⅞ yd (2.6 m) of 108" (274 cm) wide backing fabric

¾ yd (68.5 cm) of fabric to make 385" (978 cm) of 2½" (6.5 cm) bias binding

92" × 102" (234 × 259 cm) of batting

Notions

Template plastic

Erasable fabric-marking tool

TIP!

A 60-degree equilateral triangle ruler is a great alternative tool for this quilt in place of the Flower Template A.

CUT THE FABRICS

Note: The Future Flower quilt top is comprised of 18 full tumbling block flowers and four half-flowers. Four of the fabric trios make three flowers each, and the remaining four fabric trios make two flowers each. A "trio" refers to the set of three coordinating fabrics that make one tumbling block: 12 light triangles, 7 medium diamonds, and 7 dark diamonds. Cut one fabric trio at a time and keep the pieces together to avoid confusion.

1. Trace Flower Templates A, B, and C (pages 187–188) once each onto the template plastic, label each template, and cut them out on the drawn line. Use a ruler and rotary cutter to cut the straight edges and scissors to cut the curved edges.

2. From each of 4 light-value fabrics, cut four 4" (10 cm) × WOF (width of fabric) strips.

   Using Template A, sub cut each WOF strip into 12 triangles, making 42 triangles of each color (**Figure 1**, page 60). Cut a total of 168 triangles.

3. From each of the 4 corresponding medium-value fabrics, cut three 4" (10 cm) × WOF strips.

Using the reverse side of Template B, sub cut each WOF strip into 7 diamonds to make 21 diamonds of each color **(Figure 2)**. Cut a total of 84 diamonds.

4. From each of the 4 corresponding dark-value fabrics, cut three 4" (10 cm) × WOF strips.

    Using Template B, sub cut each strip into 7 diamonds to make 21 diamonds of each of color **(Figure 3)**. Cut a total of 84 diamonds.

5. From each of the 4 remaining light-value fabrics, cut three 4" (10 cm) × WOF strips.

    Using Template A, sub cut each strip into 12 triangles to make 36 triangles of each color, alternating the direction of the template across the strip (see **Figure 1**). Cut a total of 144 triangles.

6. From each of the 4 remaining medium-value fabrics, cut two 4" (10 cm) × WOF strips.

    Using the reverse side of Template B, sub cut each strip into 7 diamonds to make 14 diamonds of each color (see **Figure 2**). Cut a total of 56 diamonds.

7. From each of the 4 remaining dark-value fabrics, cut two 4" (10 cm) × WOF strips.

    Using Template B, sub cut each strip into 7 diamonds to make 14 diamonds of each color (see **Figure 3**). Cut a total of 56 diamonds.

8. From the light blue fabric, cut sixteen 4" (10 cm) × WOF strips.

    Using Template C, sub cut each of the 16 WOF strips into 5 trapezoids to make 80 trapezoids for

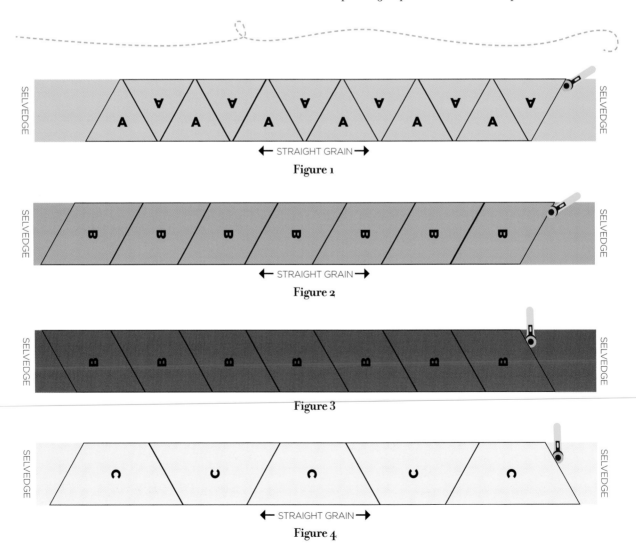

Figure 1

Figure 2

Figure 3

Figure 4

the background, alternating the direction of the template across the strip (**Figure 4**).

9. From the medium blue fabric, cut four 4" (10 cm) × WOF strips.

   Using Template A, sub cut each strip into 12 triangles to make 48 top and bottom setting triangles, alternating the direction of the template across the strip (see **Figure 1**).

SEW THE FLOWER COLUMNS

Note: The Future Flower Garden quilt top is assembled in columns to avoid Y seams. Each flower is made up of a center tumbling block surrounded by 6 tumbling block petals. Sew each flower at a time into columns. The fabrics that make the petals of one flower will be used as the center of another flower.

10. Choose fabrics for 1 flower. For the 6 flower petals of one coordinating color set, choose 12 light-value triangles, 6 medium-value diamonds, and 6 dark-value diamonds.

    For the first flower's center, choose a contrasting (but coordinating) trio of 2 light-value triangles, 1 medium-value diamond, and 1 dark-value diamond.

11. Following **Figure 5**, place 1 light-value triangle at the top edge of 1 medium-value diamond, right sides together, and sew. Place a second light-value triangle on a dark-value diamond, right sides together, and sew.

12. Repeat Step 10 until 7 light-value triangles have been sewn to all 7 medium-value diamonds in the color set and 7 more light-value triangles have been sewn to all 7 dark-value diamonds.

13. Assemble the flower into six columns (**Figure 6**, page 62). Keep the finished flower columns together, including the individual sewn units in Columns 1 and 6, until you assemble the quilt top.

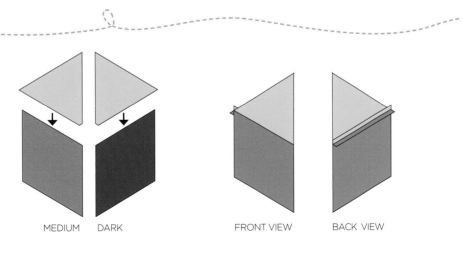

MEDIUM DARK

FRONT VIEW BACK VIEW

Figure 5

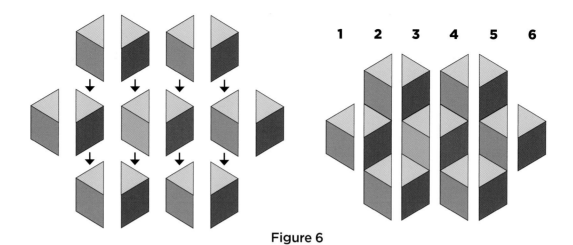

Figure 6

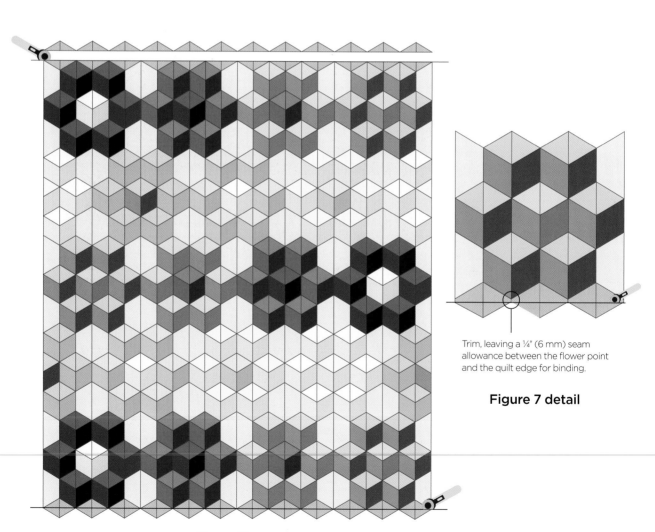

Trim, leaving a ¼" (6 mm) seam allowance between the flower point and the quilt edge for binding.

Figure 7 detail

Figure 7

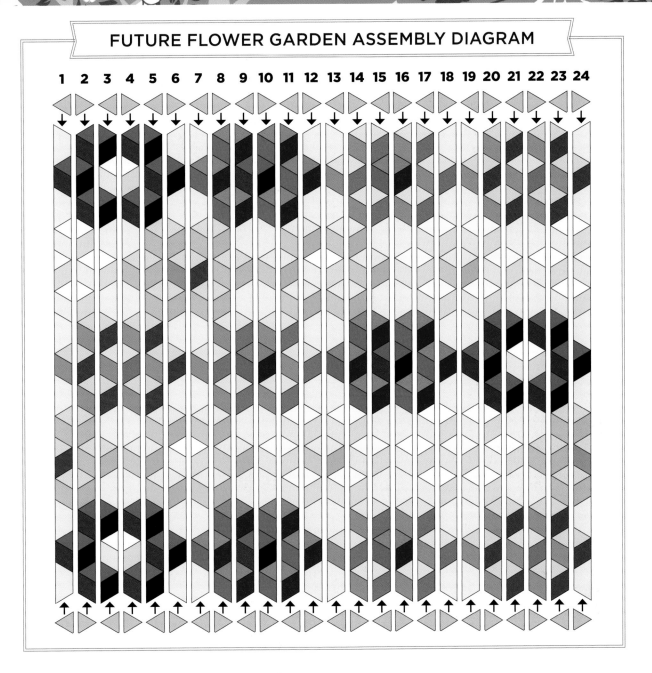

FUTURE FLOWER GARDEN ASSEMBLY DIAGRAM

1 2 3 4 5 6 7 8 9 10 11 12 13 14 15 16 17 18 19 20 21 22 23 24

Complete the Flower Columns

14. Repeat Steps 1–4 to complete 19 more flower sets, each one a different coordinated color combination.

15. Lay out the flower columns and the background trapezoids according to the Future Flower Garden Assembly Diagram to complete the 24 columns. Sew 1 medium blue setting triangle to the top of each column and 1 setting triangle to the bottom.

See *Tips for Sewing Triangles, Diamonds, and Trapezoids* (page 64) for more information on joining angled pieces.

ASSEMBLE THE QUILT TOP

16. Beginning at Column 1, sew each column to the next until all 24 columns are joined.

17. Using a rotary cutter and a ruler, carefully trim away the top and bottom points of the setting triangles, leaving a clean straight edge and a ¼" (6 mm) seam allowance beyond the flower points **(Figure 7)**.

PIECE THE BACKING

18. To make the quilt backing from 40"/42" (102 × 107 cm) backing fabric, trim the selvedges. Cut the trimmed backing yardage into 3 equal

TRIANGLE TO DIAMOND

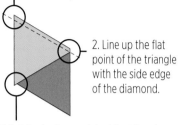

1. Line up the point of the triangle and the point of the diamond.

2. Line up the flat point of the triangle with the side edge of the diamond.

3. Let the bottom point of the triangle extend past the bottom edge of the diamond by the width of one seam allowance.

SETTING TRIANGLE TO BACKGROUND TRAPEZOID

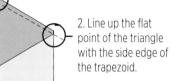

1. Line up the point of the triangle and the point of the trapezoid.

2. Line up the flat point of the triangle with the side edge of the trapezoid.

TRAPEZOID TO TRAPEZOID
(A half-tumbling block forms a trapezoid.)

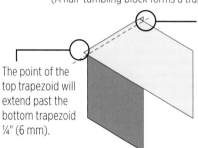

1. Stitch from one intersection directly through the other intersection of the two trapezoids.

The point of the top trapezoid will extend past the bottom trapezoid ¼" (6 mm).

The point of the bottom trapezoid will extend past the top trapezoid ¼" (6 mm).

---

pieces each measuring 96" (244 cm) WOF (**Figure 8**, page 64).

19. Place two backing pieces right sides together and sew along the 96" (244 cm) edge, then sew the third backing piece, right sides together, along the bottom edge (**Figure 9**).

Backing should measure about 96" × 123" (244 × 312 cm).

FINISH THE QUILT

20. Follow the instructions for preparing the quilt top for quilting on page 10.

21. Follow the quilting instructions on page 65.

22. To complete the quilt, follow the bias binding instructions on page 183.

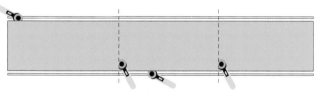

Figure 8

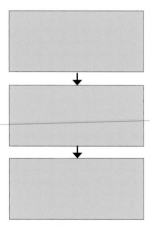

Figure 9

QUILTING 3D SHAPES

If the tumbling block is all about color placement, Tula certainly nailed it with this quilt. Combining tumbling blocks to make a larger flower-shaped block really shows how versatile this 3D block is! For this quilt, I quilted a dot-to-dot design that uses the corners of the block as reference points. The result is quick and easy quilting that really enhances the quilt pattern.

In this quilt, the print blocks aren't the whole story. The quilting in the solid hexagon background blocks impacts the quilt as well. Use the quilting in these blocks to highlight, or frame, your favorite blocks. Try stitching geometric designs that point to the center of the block or frame a block with a quilting design.

DOT TO DOT

I love that this design starts and stops at the same point. That means you can get in, quilt the block, and return to the same point without stopping, then moving on to the next block. I also love how it combines curvy lines with straight lines to provide a top and bottom to the design, similar to the quilt block itself. It's pretty and efficient—talk about a win/win!

1. Pick a complete tumbling-block hexagon. Starting in the upper left corner, quilt a diagonal line to the bottom corner and back up to the right corner, opposite the starting point **(Figure 1)**.

2. Still on the right side of the hexagon, quilt a line that angles down, stopping ½" (1.3 cm) away from the bottom right corner. Angle left and down, stopping at the bottom corner **(Figure 2)**.

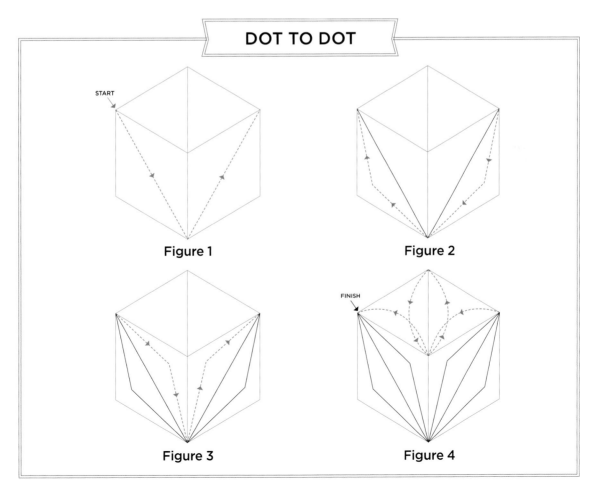

Figure 1

Figure 2

Figure 3

Figure 4

Repeat on the left side, mirroring the angled line.

3. Repeat Step 2 above the diagonal line, starting at the top left corner of the hexagon, angling toward the center point, and ending at the bottom point. Mirror that line on the right side (**Figure 3**, page 65).

4. Quilt the top diamond of the hexagon in continuously curved lines. Start at the top right corner, stitching a continuous line that curves down, up to the top corner and back down to the center, and then to the top left corner (**Figure 4**, page 65).

If you prefer quilting that is purely geometric, you can replace the curvy top with the same quilting as the sides.

FRAMED TRIANGLES

A framed triangle design is really easy to quilt. You can start from any point on a tumbling-block hexagon and stitch around the center, using it to focus attention on a favorite block. Or you could tweak the design to frame and highlight a particular block. Just quilt one side of the hexagon and alternate the direction so that it frames a single block.

1. Start at the top corner of the hexagon, stitch a straight, diagonal line to the bottom right corner, stitch straight across the hexagon to the bottom left corner, and then stitch a straight, diagonal line up to the starting point **(Figure 5)**.

Dot-to-dot quilting highlights the 3D shapes of a hexagon quilt.

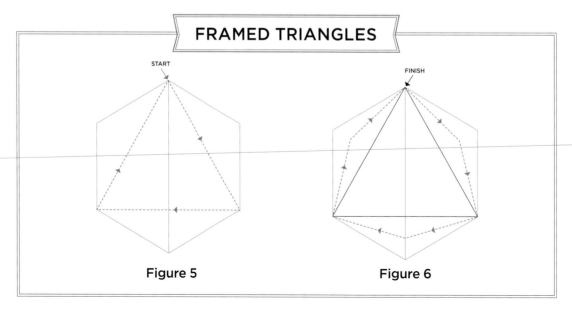

FRAMED TRIANGLES

START

FINISH

Figure 5

Figure 6

2. Starting again at the top corner of the hexagon, quilt a line that angles down to the right, stopping ½" (1.3 cm) away from the top right corner. Angle left and down, stopping at the bottom right corner **(Figure 6)**.

Stitch a line to the left, angling down midway between the straight quilting line above and the bottom corner of the hexagon, then angle back up to the bottom left corner.

Stitch an angled line on the left side of the hexagon that mirrors the first angled line in this step.

To give the blocks even more depth and interest, you can fill in the centers of them with a dense free-motion quilting design. You could quilt leaves (see page 44 for instructions), pebbles (page 42), or swirls (page 41), just as I did.

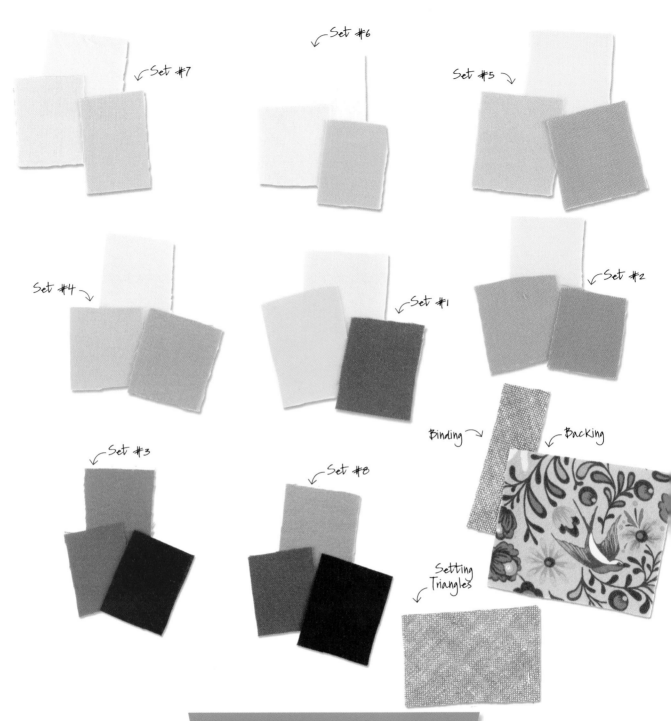

Set #7

Set #6

Set #5

Set #4

Set #1

Set #2

Binding

Backing

Set #3

Set #8

Setting
Triangles

CHOOSING FABRICS

I adore a tumbling block. It is both classic and modern all at the same time. In the Future Flower Garden quilt, I took an updated approach to a traditional layout. In The Tumbler quilt, I let the tumbling block stand on its own and used solid color to create a secondary design.

This hexagon quilt uses all solid fabrics to create a clever ombré effect fading from light to dark, to create a secondary design. The Tumbler uses 24 fabrics in eight sets of three related solid hues, ranging through all of the warm colors of the rainbow.

When I selected the medium-value solids, I began with a deep plum and worked my way through red to orange to yellow and finished just as the yellow was starting to turn to green.

THE
TUMBLER

Finished quilt size: 56" × 62"
(142 × 157.5 cm)

Templates: Flower A, B, C

Fabrics

⅓ yd (30 cm) each of 8 light-value solids*

¼ yd (23 cm) each of 8 medium-value solid*

¼ yd (23 cm) each of 8 dark-value solids*

½ yd (45.5 cm) of medium gray

Choose a total of 24 solids that are divided into 8 different-colored sets of three matching values.

Backing, Binding & Batting

4 yd (3.6 m) of 40"/42" (102/107 cm) wide backing fabric or

1¾ yd (160 cm) of 108" (274 cm) wide backing fabric

½ yd (45.5 cm) of fabric to make 250" (635 cm) of 2½" (6.5 cm) bias binding

64" × 70" (162.5 × 178 cm) of batting

Notions

Template plastic

Erasable fabric-marking tool

CUT THE FABRICS

Note: Each set of three matching colors has 40 pieces: 20 light triangles, 10 medium diamonds, and 10 dark diamonds.

1. Trace Flower Templates A and B (pages 187–188) once each onto the template plastic, label each template, and cut them out on the drawn line. Use a ruler and rotary cutter to cut the straight edges and scissors to cut the curved edges.

   From each of the 8 light-value fabrics, cut two 4" (6 mm) × WOF (width of fabric) strips. Cut a total of 16 strips.

   Using Template A, sub cut each (WOF) strip into 10 triangles to make a total of 20 triangles of each color, alternating the direction of the template across the strip (see **Figure 1**, page 60).

> ## Tip!
> Use large sandwich bags to keep each fabric trio of 40 pieces together until you are ready to sew.

2. From each of the 8 medium-value fabrics, cut two 4" (6 mm) × WOF strips. Cut a total of 16 strips.

   Using the reverse side of Template B, sub cut each WOF strip into 10 diamonds to make a total of 20 diamonds of each color (see **Figure 2**, page 60).

3. From each of the 8 dark-value fabrics, cut two 4" (6 mm) × WOF strips. Cut a total of 16 strips. Using Template B, sub cut each WOF strip into 10

diamonds to make a total of 20 diamonds of each color.

4. From the medium gray fabric, cut three 4" (6 mm) × WOF strips.

Using Template A, sub cut each WOF strip into 11 triangles to make a total of 32 triangles. Alternate the direction of the template across the strip.

SEW HALF-TUMBLING BLOCKS

5. Choose a fabric trio: 20 light-value triangles, 10 medium-value diamonds, and 10 dark-value diamonds.

With right sides together, sew 10 light-value triangles to the top edge of 10 medium-value diamonds (see **Figure 5**, page 61).

6. With right sides together, sew the 10 remaining light-value triangles to the top edge of 10 dark-value diamonds.

Set aside these 20 half-tumbling blocks, keeping the coordinating halves together.

7. Repeat Steps 1–3 to create the remaining 7 sets of half-tumbling blocks. Sew a total of 160 half-tumbling blocks.

8. Lay out the half-tumbling blocks in columns according to The Tumbler Assembly Diagram, then join each of the 16 columns individually (see **Figure 6**, page 62).

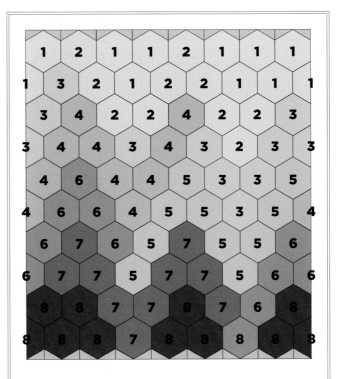

Tip!

The Tumbler quilt is built on the blending of colors, slowly changing from deep plum to light cream. Slight changes in color can make laying out the blocks confusing.

Keep the half-tumbling blocks in their coordinating sets and number each set. Follow this layout diagram to arrange the quilt top by block, then sew it together by column. The gray numbers represent single blocks that are split between the left and the right sides of the quilt.

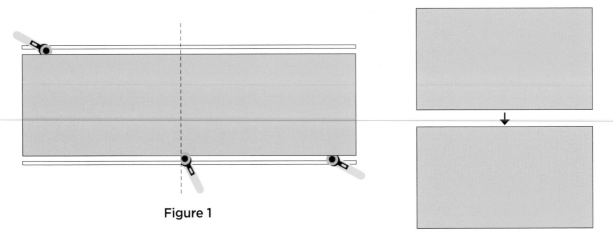

Figure 1

Figure 2

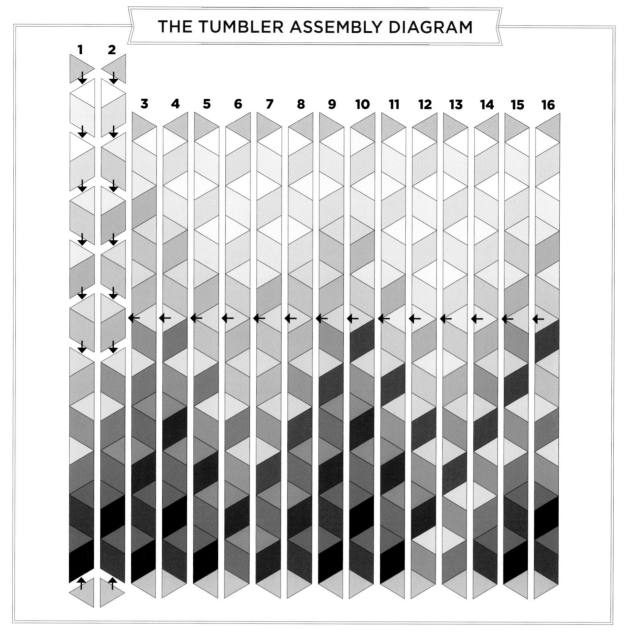

9. Sew 1 setting triangle to the top and 1 to the bottom of each column.

10. Beginning at Column 1, sew each column to the next until all 16 columns are joined.

11. Using a rotary cutter and a ruler, carefully trim away the top and bottom points of the setting triangles, leaving a clean straight edge and a ¼" (6 mm) seam allowance beyond the tumbling-block points.

PIECE THE BACKING

12. To make the backing, trim the selvedge off of the backing yardage. Cut the trimmed backing yardage in half to create two 72" (183 xm) × WOF pieces **(Figure 1)**.

13. Place the 2 backing pieces right sides together and sew along the 72" (183 cm) edge **(Figure 2)**.

Backing should measure about 72" × 84" (183 × 213 cm).

FINISH THE QUILT

14. Follow the instructions for preparing the quilt top for quilting on page 10.

15. Follow the quilting instructions on page 72.

16. To complete the quilt, follow the bias binding instructions on page 183.

QUILTING IN DIFFERENT DENSITIES

I love that the fabrics in The Tumbler show off the flow of color values in the pattern. Instead of focusing on a single block, I used the quilting to highlight specific colors, resulting in some interesting secondary patterns. Try combining parts of the blocks to make a secondary design with stitching, such as a star shape.

When quilting, you might consider the overall texture or highlight specific blocks. I quilted geometric designs in the darker red blocks, then switched to a wavy filler design in the rest of the quilt. This both switches up the texture of the quilting and makes the red blocks stand out.

DENSE LINES

To really show off the 3D look of the tumbling blocks, I quilted designs of straight lines of different densities within the blocks. When stitching this on your quilt, use the color placement of the fabric to determine where to put the designs. The densest design goes on the darkest fabric; least dense on the lighter fabric.

1. From one side of the darkest color in one block, quilt the densest back-and-forth line pattern that echoes the side of the block. Continue quilting until you reach the bottom corner of the block (**Figure 1**).

2. Travel up the middle seam of the block, between the darkest and the medium colors, ½" (1.3 cm). Echo quilt the bottom side of the block until you

TIP!

I like to quilt the back-and-forth lines ⅛" (3 mm) apart, but you could quilt them farther apart if you would like. To keep the overall effect, increase the spacing between the lines on the rest of the designs.

DENSE LINES

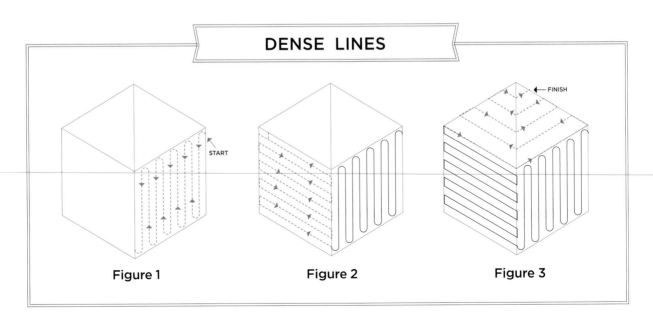

Figure 1　　　　Figure 2　　　　Figure 3

3 TIPS FOR QUILTING TUMBLING BLOCKS

The tumbling block has to be one of the most striking quilt blocks to work with. Three small diamond shapes result in a block that pops off the quilt with a 3D illusion. The block can take different forms and layouts, but no matter the differences, you can find a perfect design for highlighting the shape.

1. Use contrast to emphasize the Illusion.

Quilting doesn't need to be complex to create an interesting look. One of my favorite ways to quilt tumbling blocks is to use straight line patterns of different densities. Not only does it help the 3D look of the block stand out, but it helps certain blocks pop out from the rest of the quilt.

2. Follow the points of the blocks.

I am not a big fan of marking out the quilting designs. Instead, I like to use the points of the block as reference points to create intricate-looking designs. Dot-to-dot quilting, as I like to call it, is perfect for the corners of tumbling blocks.

3. Fill with a hexagon shape.

Instead of quilting the individual parts of the tumbling block, you can quilt them all together as a hexagon. I prefer doing this in blocks pieced with busy fabrics, because the quilting will be less visible.

Changing the density of your quilting design keeps the work interesting.

reach the left edge of the block. Travel up the side of the block ½" (1.3 cm) and echo again. Continue quilting straight parallel lines until you reach the top left corner of the block **(Figure 2)**.

3. Between the medium and the lightest colors, travel along the top left edge of the block ½"–¾" (1.3–2 cm) and echo the bottom two sides of the top block. Continue echoing and traveling until it is filled in, stitching to make the least dense lines in the block[space]**(Figure 3)**.

GREEN

Green is a real outdoorsy type. Green loves the smell of fresh grass and spring leaves and can often be spotted high up in the trees on a warm summer day. He's always keeping the peace between the two sides of the spectrum, mingling effortlessly with both the warm and the cool kids, while not truly being a core member of either clique.

The other colors love the way Green reflects their best qualities; Yellow brings out Green's warmer lime tones and a touch of Blue adds a minty hue, although too much Blue turns him a little teal in the cheeks. Green is a team player, forever taking his place in the middle of the rainbow, happy to have a spot in the spectrum.

GREEN QUILT TECHNIQUES

Understanding a Hexagon

A hexagon can be broken down into a series of 60-degree triangles. In the Big Hex quilt, the scattered triangles come together to form one central hexagon. Inside the large hexagon, smaller hexagons pop up. This is truly a pattern within a pattern.

Prints for whole triangles

pine   olive   spring   citron   bleached   natural   white   light mint

Background

Backing →

Binding ↓

macaw   dark gray   mountain   sunset

Solids for pieced triangles

CHOOSING FABRICS

For the Big Hex, I chose my fabrics in three parts: the whole triangles, the pieced triangles, and the background.

The whole triangles make a field of uninterrupted space where larger prints can really shine. I chose larger prints that use shades of green as their unifying color, either as a background or a main design element to dictate the palette for the remaining smaller print and solid fabrics.

For the pieced triangles, I needed fabrics that could be cut up many times without losing their beauty. I selected smaller graphic prints and solids. I also wanted to pull a contrasting color from my larger prints that would break away from the shades of green that make up the majority of the quilt top. I pulled the orange from the small tufts on the fox's tail and head. The orange repeats in the lime green and sky blue floral print and in the binding as a small solitary stripe.

The background fabrics posed a unique opportunity to play with texture.

The pattern of the background, while soft and very subtle, can so often be overlooked in a quilt. I chose natural linen with a white polka dot that is only visible when you are right on top of it, a similarly subtle white-on-white print, a very soft mint green with a tiny gold line detail, and a natural-colored solid to break up the prints.

THE BIG HEX

Finished quilt size: 78″ × 75½″
(198 × 192 cm)

Template: Hex A

Fabrics

¼ yd (23 cm) each of 8 green large prints for whole triangles

⅓ yd (30 cm) each of 8 green small prints and solids for pieced triangles

1 yd (91.5 cm) each of 4 light and neutral colors for background

Backing, Binding & Batting

5 yd (4.5 m) of 40″/42″ (102/107 cm) wide backing fabric or 2¼ yd (2 m) of 108″ (274 cm) wide backing fabric

⅝ yd (57 cm) of fabric to make 288″ (731.5 cm) of 2½″ (6.5 cm) bias binding

82″ × 80″ (208 × 203 cm) of batting

Notions

Template plastic

Erasable fabric-marking tool

TIP!

A 60-degree equilateral triangle ruler (at least 8″ [20.5 cm] from blunt tip to bottom edge) is a great alternative for Template Hex A. Follow the pattern instructions and substitute Template A with the ruler. Line up the blunt tip with the strip's top edge and the 8″ (20.5 cm) line on the ruler with the strip's bottom edge. Then rotate the ruler as you would the template to create alternating triangles.

CUT THE FABRICS

1. Trace Hex Template A (page 189) once each onto the template plastic, label each template, and cut them out on the drawn line. Use a ruler and rotary cutter to cut the straight edges and scissors to cut the curved edges.

2. From each of the eight ¼ yd (23 cm) green large print pieces, cut one 8″ (20.5 cm) × WOF (width of fabric) strip.

3. Using Template Hex A or a 60-degree equilateral triangle ruler, sub cut 6 triangles from each of the 8 WOF strips by rotating the template (**Figure 1**, page 79). Cut a total of 48 triangles.

4. From the eight ⅓ yd (30 cm) smaller prints and solids, prepare the following 4 different pieced triangle sets:

Lime, mint, and turquoise make for unexpected green combinations.

PIECED TRIANGLE SET A

Select 2 coordinating fabrics and cut from each:

» One 5¼" (13.5 cm) × WOF strip
» One 3¼" (8.5 cm) × WOF strip

PIECED TRIANGLE SET B

Select 2 coordinating fabrics and cut from each:

» Two 2¼" (5.5 cm) × WOF strips
» Two 2½" (6.5 cm) × WOF strips

PIECED TRIANGLE SET C

Select 2 coordinating fabrics and cut from each:

» Two 4¼" (11 cm) × WOF strips

PIECED TRIANGLE SET D

Select 2 coordinating fabrics and cut from each:

» One 2¼" (5.5 cm) × WOF strip
» One 1½" (3.8 cm) × WOF strip
» One 5¼" (13.5 cm) × WOF strip

5. From each of the four 1 yd (91.5 cm) background fabrics, cut four 8" (20.5 cm) × WOF strips. Cut a total of 16 background strips.

6. Using Template A or a 60-degree equilateral triangle ruler, sub cut 6 triangles from each of the 16 strips by rotating the template (**Figure 1**). Cut a total of 96 background triangles.

MAKE PIECED TRIANGLE SET A

7. Sew one 5¼" (13.5 cm) × WOF strip to the 3¼" (8.5 cm) × WOF strip of coordinating fabric (**Figure 2**).

Alternating fabrics, sew the remaining 5¼" (13.5 cm) × WOF strip to the remaining 3¼" (8.5 cm) × WOF strip of coordinating fabric (**Figure 3**).

8. Sub cut each strip set into 6 triangles by rotating the template. Cut a total of 12 pieced triangles A.

MAKE PIECED TRIANGLE SET B

9. Sew one 2¼" (5.5 cm) × WOF strip to the 2½" (6.5 cm) × WOF strip of coordinating fabric (**Figure 4**).

Alternating fabrics, join a 2½" (5.5 cm) × WOF strip, then join a coordinating 2¼" (5.5 cm) × WOF strip to the same unit.

10. Repeat Step 4 to create a second identical strip set (**Figure 5**).

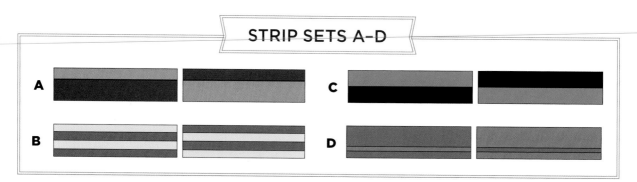

STRIP SETS A–D

A

B

C

D

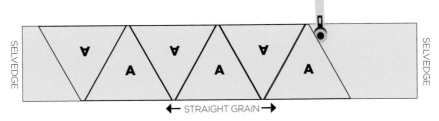

Figure 1

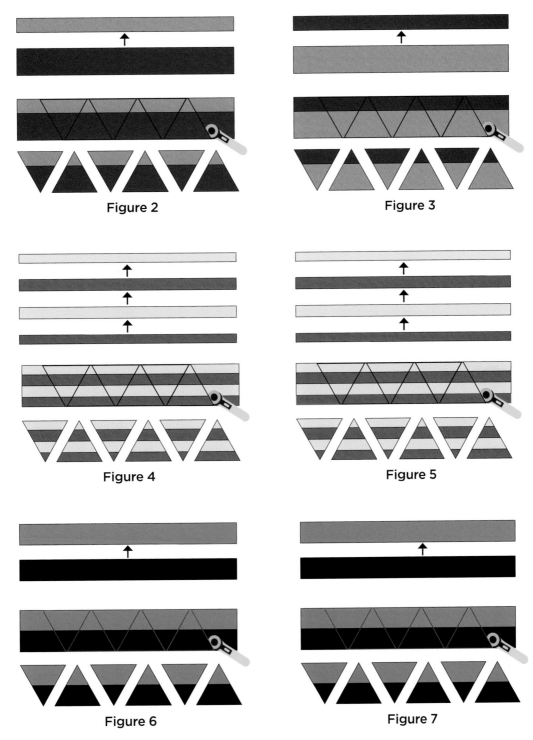

Figure 2

Figure 3

Figure 4

Figure 5

Figure 6

Figure 7

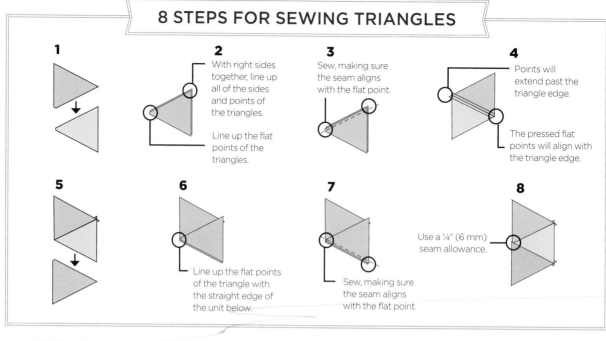

8 STEPS FOR SEWING TRIANGLES

1

2
With right sides together, line up all of the sides and points of the triangles.

Line up the flat points of the triangles.

3
Sew, making sure the seam aligns with the flat point.

4
Points will extend past the triangle edge.

The pressed flat points will align with the triangle edge.

5

6
Line up the flat points of the triangle with the straight edge of the unit below.

7
Sew, making sure the seam aligns with the flat point.

8
Use a ¼" (6 mm) seam allowance.

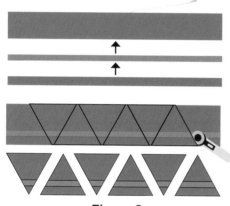

Figure 8

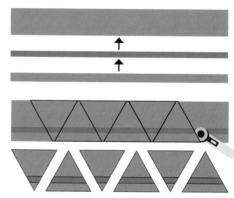

Figure 9

11. Sub cut each strip set into 6 triangles by rotating the template. Cut a total of 12 pieced triangles B.

MAKE PIECED TRIANGLE SET C

12. Sew one 4¼" (11 cm) × WOF strip to the 4¼" (11 cm) × WOF strip coordinating fabric (**Figure 6**, page 79).

13. Repeat Step 7 to create an identical strip set (**Figure 7** page 79).

14. Sub cut each strip set into 6 triangles by rotating the template. Cut a a total of 12 pieced triangles C.

MAKE PIECED TRIANGLE SET D

15. Sew one 5¼" (5.5 cm) × WOF strip to the 1½" (3.8 cm) × WOF strip of coordinating fabric (**Figure 8**).

Alternating fabrics, join a 2¼" (13.5 cm) × WOF strip to the same unit.

16. Repeat Step 10 to create a second strip set with the remaining strips, alternating the colors of the fabrics (**Figure 9**).

17. Sub cut each strip set into 6 triangles by rotating the template. Cut a total of 12 pieced triangles D.

ASSEMBLE THE QUILT TOP

18. Follow the Big Hex Assembly Diagram on page 82 to complete the quilt top, first sewing together each of the 10 columns.

Refer to **Figure 10** when lining up the triangles to join them. Each column consists of 19 triangles. Pay special attention to the placement of the background

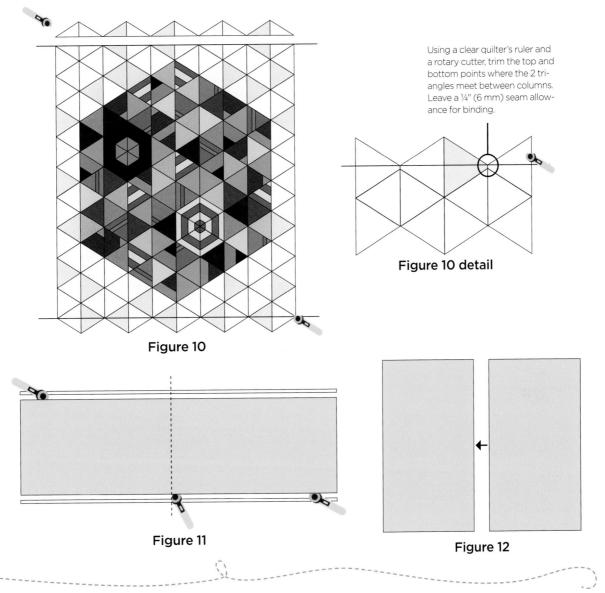

Using a clear quilter's ruler and a rotary cutter, trim the top and bottom points where the 2 triangles meet between columns. Leave a ¼" (6 mm) seam allowance for binding.

Figure 10 detail

Figure 10

Figure 11

Figure 12

and foreground triangles as well as the orientation of the pieced triangles.

19. Sew all 10 columns together to assemble the quilt top.

20. Trim off the top and bottom points, leaving a ¼" (6 mm) seam allowance and a straight clean edge (**Figure 10** detail).

PIECE THE BACKING

21. To make the backing from 40"/42" (102/107 cm) backing fabric, trim the selvedge. Cut the trimmed backing yardage in half to create two 90" (229 cm) WOF pieces (**Figure 11**).

22. Place the 2 backing pieces right sides together and sew along the 81" (206 cm) edge(**Figure 12**).

The backing should measure about 90" × 82" (229 × 213 cm).

FINISH THE QUILT

23. Follow the instructions for preparing the quilt top for quilting on page 10.

24. Follow the quilting instructions on page 83.

25. To complete the quilt, follow the bias binding instructions on page 183.

BIG HEX ASSEMBLY DIAGRAM

QUILTING TRIANGLE BLOCKS

Even though this entire quilt is made out of triangle blocks, the color placement of the fabrics helps provide a clear distinction between the center and background blocks. Using the quilting to enhance those areas is an impactful way to quilt your Big Hex.

The quilting in the center of the quilt can help it shine, but using the quilting in the background to frame it is an easy way to enhance the pattern even more. I also like how the quilting changes the shape of the center hex slightly, making it more jagged around the edges. Because the quilt is pieced with triangles, you can use the blocks as a guide for the quilting, which means no marking!

With all of the different blocks in the center of the Big Hex, it can be a little overwhelming to decide what design to quilt. One of my favorite things to do is to use the quilting to highlight just my favorite blocks and then fill in the rest of the area with an allover design.

POINTED Vs

This design is easy to stitch, but it takes a little planning to decide which background blocks to quilt it in. Use the pieced blocks in the center as a guide—the design should always be touching one of them.

1. From the left bottom corner of the first background triangle, quilt a straight diagonal line that goes 2" (5 cm) or so away from the upper corner and down to the opposite corner **(Figure 1)**.

2. Alternating directions, repeat two more times, echoing the first line of stitching within the triangle 2" (5 cm) from the previous line **(Figure 2)**.

3. This design ends at the corner opposite from your starting point, so you can easily quilt from block to

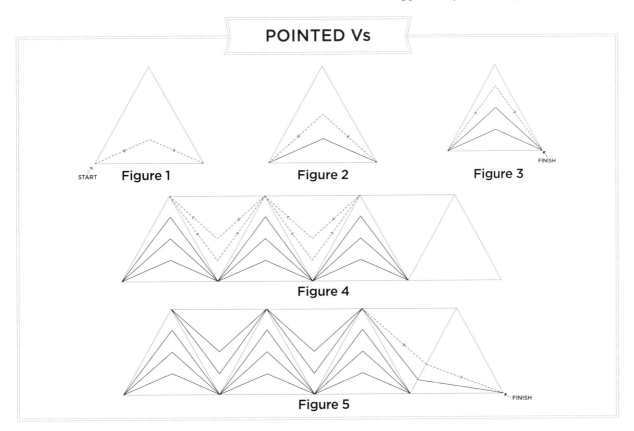

POINTED Vs

START **Figure 1**

Figure 2

FINISH **Figure 3**

Figure 4

FINISH **Figure 5**

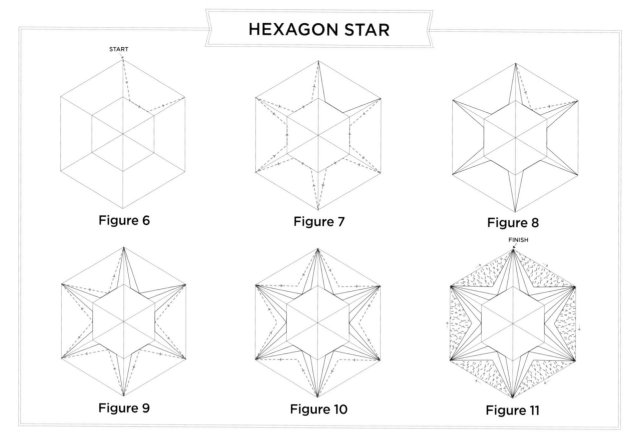

HEXAGON STAR

Figure 6

Figure 7

Figure 8

Figure 9

Figure 10

Figure 11

block without stopping (**Figure 3**, page 83). Repeat Steps 1–3 to quilt a row of blocks.

4. To add detail to the background, quilt the same pattern in the next row of triangles, stitching only 2 echo lines. Orient the pointed Vs in the opposite direction of the first set of pointed Vs (**Figure 4**, page 83).

5. To make the quilting wrap around the big hexagon shape, combine the 2 corner triangles and quilt them like one large diamond. Starting at the top of the last triangle in the row, quilt a straight diagonal line to the seam between the corner triangles, then angle out to the far right corner of the second corner triangle (**Figure 5, page 83**).

After quilting the pointed Vs, quilt the rest of the background with an allover design, such as swirls (see page 41 for instructions). The contrast between the swirls and straight lines helps the pointed Vs show up a little more, even on busier fabric.

HEXAGON STAR

I quilted one of the hexagon blocks in the center of the quilt with a geometric quilting design that uses the point of the block as a guide. It has a little traveling along the seam of the block, but the extra effort is what really adds interest to the design.

1. Starting at the top left corner of a hexagon block, quilt a diagonal line that ends 1" (2.5 cm) away from the same corner of the inner hexagon. Travel along the horizontal seam, stopping 1" (2.5 cm) away from the next corner. Quilt another diagonal line to the top right outer corner (**Figure 7**).

2. Repeat on each side of the block until you return to the starting point, stitching a six-pointed star shape within the hexagon (**Figure 8**).

3. Starting at the same top left corner of the hexagon block, quilt a diagonal line to the midpoint of the inner block and up to the next corner (**Figure 9**).

4. Repeat, moving from left to right around the block, echo stitching the star shape around the hexagon shape, ending at the starting point (**Figure 10**).

5. Repeat Step 3, echoing the diagonal lines previously quilted, resulting in another six-pointed star shape (**Figure 11**).

6. If you like a lot of quilting like I do, try adding another step. Work your way around the block, quilting a wishbone design (see page 21 for instructions), filling in the space between the edge of the block and the straight lines you've already stitched (**Figure 12**).

THE MINI HEX

The Mini Hex is a smaller, more uniform version of the Big Hex quilt. In the Mini Hex, I used mostly green solids in the center and a printed fabric as the background. When working with many smaller pieces, the solids allow the piecing to show and create a bolder, graphic statement overall.

Finished mini-quilt size: 26" × 30" (66 × 76 cm)

Template: Hex B

Fabrics
⅙ yd (15 cm) each of 8 green fabrics, mostly solids

¾ yd (68.5 cm) of green print fabric for the background

Backing, Batting & Binding
1 yd (91.5 cm) 4"/42" (112/114.5 cm) wide backing fabric

⅓ yd (30 cm) of fabric to make 122" (310 cm) of 2½" (6.5 cm) bias binding

34" × 38" (86.5 × 96.5 cm) of batting

Notions
Template plastic

Erasable fabric-marking tool

TIP!

A 60-degree equilateral triangle ruler (at least 8" [20.5 cm] from blunt tip to bottom edge) is a great alternative for Template B. Follow the pattern instructions and substitute Template B with the ruler. Line up the blunt tip with the strip's top edge and the 8" (20.5 cm) line on the ruler with the strip's bottom edge. Then rotate the ruler as you would with the template to create alternating triangles.

CUT THE FABRICS

1. From each of the eight ⅙ yd (15 cm) pieces, cut two 1¾" (4.5 cm) × WOF (width of fabric) strips. Cut a total of 16 strips.

2. From the background fabric, cut:
   » Four 6" × 14" (15 × 35.5 cm) rectangles
   » Three 3⅓" (8.5 cm) × WOF strips

SEW THE BLOCK

3. Sew one 1¾" (4.5 cm) × WOF strip to a coordinating 1¾" (4.5 cm) × WOF strip to create a strip set, then press the seam open (**Figure 1**, page 86).

4. Sub cut the strip set into 12 triangles by rotating the template across the length of the strip.

Curved quilting lines offset geometric piecing.

Separate the 12 triangles into two stacks with 6 identical triangles in each.

5. Combine the remaining 1¾" (4.5 cm) × WOF strips to create 7 more different strip sets.

6. Repeat Steps 1 and 2 to create 16 triangle stacks, each stack with 6 identical triangles.

ASSEMBLE THE QUILT TOP

7. Lay out the triangles according to the Mini Hex Center Assembly Diagram on page 88. Pay special attention to the color placement and orientation of each triangle.

8. Join each column first (see 8 Steps for Joining Triangles, page 80). Beginning at one end, sew each column to the next until the center of Mini Hex is complete. Press each seam open.

JOIN THE BACKGROUND

9. Center one 6" × 14" (15 × 35.5 cm) rectangle, right sides together, on the top left angled edge of the center hexagon and sew **(Figure 2)**. Press the seam toward the rectangle.

10. Align the edge of a ruler with the top right edge of the center hexagon and trim away excess background fabric **(Figure 3)**.

11. Center a second 6" × 14" (15 × 35.5 cm) rectangle, right sides together, on the top right angled edge of the center hexagon and sew **(Figure 4)**. Press the seam toward the rectangle.

12. Repeat Steps 9–11 to sew 2 more background rectangles to the bottom angled edges of the center hexagon **(Figure 5)**.

13. Trim the block to 24½" × 20½" (61 × 52 cm) **(Figure 6)**.

14. Sew the three 3½" (9 cm) × WOF background strips together end to end to create one long strip.

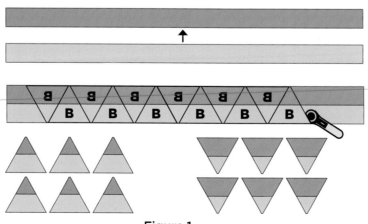

Figure 1

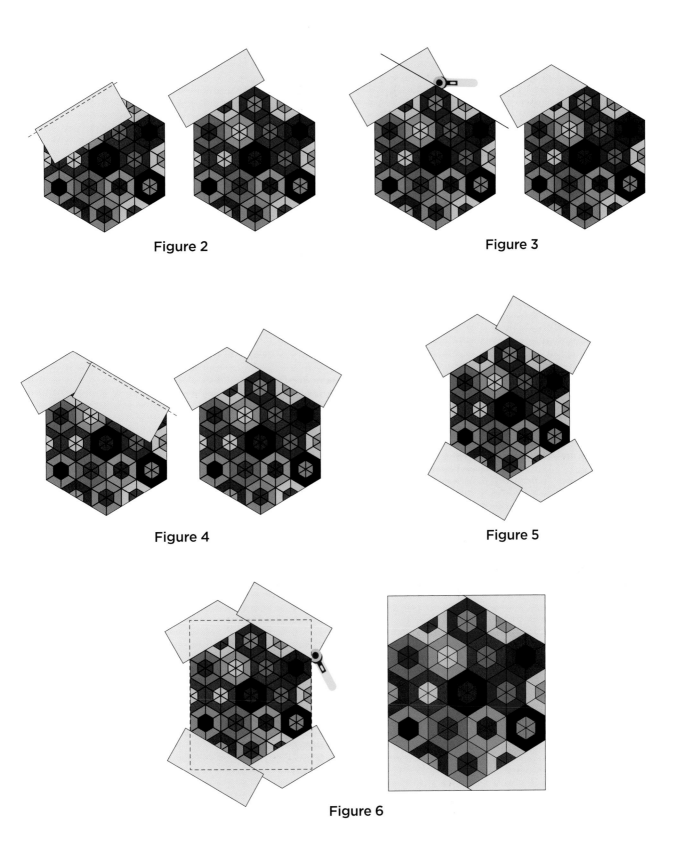

Figure 2

Figure 3

Figure 4

Figure 5

Figure 6

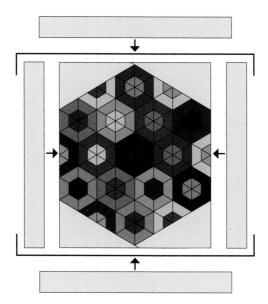

Figure 7

15. From the long background strip, cut two
    3½" × 24½" (9 × 62 cm) and two 3½" × 26½"
    (9 × 66 cm) rectangles.

16. Sew one 3½" × 24½" (9 × 62 cm) rectangle to
    the left side and one to the right side of the Mini
    Hex. Press seams toward the background fabric
    (Figure 7).

17. Sew one 3½" × 26½" (9 × 66 cm) rectangle to the
    top and one to the bottom of the Mini Hex. Press
    seams toward the background fabric.

FINISH THE QUILT

18. Follow the instructions for preparing the quilt top
    for quilting on page 10.

19. Follow the quilting instructions on page 89.

20. To complete the quilt, follow the bias binding
    instructions on page 183.

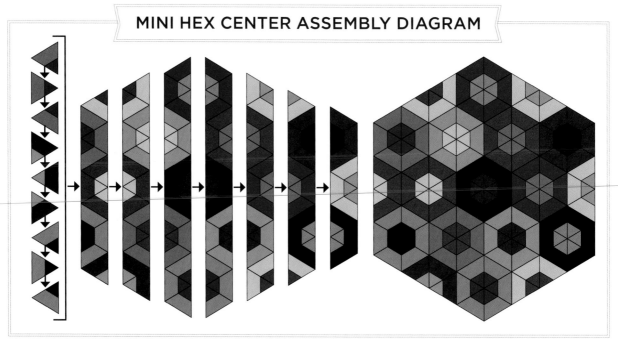

MINI HEX CENTER ASSEMBLY DIAGRAM

QUILTING HEXAGON BLOCKS

Sometimes all you need to do is give your quilting a little flip. Changing the orientation of a quilting design can add a fun effect to your quilt, which is the case with the Mini Hex quilt. This design rotates around the center block, really drawing the eye to the middle of the quilt. But my favorite thing about it is that you can quilt the whole block without stopping.

HEXAGON FLOWER

1. Starting ½" (1.3 cm) away from the left corner of the first hexagon block, quilt a line that echoes five sides of the block **(Figure 1)**.

2. Travel along the bottom edge of the block ¼" (6 mm), then echo the line quilted in Step 1, stopping at the bottom edge of the block **(Figure 2)**.

3. Quilt a diagonal line to the center of the bottom side of the inner hexagon. Stitch in the ditch of the inner hexagon, stopping at the last corner **(Figure 3)**.

4. Quilt a continuous curve flower inside one wedge of the inner hexagon, starting at the right corner of the wedge, curving to the center of the block, and stitching to the left corner **(Figure 4)**.

5. Repeat, stitching curved petal shapes around each seam between wedges, working clockwise around the center of the hexagon. Quilt along the bottom edge of the center hexagon, then stitch a diagonal

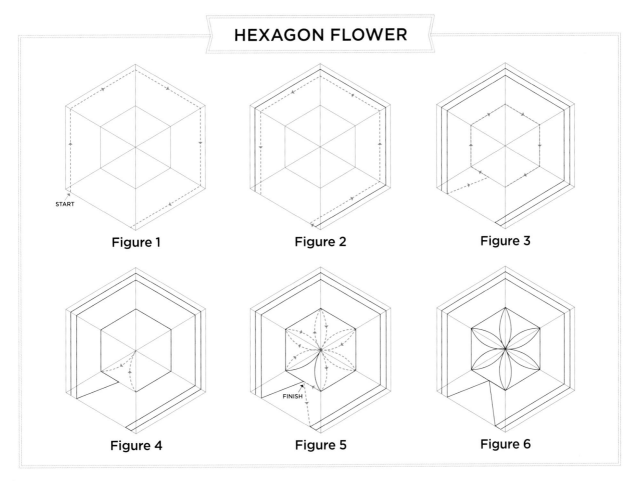

HEXAGON FLOWER

Figure 1

Figure 2

Figure 3

Figure 4

Figure 5

Figure 6

line to the outside of the hexagon (**Figures 5 and 6**, page 89).

As you quilt each of the hexagon blocks, change the orientation of the design so that the bottom touches the block in the very center. Doing this creates interesting secondary designs.

VARIATIONS ON A FLOWER

This design can be easily tweaked to come up with some fun variations. Below are just a couple of options—experiment with them to come up with some of your own variations.

Variation #1

1. Repeat Steps 1 and 2 (page 89), but echo stitch only four sides of the hexagon block. Quilt a diagonal line to the bottom corner of the inner quilt block, then stitch a continuous curve flower shape just as in Step 4, returning to the bottom corner (**Figure 7**).

2. Stitch a straight diagonal line to the right side of the block where the echo lines meet the seam, then stitch an upside-down V shape that ends where the echo lines meet the bottom seam on the left side. Quilt along the bottom of the block to finish the design (**Figure 8**).

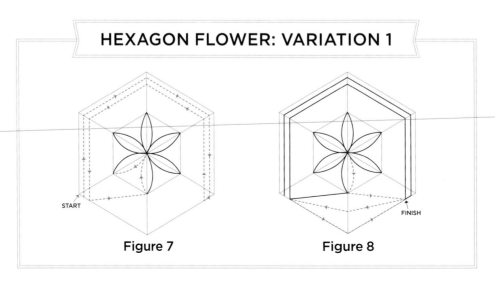

HEXAGON FLOWER: VARIATION 1

START

FINISH

Figure 7 — Figure 8

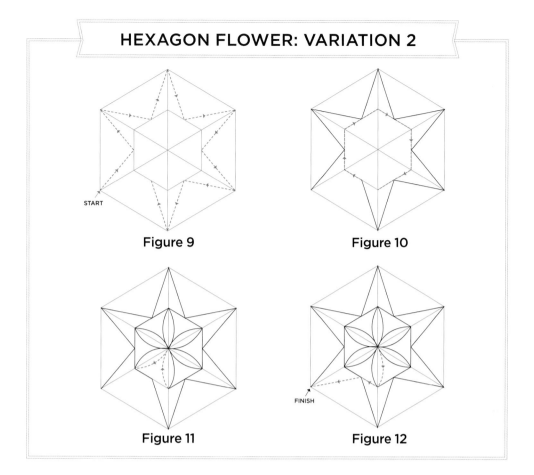

HEXAGON FLOWER: VARIATION 2

Figure 9

Figure 10

Figure 11

Figure 12

Variation #2

This is perfect for quilting the center hexagon block of the quilt. It replaces the echo lines with diagonal lines, resulting in a striking star shape.

1. Work in a clockwise direction. Starting at any outer corner of the block, quilt a straight diagonal line to the middle of the same side of the inner hexagon and onto the next outer point. Continue quilting around the block, stopping in the middle of the last side of the inner block **(Figure 9)**.

2. Travel along the seams of the inner block, stopping at the last corner **(Figure 10)**.

3. Quilt a center curve flower (see page 22 for instructions) in the center block, ending at the starting point **(Figure 11)**.

4. Stitch along the seam to the middle of the last side of the inner block, then diagonally to the starting corner in Step 1 **(Figure 12)**.

BLUE

Oh, Blue, how everyone adores you. Old people, young people, girls, boys, even babies love Blue. Like clear skies and cool water, Blue is nothing if not a pleaser. She is just so easygoing, definitely the one you want around when you need a little calming down.

Blue will stay up for hours listening to your problems, watch movies, and eat ice cream with you when you are down. Blue is always there for you when you need her most.

Blue is like your favorite pair of jeans—she goes with everything. Just her presence adds an air of coolness to the rainbow, keeping the warm colors from dominating everything. Blue is a welcome addition to a sophisticated palette.

BLUE QUILT TECHNIQUES

Sewing Squares

Let's be real: This quilt is not going to trip up anyone up. The square is the fundamental building block of most quilt tops. When the sewing is this easy—simply joining squares and rectangles—a successful quilt is all about the fabric.

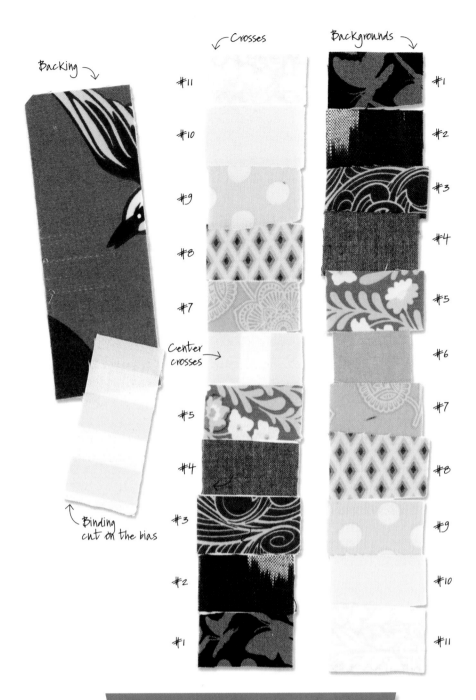

Backing ↘

Crosses ↓

Backgrounds ↘

#11

#10

#9

#8

#7

Center crosses →

#5

#4

#3

#2

#1

↖ Binding cut on the bias

#1

#2

#3

#4

#5

#6

#7

#8

#9

#10

#11

CHOOSING FABRICS

For the Plus One quilt, choose 11 fabrics that easily blend from light to dark—in this case, ranging from green to navy, plus one contrasting fabric used in the center row of crosses only. While the background stripes fade from navy to green, the crosses blend in the opposite direction, from green to navy.

I began by choosing the first and last fabrics. I wanted to make sure that there was a enough contrast between the two to have room for nine shades of blue between them. The fabrics had to be close enough in color that I would be able to get from one end of the spectrum to the other without any huge jumps in color.

PLUS ONE

Finished quilt size: 60″ × 72″ (152 × 183 cm)

Finished block size: 6″ × 6″ (15 × 15 cm)

Fabrics

¾ yd (68.5 cm) of fabric #1 (darkest blue)

⅝ yd (57 cm) of fabric #2

⅝ yd (57 cm) of fabric #3

⅝ yd (57 cm) of fabric #4

⅝ yd (57 cm) of fabric #5

⅜ yd (34.5 cm) of fabric #6

⅝ yd (57 cm) of fabric #7

⅝ yd (57 cm) of fabric #8

⅝ yd (57 cm) of fabric #9

⅝ yd (57 cm) of fabric #10

¾ yd (68.5 cm) of fabric #11 (lightest blue)

¼ yd (23 cm) of striped center cross fabric

4 yd (4 m) of 40″/42″ (102/107 cm) wide fabric or 2 yd (2 m) of 108″ (274 cm) wide backing fabric

½ yd (45.5 cm) of fabric to make 274″ (696 cm) of 2½″ (6.5 cm) bias binding

68″ × 80″ (173 × 203 cm) of batting

Tip!

When a quilt top requires specific fabric placement and a pattern contains number and letter identifiers, it can get confusing really quickly. Keep a box of sandwich bags on hand and a marker to mark what is in them. Pull out only what you need to complete each step. As you cut the fabric, place it in a bag and mark the bag "Fabric #1 Background," "Fabric #1 Cross," etc.

CUT THE FABRICS

1. From fabrics #1 and #11 each, cut:

For the background:
» Two 3½″ (9 cm) × WOF (width of fabric) strips
» Four 6½″ × 6½″ (16.5 × 16.5 cm) squares
» Two 3½″ × 6½″ (9 × 16.5 cm) rectangles
» Twenty 2½″ × 2½″ (6.5 × 6.5 cm) squares

For the crosses:
» Five 6½″ × 2½″ (16.5 × 6.5 cm) rectangles
» Ten 2½″ × 2½″ (6.5 × 6.5 cm) squares

2. From fabrics #2, #4, #8, and #10 each, cut:

For the background:
» Two 9½″ × 6½″ (24 × 16.5 cm) rectangles
» Three 6½″ × 6½″ (16.5 × 16.5 cm) squares
» Sixteen 2½″ × 2½″ (6.5 × 6.5 cm) squares

For the crosses:
- » Four 6½" × 2½" (16.5 × 6.5 cm) rectangles
- » Eight 2½" × 2½" (6.5 × 6.5 cm) squares

3. From fabrics #3, #5, #7, and #9 each, cut:

For the background:
- » Two 3½" × 6½" (9 × 16.5 cm) rectangles
- » Four 6½" × 6½" (16.5 × 16.5 cm) squares
- » Twenty 2½" × 2½" (6.5 × 6.5 cm) squares

For the crosses:
- » Five 6½" × 2½" (16.5 × 6.5 cm) rectangles
- » Ten 2½" × 2½" (6.5 × 6.5 cm) squares

4. From fabric #6, cut:

For the background:
- » Two 9½" × 6½" (24 × 16.5 cm) rectangles
- » Three 6½" × 6½" (16.5 × 16.5 cm) squares
- » Sixteen 2½" × 2½" (6.5 × 6.5 cm) squares

5. From the striped center cross fabric, cut:

For the center crosses:
- » Eight 2½" × 2½" (6.5 × 6.5 cm) squares
- » Four 2½" × 6½" (6.5 × 16.5 cm) rectangles

SEW ROWS A, C, E, G, I, AND K

6. Select sets of opposing background pieces and dark cross pieces according to the row recipes in the Plus One Assembly Diagram on page 99.

7. Sew a background 2½" × 2½" (6.5 × 6.5 cm) square to each side of a 2½" × 2½" (6.5 × 6.5 cm) cross square.

8. Repeat Steps 1 and 2 to create an identical unit.

9. Sew the two units to the top and bottom of a cross 6½" × 2½" (16.5 × 6.5 cm) rectangle (**Figure 1**).

   Make 4 more identical cross blocks (**Figure 2**).

10. Alternating cross blocks and background squares, join 5 cross blocks and 4 background 6½" × 6½" (16.5 × 16.5 cm) squares to create a partial row.

11. Sew the 3½" × 6½" (9 × 16.5 cm) background rectangles to both ends of the partial row (**Figure 3**). Press all seams away from the cross blocks.

12. Repeat Steps 6–12 for Rows C, E, G, I, and K.

SEW ROWS B, D, F, H, AND J

13. Select sets of opposing background pieces and cross pieces according to the row recipes on page 99.

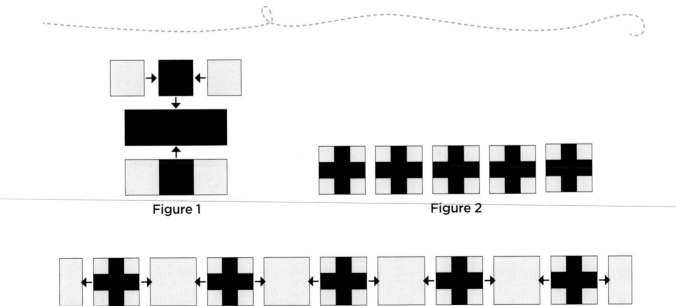

Figure 1

Figure 2

Figure 3

14. Sew a 2½" × 2½" (6.5 × 6.5 cm) background square to each side of a 2½" × 2½" (6.5 × 6.5 cm) cross square.

Repeat Steps 13 and 14 to create an identical unit.

15. Sew the two units to the top and bottom of a cross 6½" × 2½" (16.5 × 6.5 cm) rectangle (**Figure 4**).

16. Repeat Steps 10 and 11 to make a total of 4 identical cross blocks (**Figure 5**).

17. Alternating cross blocks and background squares, join 4 cross blocks and three 6½" × 6½" (16.5 × 16.5 cm) background squares to create a partial row.

18. Sew the 9½" × 6½" (24 × 16.5 cm) background rectangles to both ends of the partial row (**Figure 6**). Press all seams away from the cross blocks.

19. Repeat Steps 14–19 to make Rows D, F, H, and J.

ASSEMBLE THE QUILT TOP

20. Following the Plus One Assembly Diagram, sew the remaining fabric #11 (lightest blue fabric) 3½" (9 cm) × WOF strips end to end along the 3½" (9 cm) edge.

Trim the unit to 3½" × 60½" (9 × 153.5 cm).

21. Sew the trimmed strip to the top of Row A.

22. Sew the remaining fabric #1 (darkest blue fabric) 3½" (9 cm) × WOF strips end to end along the 3½" (9 cm) edge.

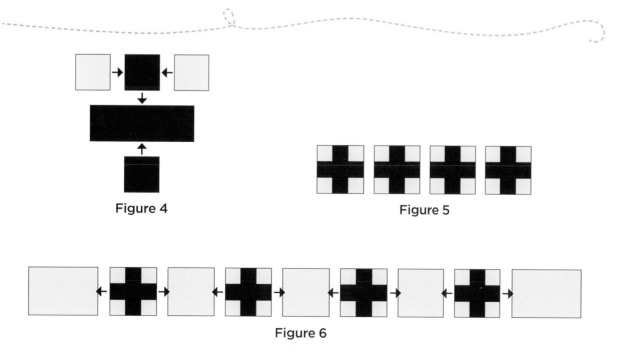

Figure 4

Figure 5

Figure 6

Trim the unit to $3\frac{1}{2}$" × $60\frac{1}{2}$" (9 × 153.5 cm).

23. Sew the trimmed strip to the bottom of Row K.

PIECE THE BACKING

24. To make the backing from 40"/42" (102/107 cm) backing fabric, trim the selvedge. Cut the trimmed backing yardage in half to create two 72" (183 cm) × WOF pieces **(Figure 7)**.

25. Place the 2 backing pieces right sides together and sew along the 72" (183 cm) edge **(Figure 8)**.

    Backing should measure about 72" × 82" (183 × 213 cm).

FINISH THE QUILT

26. Follow the instructions for preparing the quilt top for quilting on page 10.

27. Follow the quilting instructions on page 100.

28. To complete the quilt, follow the bias binding instructions on page 183.

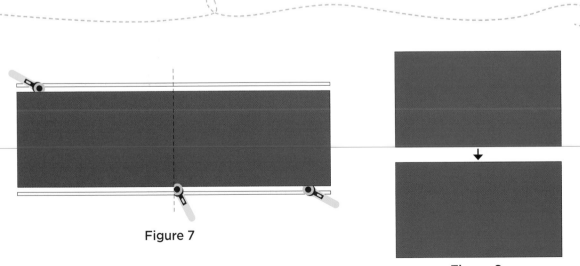

Figure 7

Figure 8

PLUS ONE ASSEMBLY DIAGRAM

ROW RECIPES

Row A
Background: Fabric #11
Cross: Fabric #1

Row B
Background: Fabric #10
Cross: Fabric #2

Row C
Background: Fabric #9
Cross: Fabric #3

Row D
Background: Fabric #8
Cross: Fabric #4

Row E
Background: Fabric #7
Cross: Fabric #5

Row F
Background: Fabric #6
Cross: Center Cross Fabric

Row G
Background: Fabric #5
Cross: Fabric #7

Row H
Background: Fabric #4
Cross: Fabric #8

Row I
Background: Fabric #3
Cross: Fabric #9

Row J
Background: Fabric #2
Cross: Fabric #10

Row K
Background: Fabric #1
Cross: Fabric #11

QUILTING SECONDARY PATTERNS

Using the quilting to create secondary patterns is such a fun way to add detail to the quilt, especially when a pattern has a regular block layout such as the Plus One quilt. I used diagonal lines and fun fillers to create interesting texture and geometric secondary designs.

When deciding where to begin quilting on a quilt, the blocks are usually the best place to start. This allows the quilting to put the focus where it belongs: on the quilt pattern.

For the plus blocks in this quilt, I quilted straight lines to emphasize their geometric shape. They also contrast with the background quilting, making the blocks stand out even more. Just like most of the designs in this book, this cross design uses the corners of the blocks as a guide, which means no marking.

PLUS CROSSES

This design quilts the block as well as some of the background space. Using the quilting to incorporate part of the background area into the block changes the look altogether. It's something that I find highly fun and amusing. Although it may look like there are a

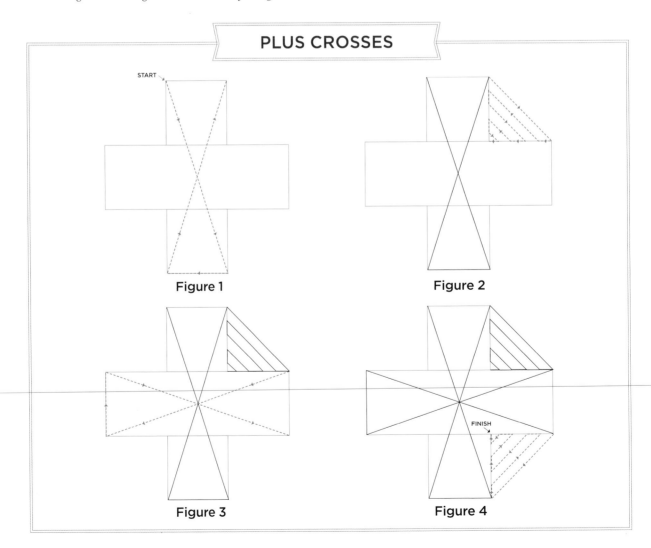

lot of steps to this design, it's really just the same two steps repeated over and over again.

1. Quilt a diagonal line from the top left corner of the vertical bar of the first cross block to the bottom right corner of the cross. Travel along the bottom edge of the cross and quilt another diagonal line to the upper right corner **(Figure 1)**.

2. Outside of the block and between the top and the right arm of the cross, stitch a diagonal line to the next outer corner. Travel along the edge of the block ¼" (6 mm), then stitch an echo line inside the previous line **(Figure 2)**.

    Continue traveling and echo stitching inside your quilted lines until this background space is filled in.

3. Travel along the edge of the block to the top corner of the horizontal bar of the right side of the cross and quilt a horizontal X across the center of the cross to the left bottom corner of the left side of the cross. Travel up the left side of the cross and stitch another diagonal line from the top left corner to the bottom right corner of the cross **(Figure 3)**.

4. Quilt a diagonal line to the bottom right corner of the block. Travel and echo the line, as in Step 2 **(Figure 4)**.

5. Repeat on the left side of the block, traveling along the edge and filling in the background spaces with traveling and echo lines.

Note: Some sides of the block will have two lines of traveling quilting. Using a thread color that blends in with the quilt top will prevent that from being too obvious. It will also keep the quilting from overwhelming the pieced design.

ADDITIONAL BLOCK DESIGNS

While I love the Plus Cross quilting design, I didn't use it on all of the quilt blocks. In specific blocks, I used the quilting to join them together in such a way that they give the quilt a medallion-style layout.

Deciding which blocks to connect with the quilting took a little planning. But the result was well worth the effort. Use your imagination! You can create so many secondary designs by connecting the blocks in different ways. Experiment to see if you can find a favorite. You could connect the blocks in the very center of the quilt or maybe connect the blocks around the outer edge.

Contrasting thread makes the back of the quilt even more interesting.

QUILTING IN THE BACKGROUND

Once the blocks were quiltied and connected, it was time to quilt the background. Because the quilt has stripes of color in the background, I used them as boundaries for the designs.

In each stripe, I quilted a different filler design. Using several different designs on a quilt is a great way to practice different designs, especially ones that are new to you. I also think that it makes the quilting process more fun. In some of the stripes that weren't already filled in with quilting, I quilted swirls (page 41 for instructions), and in others, I combined swirls with leaves (page 44) and pebbles (page 42).

How Much Is Too Much?

Using several different quilting designs always makes me happy. To continue the medallion theme of the quilting, I quilted diagonal lines between some of the blocks. It was as easy as connecting the dots (page 65)! I also had fun creating some geometric Vs (page 83) in between some of the quilting lines.

It may be too much quilting for your taste, and that is completely fine. Do what you think looks good. Having fun with the quilting is the more important part of the process, so once you get on a roll, keep on going!

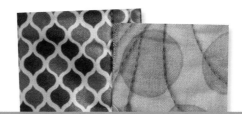

purple

Purple is so moody. Behind those heavily lidded eyes, she pulls up the end of the rainbow with just as much punch as Red and all of the subtleties of Blue.

It is almost impossible to feel indifferent toward purple. As a descendant of Red and Blue, she is often confused about who she is herself. Purple sometimes gets fed up with being the dutiful caboose on the rainbow and draws on the red that lies deep in her soul, becoming a violent shade of fuchsia.

Purple functions almost entirely on emotion. From sweet lavender days to periwinkle moments, all of the other colors know that you have to walk on eggshells around Purple and give her some space. She really only plays well with others when she is in just the right mood.

PURPLE QUILT TECHNIQUES

Sewing the Sugar Skulls

The Sugar Skull block is made almost entirely of squares and rectangles with a few half square triangles. The skulls are set into a traditional block format, so scaling the quilt up (or down) is a simple matter of adding (or subtracting) more blocks and extending (or not) the sashing strips that set the blocks together.

The Sugar Skulls quilt does not require any great feat of sewing mastery, but there are quite a few small pieces that make up the nose and teeth. If you cut carefully and your seams are consistent, the Sugar Skulls quilt will come together quite easily.

skull #1

skull #2

skull #3

skull #4

skull #5

skull #6

skull #7

skull #8

skull #9

← Background

Binding →

← Backing

CHOOSING FABRICS

Each skull is made up of one skull fabric and the background fabric. The subject of a skull evokes images of darkness, so I chose to make my Sugar Skulls out of sweet purple feminine fabrics for contrast.

I love it when two opposing things collide! I call it the Angry Cupcake aesthetic, because what is funnier than a sweet pink frosted cupcake that has the character traits of a strict headmistress? In this case, pretty purple flowers and cute lavender bunnies are cut and sewn into a big, tough skull.

SUGAR SKULLS

Finished quilt size: 55" × 61"
(138 × 155 cm)

Finished block size: 15" × 17"
(38 × 43 cm)

Fabrics
9 purple small print fat quarters each
18" × 21" (46 × 53 cm)

2¾ yd (2.5 m) of background fabric

Backing, Binding & Batting
3½ yd (3.3 m) of 40"/42"
(102/107 cm) wide fabric or 1¾
yd (1.6 m) of 108" (274 cm) wide
backing fabric

½ yd (45.5 cm) of fabric to make
242" (615 cm) of 2⅓" (6.5 cm) bias
binding

63" × 69" (160 × 175 cm) of batting

Notions
Erasable fabric-marking tool

CUT THE FABRICS

1. From each of the Sugar Skull small-print fat
   quarters, cut:
   » One 15½" × 5½" (39.5 × 14 cm) rectangle
   » One 3½" × 5½" (9 × 14 cm) rectangle
   » Two 3½" × 6½" (9 × 16.5 cm) rectangles
   » Four 3½" × 1½" (9 × 3.8 cm) rectangles
   » One 9½" × 1½" (24 × 3.8 cm) rectangle
   » One 13½" × 2½" (34.5 × 6.5 cm) rectangle
   » Eleven 1½" × 1½" (3.8 × 3.8 cm) squares

2. From the background fabric, cut:
   » Three 2½" (6.5 cm) × WOF (width of fabric) strips
     · Sub cut eighteen 2½" × 2½" (6.5 × 6.5 cm)
       squares
     · Sub cut six 2½" × 17½" (6.5 × 44.5 cm)
       rectangles
   » Two 5½" (14 cm) × WOF strips
     · Sub cut eighteen 3½" × 5½" (9 × 14 cm)
       rectangles
   » Thirteen 1½" (3.8 cm) × WOF strips
     · Sub cut nine 9½" × 1½" (24 × 3 cm)
     · Sub cut eighteen 2½" × 1½" (6.5 × 3.8 cm)
     · Sub cut eighteen 3½" × 1½" (9 × 3.8 cm)
       rectangles
     · Sub cut eighteen 6½" × 1½" (16.5 × 3.8 cm)
       rectangles
     · Sub cut ninety 1½" × 1½" (3.8 × 3.8 cm) squares
   » Three 2½" (6.5 cm) × WOF strips
   » Six 3½" (9 cm) × WOF strips

SEW THE FOREHEAD

3. Choose 1 set of fat quarter pieces to make the first
   Sugar Skull block. Draw a diagonal line on the
   wrong side of two 2½" × 2½" (6.5 × 6.5 cm) background squares (**Figure 1**, page 106).

4. Place one of the marked 2½" × 2½" (6.5 × 6.5 cm)
   background squares, right sides together, on the

upper left corner of one $15\frac{1}{2}" \times 5\frac{1}{2}"$ (39.5×14 cm) skull rectangle **(Figure 2)**.

Sew on the drawn line **(Figure 3)**. Trim the excess, leaving a $\frac{1}{4}"$ (6 mm) seam allowance **(Figure 4)**.

5. Place the second marked $2\frac{1}{2}" \times 2\frac{1}{2}"$ (6.5×6.5 cm) background square, right sides together, on the upper right corner of the $15\frac{1}{2}" \times 5\frac{1}{2}"$ (39.5×14 cm) skull rectangle **(Figure 5)**.

Sew on the drawn line **(Figure 6)**.

Trim the excess, leaving a $\frac{1}{4}"$ (6 mm) seam allowance **(Figure 7)**.

6. Press this piece—the forehead—and set it aside **(Figure 8)**.

SEW THE EYES AND NOSE

7. Sew two $3\frac{1}{2}" \times 5\frac{1}{2}"$ (9×14 cm) background rectangles to opposite sides of one $3\frac{1}{2}" \times 5\frac{1}{2}"$ (9×14 cm) skull rectangle along the $5\frac{1}{2}"$ (14 cm) edges **(Figure 9)**. This unit is the eyes of the sugar skull.

8. Sew two $1\frac{1}{2}" \times 1\frac{1}{2}"$ (3.8×3.8 cm) background squares to opposite sides of one $1\frac{1}{2}" \times 1\frac{1}{2}"$ (3.8×3.8 cm) skull square **(Figure 10)**.

9. Sew one $3\frac{1}{2}" \times 1\frac{1}{2}"$ skull rectangle to the left edge and one to the right edge of the unit created in the previous step **(Figure 11)**. This unit is the nose.

10. Join the eyes to the top of the nose **(Figure 12)**.

11. Sew one $3\frac{1}{2}" \times 6\frac{1}{2}"$ skull rectangle to the left and one to the right edge of the eyes and nose unit. **(Figure 13)**.

SEW THE TEETH

12. Sew five $1\frac{1}{2}" \times 1\frac{1}{2}"$ (3.8×3.8 cm) skull squares and four $1\frac{1}{2}" \times 1\frac{1}{2}"$ (3.8×3.8 cm) background squares, alternating skull and background, to make a row of upper teeth **(Figure 14)**.

Repeat to make an identical set for the lower teeth.

13. Sew one $9\frac{1}{2}" \times 1\frac{1}{2}"$ (24×3.8 cm) skull rectangle to the top edge of the upper teeth, then sew one

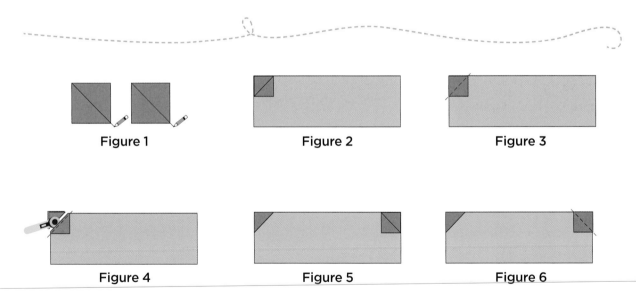

Figure 1   Figure 2   Figure 3

Figure 4   Figure 5   Figure 6

Figure 7   Figure 8   Figure 9

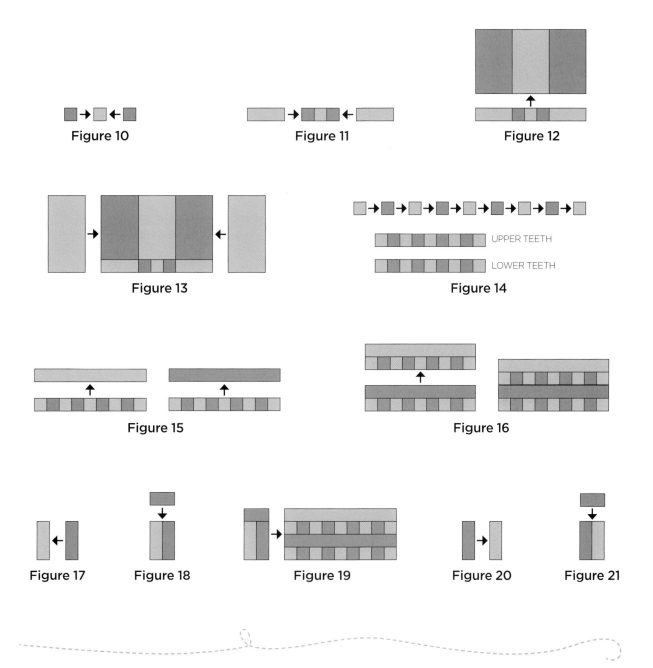

Figure 10

Figure 11

Figure 12

Figure 13

Figure 14

UPPER TEETH

LOWER TEETH

Figure 15

Figure 16

Figure 17

Figure 18

Figure 19

Figure 20

Figure 21

$9\frac{1}{2}$" × $1\frac{1}{2}$" (24 × 3.8 cm) background rectangle to the top edge of the lower teeth **(Figure 15)**.

14. Sew the lower teeth to the upper teeth **(Figure 16)**.

SEW THE JAW

15. Sew one $1\frac{1}{2}$" × $3\frac{1}{2}$" (3.8 × 9 cm) background rectangle to the right edge of one $1\frac{1}{2}$" × $3\frac{1}{2}$" (3.8 × 9 cm) skull rectangle **(Figure 17)**.

    Join one $2\frac{1}{2}$" × $1\frac{1}{2}$" (6.5 × 3.8 cm) background rectangle to the top edge **(Figure 18)**.

16. Sew the unit created in Step 13 to the left side of the teeth unit **(Figure 19)**.

17. Sew one $1\frac{1}{2}$" × $3\frac{1}{2}$" (3.8 × 9 cm) background rectangle to the left edge of one $1\frac{1}{2}$" × $3\frac{1}{2}$" (3.8 × 9 cm) skull rectangle **(Figure 20)**.

    Join one $2\frac{1}{2}$" × $1\frac{1}{2}$" (6.5 × 3.8 cm) background rectangle to the top edge **(Figure 21)**.

18. Sew the unit created in Step 15 to the right side of the teeth unit **(Figure 22**, page 108) to make the jaw.

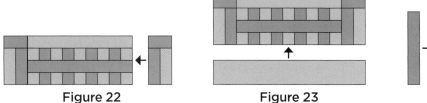

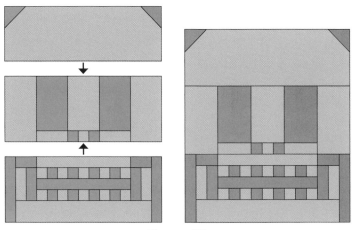

Figure 22   Figure 23   Figure 24

Figure 25

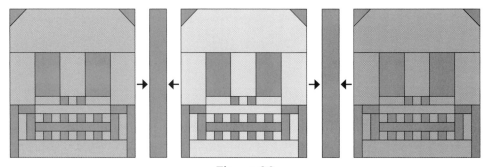

Figure 26

19. Sew one 13½" × 2½" (34.5 × 6.5 cm) skull rectangle to the bottom edge of the jaw unit **(Figure 23)**.

20. Sew one 1½" × 6½" (3.8 × 16.5 cm) background rectangle to the right edge and one to the left edge of the jaw **(Figure 24)**.

SEW THE SKULL

21. Sew the forehead unit to the top edge of the eye and nose unit, then sew the jaw unit to the bottom edge **(Figure 25)**.

The block should measure about 15½" × 17½" (39.5 × 44.5 cm).

22. Repeat Steps 3–21 to make a total of 9 Sugar Skull blocks.

ASSEMBLE THE QUILT TOP

23. Follow the Sugar Skulls Assembly Diagram on page 110 to assemble the quilt top. Sew the first row by alternating 3 skull blocks and two 2½" × 17½" (6.5 × 44.5 cm) background rectangles **(Figure 26)**.

Repeat to make 2 more rows.

24. Sew three 2½" (6.5 cm) × WOF strips together end to end along the 2½" (6.5 cm) edge to make one long strip.

Cut the strip into two 2½" × 49½" (6.5 × 125.5 cm) lengths.

25. Join one 2½" × 49½" (6.5 × 125.5 cm) strip each to the top and bottom of the center row.

26. Sew the top row to the top edge of the center row, then sew the bottom row to the bottom edge of the center row.

27. Sew the six 3½" (9 cm) × WOF background strips together end to end along the 3½" (9 cm) edge.

    Cut the strip into four 3½" × 55½" (9 × 141 cm) lengths.

28. Sew one 3½" × 55½" (9 × 141 cm) strip each to the top, bottom, and sides of the quilt top.

PIECE THE BACKING

29. To make the backing from 40"/42" (102/107 cm) backing fabric, trim the selvedge. Cut the trimmed backing yardage in half to create two 63" (160 cm) x WOF pieces **(Figure 27)**.

30. Place the 2 backing pieces right sides together and sew along the 63" (160 cm) edge **(Figure 28)**.

    Backing should measure about 63" × 82" (160 × 208 cm).

FINISH THE QUILT

31. Follow the instructions for preparing the quilt top for quilting on page 10.

32. Follow the quilting instructions on page 111.

33. To complete the quilt, follow the bias binding instructions on page 183.

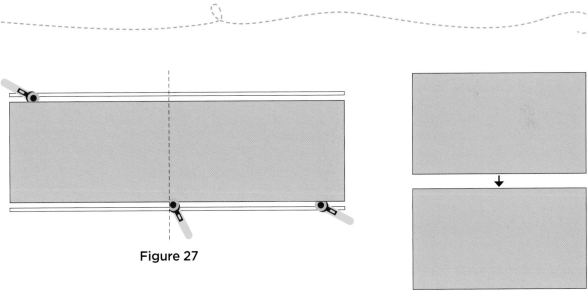

Figure 27

Figure 28

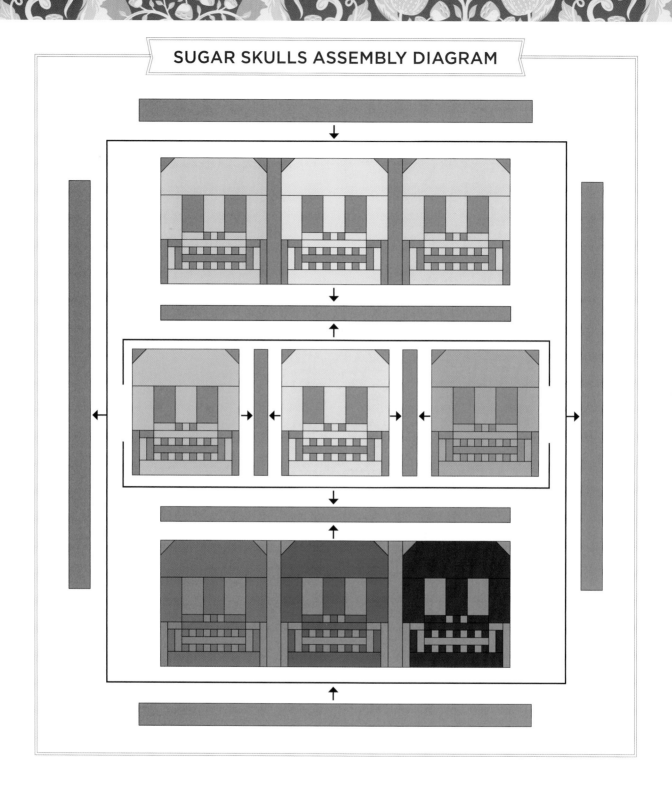

QUILTING WITH PERSONALITY

This quilt shows why I love working with Tula so much! Who else would give me a skull quilt to machine quilt? Unable to decide on just one quilting design, I combined fancy stitching with funny designs that add detail—both of which are so very appropriate for Tula Pink.

I love using the quilting to add details and tell a story. Not only is it a lot of fun to do, but it can enhance your quilt with a touch of whimsy. I used the quilting in the skulls' eyes to show personality. In my mind, these skulls aren't looking out, they are looking around at each other. Using straight or curved lines inside the eyes, I gave each skull pupils to make it seem as if they are looking at different things.

All of them are looking around, except one . . . that poor guy didn't make it!

Sticking with the same story, the skulls are also expressing different emotions. How does one give skull quilt blocks emotions? With eyebrows, of course! Some are mad, some are happy, others are surprised.

FEATHERS

Around the outside of the quilt, I decided to take a break from the funny quilting and add some fancy quilting by using a contrasting feather motif and quilting swirls (see page 41 for instructions). Try quilting the feathers so that the design weaves in front of and behind the blocks. This adds depth to the quilt and is an unusual way to use a quilting design.

Mark a gently curving line around the outer area of the quilt. Draw it so that it falls on some of the skulls and avoids some of them. When you start quilting, decide which blocks you want the feather to overlap. For those, quilt the feather directly on top of the block.

For the blocks where you want the quilting to go behind the block, you just need to add a bit of

traveling. Quilt the feather as normal. When a part of the feather runs into the block, travel along the edge of the block about ½" (1.3 cm) and then return to the spine. It will look as though the block is in front of the feather (**Figure 1**, page 112).

1. Begin anywhere on your quilt—this design is not dependent on the quilt blockStitch a gently curving line as the spine of your feather, moving from the top to the bottom of the feather (**Figure 2**, page 112).

2. From the bottom of the feather, quilt a line that extends out from the feather and curves back into the spine, resembling a petal. It can extend out as far or as close as you would like (**Figure 3**, page 112).

3. Travel along the spine ½" (1.3 cm) and quilt a line that curves out and down so that it touches the first part of the feather (**Figure 4**, page 112).

    Travel back around the curve you just quilted, then stitch a line that curves out and returns back to the spine. The petals of the feather should be roughly the same size.

4. Repeat Step 3, quilting the individual parts of the feather up the spine until you reach the top. After you stitch the last petal, stitch a gently curving line

Feminine swirls add whimsy to this quilt full of contradictions.

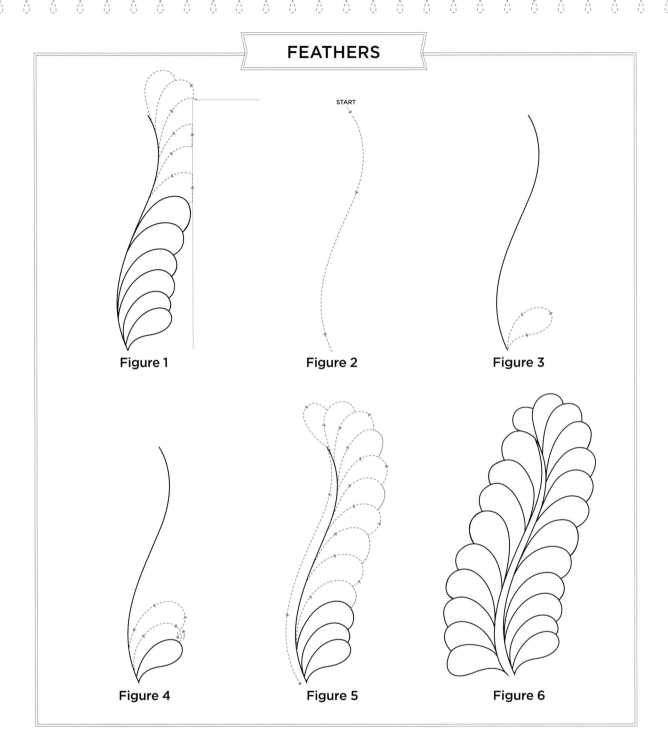

FEATHERS

Figure 1

START

Figure 2

Figure 3

Figure 4

Figure 5

Figure 6

to the bottom of the feather that echoes the first line of the spine **(Figure 5)**.

5. Repeat quilting petals on the other side of the spine **(Figure 6)**.

EYES AND TEETH

Quilting inside the blocks was so much fun. I kept the quilting basic because I didn't want it to overwhelm the skulls. I echo stitched around the inside of the blocks and around the teeth. I also used straight and curved lines to create different expressions on each one. It's amazing how much it changed the look of the skulls—experiment to find the expressions you want to give your skulls.

I also played with different-colored threads. While most of the quilting blends into the quilt top, I wanted the pupils of the skulls' eyes to really pop out from the block. Using a slightly thicker thread (30 wt) and a contrasting color, such as purple, will make the eyes shine.

SINGLE SUGAR SKULL

Sometimes an entire skull quilt is more than a person really needs. A single skull block can make a suprising little wall hanging or mini quilt.

The elaborately detailed backing print and coordinating binding stripe set the color palette for the block. I found two contrasting solids that matched a few of the individual colors from the prints. I threw a small piece of metallic gold in for the tooth because, well, it's a skull and I was getting a distinct pirate vibe from this little guy.

Finished mini-quilt size: 21" × 23" (53.5 × 58.5 cm)

Finished block size: 15" × 17" (38 × 43 cm)

Fabrics
1 magenta fat quarter (18" × 21" [45.5 × 53.5 cm])

½ yd (45.5 cm) of plum solid

2" × 2" (5 × 5 cm) scrap of gold fabric (optional)

Backing, Binding & Batting
⅞ yd (80 cm) of 40"/42" (102/107 cm) wide fabric

¼ yd (23 cm) of binding to make 98" (249 cm) of 2½" (6.5 cm) bias binding

29" × 31" (73.5 × 79 cm) of batting

CUT THE FABRICS

1. Following the skull fat quarter cutting diagram on page 114, cut:
   » One 15½" × 5½" (39.5 × 14 cm) rectangle
   » One 3½" × 5½" (9 × 14 cm) rectangle
   » Two 3½" × 6½" (9 × 16.5 cm) rectangles
   » Four 3½" × 1½" (9 × 3.8 cm) rectangles
   » One 9½" × 1½" (24 × 3.8 cm) rectangle
   » One 13½" × 2½" (34.5 × 6.5 cm) rectangle
   » Eleven 1½" × 1½" (3.8 × 3.8 cm) squares or 10 magenta squares and 1 gold square

2. Following the background fabric cutting diagram on page 114, cut:
   » Two 2½" × 2½" (6.5 × 6.5 cm) squares
   » Two 3½" × 5½" (9 × 14 cm) rectangles
   » One 1½" × 9½" (24 × 3.8 cm) rectangle
   » Two 2½" × 1½" (6.5 × 3.8 cm) rectangles
   » Two 3½" × 1½" (9 × 3.8 cm) rectangles
   » Two 6½" × 1½" (16.5 × 3.8 cm) rectangles
   » Ten 1½" × 1½" (3.8 × 3.8 cm) squares
   » Two 3½" × 17½" (9 × 44.5 cm) rectangles

   » Two 3½" × 21½" (9 × 54.5 cm) rectangles

SEW THE SKULL

3. Follow Steps 3–21 from the Sugar Skulls Quilt instructions on pages 105–108 to make 1 skull block.

   Optionally, switch one of the magenta skull 1½" × 1½" (3.8 × 3.8 cm) squares that make up the teeth for a metallic gold square of the same size for a little extra pirate flavor.

ASSEMBLE THE BLOCK

4. Sew one 3½" × 17½" (9 × 44.5 cm) background rectangle to the right side and one to the left side of the skull block (**Figure 1**, page 114).

5. Sew one 3½" × 21½" (9 × 54.5 cm) background rectangle to the top edge and one to the bottom edge of the skull block (**Figure 2**, page 114).

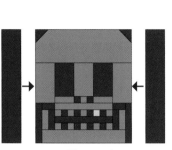

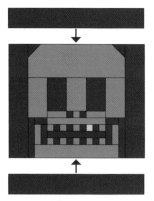

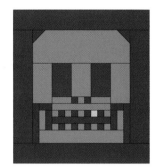

Figure 1   Figure 2   Figure 3

Block should measure about 23½" × 21½" (59.5 × 54.5 cm) **(Figure 3)**.

FINISH THE QUILT

6. Follow the instructions for preparing the quilt top for quilting on page 10.

7. Follow the quilting instructions on page 115.

8. To complete the quilt, follow the bias binding instructions on page 183.

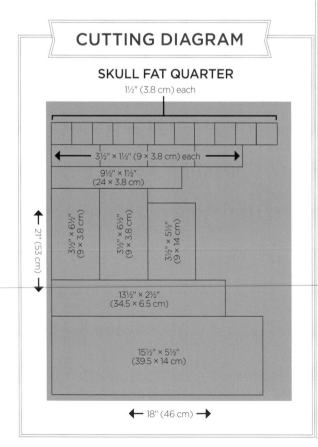

CUTTING DIAGRAM

SKULL FAT QUARTER

1½" (3.8 cm) each

3½" × 1½" (9 × 3.8 cm) each

9½" × 1½" (24 × 3.8 cm)

3½" × 6½" (9 × 3.8 cm)

3½" × 6½" (9 × 3.8 cm)

3½" × 5½" (9 × 14 cm)

2" (53 cm)

13½" × 2½" (34.5 × 6.5 cm)

15½" × 5½" (39.5 × 14 cm)

← 18" (46 cm) →

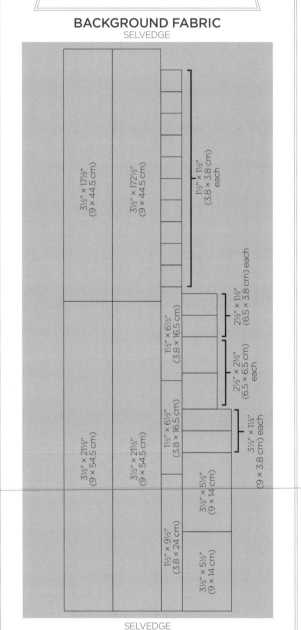

CUTTING DIAGRAM

BACKGROUND FABRIC

SELVEDGE

3½" × 17½" (9 × 44.5 cm)

3½" × 172½" (9 × 44.5 cm)

1½" × 1½" (3.8 × 3.8 cm) each

2½" × 1½" (6.5 × 3.8 cm) each

1½" × 6½" (3.8 × 16.5 cm)

2½" × 2½" (6.5 × 6.5 cm) each

1½" × 6½" (3.8 × 16.5 cm)

3½" × 1½" (9 × 3.8 cm) each

3½" × 21½" (9 × 54.5 cm)

3½" × 21½" (9 × 54.5 cm)

1½" × 9½" (3.8 × 24 cm)

3½" × 5½" (9 × 14 cm)

3½" × 5½" (9 × 14 cm)

SELVEDGE

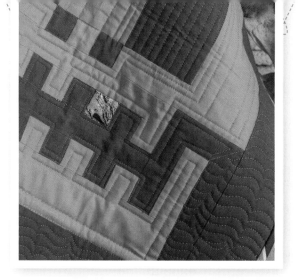

QUILTING SIMPLE

A skull with a gold tooth? Be still, my beating heart! When you want to highlight a quilt block and finish it quickly, echo quilting is the perfect option. Using straight lines to echo parts of the quilt block keeps the quilting from becoming too distracting—and it is easy to do.

Keeping it simple was my motto with the quilting designs on this mini quilt. In the background, rows of brackets help draw the eye to the center of the quilt without overwhelming it.

BRACKETS

The brackets design packs more of a punch than basic straight-line quilting, but the shape can be a little tricky to quilt. If yours doesn't seem to look quite right, try drawing it a few times to get the hang of it. The brackets don't have to be any particular size. Just quilt them in a way that feels natural to you. The most important thing is that you keep them as consistent as possible.

1. Starting from one side of the quilt, quilt a bracket so that it is parallel to the bottom of the quilt **(Figure 1)**.

2. Continue quilting brackets in a row until you reach the skull block in the middle **(Figure 2)**.

3. Travel down along the edge of the block ½" (1.3 cm) and echo the row of brackets back to the side you started from **(Figure 3)**.

4. Repeat Steps 1–3, filling in the background of the skull.

Brackets are a simple but fun background quilting design..

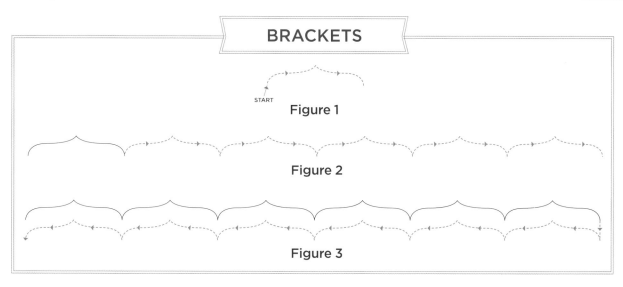

BRACKETS

START

Figure 1

Figure 2

Figure 3

COOL

When Green, Blue, and Purple get together, they create an aura of effortless ease around them. They embody that unattainable "it" factor that you can't quite put your finger on. They are moody and brooding, reflecting an air of quiet mystery that is at once soothing and somehow darkly dangerous.

The cool colors spend their weekends at obscure film festivals and slam poetry nights, preferring to avoid the nightclubs and pounding DJ sets that the warm colors love so much.

COOL QUILT TECHNIQUES

Sewing Rectangles

Sometimes the best quilts are the ones that look impressive, but require very little of the maker. The Patina quilt is a collection of rectangles sewn into strips. As the quilt builds, the design emerges, looking more like a painting or a weaving than a quilt. Accurate cutting and consistent seam allowances are the only tools you need to make this simple quilt a stunner.

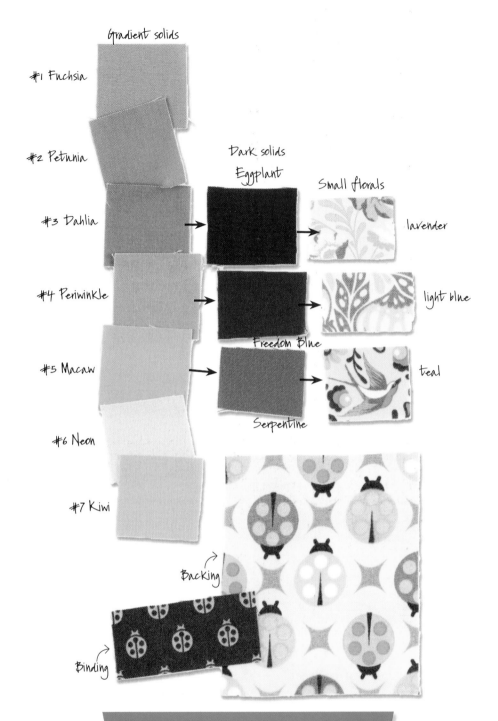

Gradient solids

#1 Fuchsia

#2 Petunia

Dark solids
Eggplant

Small florals

#3 Dahlia

lavender

#4 Periwinkle

light blue

#5 Macaw

Freedom Blue

teal

#6 Neon

Serpentine

#7 Kiwi

Backing

Binding

CHOOSING FABRICS

When choosing fabrics, look for a gradient blend from purple to blue to green for the seven main fabrics, which give the quilt its overall effect. For the three dark fabrics that surround the center crosses, I selected the darkest teal, navy, and purple solids

that I could find from Free Spirt's Designer solids line. These dark colors act as a frame for the center crosses.

The center cross fabric in the small floral prints are the least-used fabrics, so make them count! I chose small prints that best

embodied many of the solid colors in their immediate sections of the quilt top. Even these prints follow the gradient created by the original seven colors. The fabric selection and placement are what give the Patina quilt a gorgeous ombré effect.

PATINA

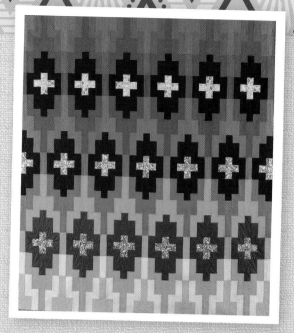

Finished quilt size: 74" × 82"
(188 × 208 cm)

Fabrics

⅓ yd (30 cm) of Fuchsia solid

⅝ yd (57 cm) of Petunia solid

1⅛ yd (103 cm) of Dahlia solid

1¼ yd (114 cm) of Periwinkle solid

1⅛ yd (103 cm) of Macaw solid

⅝ yd (57 cm) of Neon solid

⅓ yd (30 cm) of Kiwi solid

¾ yd (68.5 cm) of Eggplant solid

⅜ yd (57 cm) of Freedom Blue solid

¾ yd (68.5 cm) of Serpentine solid

¼ yd (23 cm) of lavendar small floral

¼ yd (23 cm) of light blue small floral

¼ yd (23 cm) of teal small floral

Backing, Binding & Batting

5 yd (4.5 m) of 40"/42" (102/107 cm) wide fabric or 2⅓ yd (2.1 m) of 108" (274 cm) wide backing fabric

⅔ yd (61 cm) of fabric to make 328" (833 cm) of 2½" (6.5 cm) bias binding

82" × 88" (208 × 223.5 cm) of batting

CUT THE FABRICS

1. From each of the Fuchsia and Kiwi solids, cut four 2½" (6.5 cm) × WOF (width of fabric) strips.

From each set of 4 strips, sub cut:
» Seven 2½" × 10½" (6.5 × 26.5 cm) rectangles
» Twelve 2½" × 4½" (6.5 × 16.5 cm) rectangles

2. From each of the Petunia and Neon solids, cut six 2½" (6.5 cm) × WOF strips.

From each set of 6 strips, sub cut:
» Thirty-one 2½" × 6½" (6.5 × 16.5 cm) rectangles

3. From each of the Dahlia and Macaw solids, cut fourteen 2½" (6.5 cm) × WOF strips.

From each set of 14 strips, sub cut:
» Twelve 2½" × 10½" (6.5 × 26.5 cm) rectangles
» Fifty-five 2½" × 6½" (6.5 × 16.5 cm) rectangles

4. From the Periwinkle solid, cut fourteen 2½" (6.5 cm) × WOF strips.

From the 14 strips, sub cut:
» Fourteen 2½" × 10½" (6.5 × 26.5 cm) rectangles
» Fifty-four 2½" × 6½" (6.5 × 16.5 cm) rectangles

5. From each of the Eggplant and Serpentine solids, cut nine 2½" (6.5 cm) × WOF strips.

From each set of 9 strips, sub cut:
» Forty-eight 2½" × 6½" (6.5 × 16.5 cm) rectangles

6. From the Freedom Blue solid, cut nine 2½" (6.5 cm) × WOF strips.

From the 9 strips, sub cut:
» Fifty 2½" × 6½" (6.5 × 16.5 cm) rectangles

7. From each of the lavender floral and the teal floral prints, cut three 2½" (6.5 cm) × WOF strips.

From each set of 3 strips, sub cut:

» Twelve $2\frac{1}{2}$" × $2\frac{1}{2}$" (6.5 × 6.5 cm) squares
» Six $2\frac{1}{2}$" × $6\frac{1}{2}$" (6.5 × 16.5 cm) rectangles

8. From the light blue floral print, cut three $2\frac{1}{2}$"
   (6.5 cm) × WOF strips.

From the 3 strips, sub cut:

» Twelve $2\frac{1}{2}$" × $2\frac{1}{2}$" (6.5 × 6.5 cm) squares
» Seven $2\frac{1}{2}$" × $6\frac{1}{2}$" (6.5 × 16.5 cm) rectangles

SEW COLUMN A (MAKE 7)

Note: Each sewn column should measure about
$2\frac{1}{2}$" × $82\frac{1}{2}$" (6.5 × 209.5 cm).

9. Follow the Column A Assembly Diagram to lay out
   the 11 pieces in the correct color order.

   Beginning at the top of the column, place the first
   2 rectangles right sides together and sew across the
   $2\frac{1}{2}$" (6.5 cm) edge.

10. Continue joining rectangles until the column is
    complete.

11. Repeat Steps 9 and 10 to make 6 more Column A
    units.

SEW COLUMN B (MAKE 12)

12. Follow the Column B Assembly Diagram to lay out
    the 15 pieces in the correct color order.

    Beginning at the top of Column B, place 2

rectangles right sides together and sew across the
$2\frac{1}{2}$" (6.5 cm) edge.

13. Continue joining rectangles until the column is
    complete.

14. Repeat Steps 12 and 13 to make 11 more Column B
    units.

SEW COLUMN C (MAKE 12)

15. Follow the Column C Assembly Diagram to lay out
    each of the 15 pieces in the correct color order.

    Beginning at the top of the column, place 2
    rectangles right sides together and sew across
    the $2\frac{1}{2}$" (6.5 cm) edge.

16. Continue joining rectangles until the column is
    complete.

17. Repeat Steps 15 and 16 to make 11 more Column C
    units.

> **TIP!**
>
> When joining the columns, pin at the top
> and bottom of each column and at each
> aligning seam. Pinning will insure that the
> columns consistently line up throughout the
> quilt top, and any minor variation in length,
> due to slight cutting or seam allowance
> irregularities, is evenly distributed across
> the length of each column.

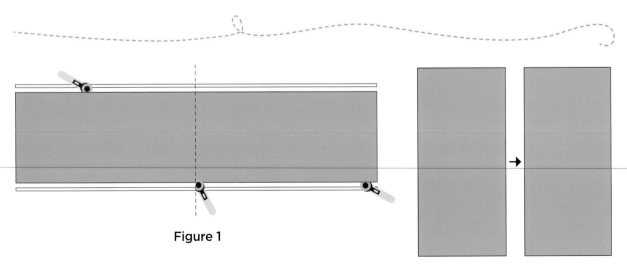

Figure 1

Figure 2

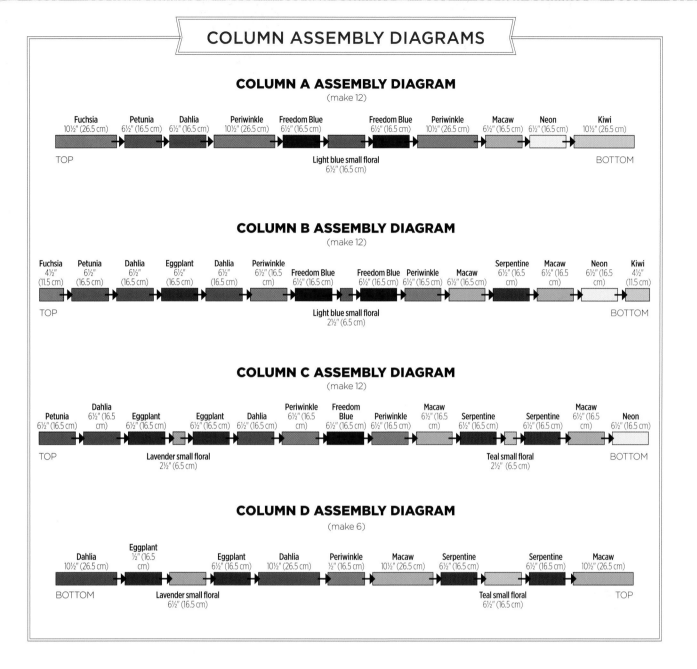

COLUMN ASSEMBLY DIAGRAMS

COLUMN A ASSEMBLY DIAGRAM
(make 12)

| Fuchsia 10½" (26.5 cm) | Petunia 6½" (16.5 cm) | Dahlia 6½" (16.5 cm) | Periwinkle 10½" (26.5 cm) | Freedom Blue 6½" (16.5 cm) | Freedom Blue 6½" (16.5 cm) | Periwinkle 10½" (26.5 cm) | Macaw 6½" (16.5 cm) | Neon 6½" (16.5 cm) | Kiwi 10½" (26.5 cm) |

TOP

Light blue small floral 6½" (16.5 cm)

BOTTOM

COLUMN B ASSEMBLY DIAGRAM
(make 12)

| Fuchsia 4½" (11.5 cm) | Petunia 6½" (16.5 cm) | Dahlia 6½" (16.5 cm) | Eggplant 6½" (16.5 cm) | Dahlia 6½" (16.5 cm) | Periwinkle 6½" (16.5 cm) | Freedom Blue 6½" (16.5 cm) | Freedom Blue 6½" (16.5 cm) | Periwinkle 6½" (16.5 cm) | Macaw 6½" (16.5 cm) | Serpentine 6½" (16.5 cm) | Macaw 6½" (16.5 cm) | Neon 6½" (16.5 cm) | Kiwi 4½" (11.5 cm) |

TOP

Light blue small floral 2½" (6.5 cm)

BOTTOM

COLUMN C ASSEMBLY DIAGRAM
(make 12)

| Petunia 6½" (16.5 cm) | Dahlia 6½" (16.5 cm) | Eggplant 6½" (16.5 cm) | Eggplant 6½" (16.5 cm) | Dahlia 6½" (16.5 cm) | Periwinkle 6½" (16.5 cm) | Freedom Blue 6½" (16.5 cm) | Periwinkle 6½" (16.5 cm) | Macaw 6½" (16.5 cm) | Serpentine 6½" (16.5 cm) | Serpentine 6½" (16.5 cm) | Macaw 6½" (16.5 cm) | Neon 6½" (16.5 cm) |

TOP

Lavender small floral 2½" (6.5 cm)

Teal small floral 2½" (6.5 cm)

BOTTOM

COLUMN D ASSEMBLY DIAGRAM
(make 6)

| Dahlia 10½" (26.5 cm) | Eggplant ½" (16.5 cm) | Eggplant 6½" (16.5 cm) | Dahlia 10½" (26.5 cm) | Periwinkle ½" (16.5 cm) | Macaw 10½" (26.5 cm) | Serpentine 6½" (16.5 cm) | Serpentine 6½" (16.5 cm) | Macaw 10½" (26.5 cm) |

BOTTOM

Lavender small floral 6½" (16.5 cm)

Teal small floral 6½" (16.5 cm)

TOP

SEW COLUMN D (MAKE 6)

18. Follow the Column D Assembly Diagram to lay out each of the 12 pieces in the correct color order.

    Beginning at the top of the column, place 2 rectangles right sides together and sew across the 2½" (6.5 cm) edge.

19. Continue joining rectangles until the column is complete.

20. Repeat Steps 18 and 19 to make 5 more Column D strips.

ASSEMBLE THE QUILT TOP

21. Working from left to right, sew all of the A, B, C, and D columns together according to the Patina Assembly Diagram on page 122.

PIECE THE BACKING

22. To make the backing from 40"/42" (102/107 cm) backing fabric, trim the selvedges. Cut the trimmed backing yardage in half to create two 90" (229 cm) × WOF pieces **(Figure 1)**.

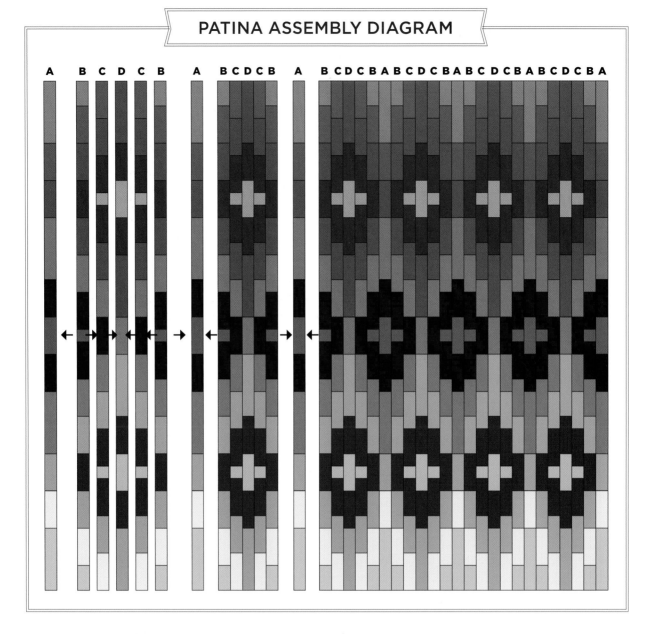

23. Place the 2 backing pieces right sides together and sew along the 90" (229 cm) edge **(Figure 2)**.

Backing should measure about 82" × 90" (208 × 229 cm).

FINISH THE QUILT

24. Follow the instructions for preparing the quilt top for quilting on page 10.

25. Follow the quilting instructions on page 123.

26. To complete the quilt, follow the bias binding instructions on page 183.

QUILTING WITH STRAIGHT LINES

Sometimes quilters feel as though they need to learn several different quilting designs before they can work on their quilt tops. That couldn't be further from the truth. Just knowing a few basic designs and using them in interesting ways can look stunning on a quilt, like

on Patina. Repeated simple quilted swirls and straight lines enhance the quilt pattern. Instead of worrying about learning a new design, think of interesting ways to use the ones you already know!

QUILTING INSIDE THE BLOCK

To make the fabric in the center of the block stand out, I quilted diagonal lines that all but point right to them. This is also a nice contrast from the swirl design in the rest of the areas. It has even more dimension than other geometric designs I have used in this book.

PATINA ARROWS

This arrow design is actually really easy to quilt—you just work your way around the block, going from point to point. It only consists of diagonal lines! If you get

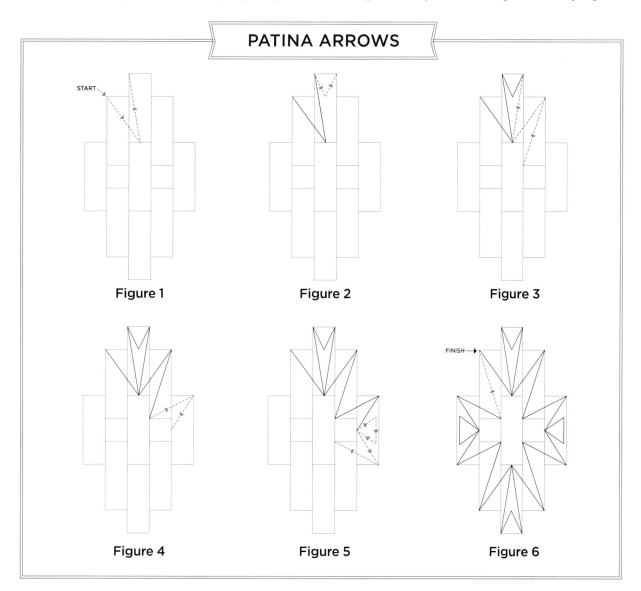

PATINA ARROWS

Figure 1

Figure 2

Figure 3

Figure 4

Figure 5

Figure 6

stuck, take a moment to think through your next step or two. You don't have to do it in the order shown, either. Whatever corner of the block you find yourself at is the best place to start.

NOTE: For this design, we consider the five columns that make up the center of each ombré design a single block.

1. Starting in the top left corner of the second column, quilt a diagonal line to the center of the top of the middle floral column. Quilt back up to the topmost left corner of the block, making an arrow shape (**Figure 1**, page 123).

2. Echo the diagonal line, quilting a small arrow shape in the top of the center column of the block, ending in the topmost right corner (**Figure 2**, page 123).

3. Quilt another diagonal line to the center of the top of the middle floral column, creating the point of an arrow. Quilt another diagonal line from the center to the top right corner of the fourth column, mirroring the diagonal line in Step 1. Finish with

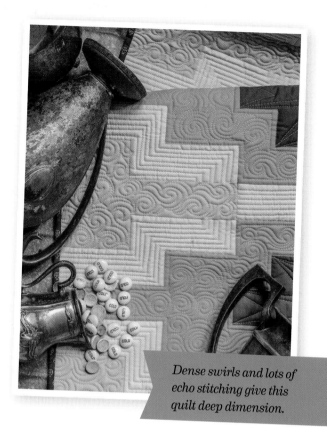

Dense swirls and lots of echo stitching give this quilt deep dimension.

ECHO QUILTING

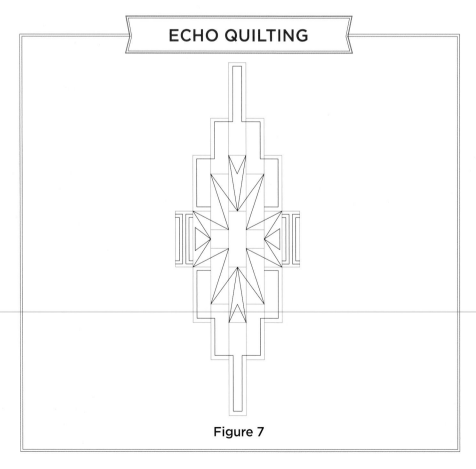

Figure 7

Echo quilting can be a little tricky, especially if you are a beginner quilter. But it doesn't take long to master. Here a few tips to help make your echoing shine.

1. Focus on quilting a smooth line, not necessarily a perfect one.

When quilting, it may be tempting to adjust your quilting midline to keep the spacing perfect. But a line that is quilted smoothly will appear perfectly spaced, even if it isn't!

2. Look ahead of where you are quilting.

Don't look at the needle; instead look ahead 1"–2" (2.5-5 cm) and trust your hands to bring you smoothly to that point.

3. Use the foot of the machine as a guide.

To keep the spacing as consistent as possible, line the foot of your machine along the previous quilted line. This will help prevent your lines from getting too close or too far apart.

4. Don't tense up!

Sometimes you might feel that if you just focused more or tried harder, the quilting would look just a little better. Instead, relax, take a breath, and go for it.

another diagonal line to the right floral piece (**Figure 3**, page 123).

4. Quilt a diagonal line to the top right corner of the last column and then back to the left center of the small floral piece in the fourth column (**Figure 4**, page 123).

5. Quilt a small triangular shape in the middle of the last column, returning to the center of the small floral piece. Quilt a diagonal line that goes to the bottom right corner of the last column and then on to the bottom left corner of the small floral piece (**Figure 5**, page 123).

6. Continue quilting the same arrow and diamond shapes around the center of the block, mirroring the stitching in Steps 1–5 (**Figure 6**, page 123).

PATINA ARROWS VARIATION

If you like more quilting on your quilts, you could add echo lines inside some of the arrows.

PUT A SWIRL ON IT

Combining straight lines with free-motion quilting designs is an easy way to add more interest to your quilt. In the rest of the Patina blocks, I quilted a dense swirl design (see page 41 for instructions). I love the way it looks with the echo quilting! It doesn't have to be swirls, of course; just choose a filler that has a different look from the straight lines for a nice contrast. Pebbles (page 42) or leaves (page 44) would look nice as well.

ECHO QUILTING

If I have said it once, I have said it a million times: Echoing the sides of a quilt block can really highlight the quilt pattern. In fact, I like to say that echoing is your best quilting friend. You can achieve many different looks by switching up how you place the echo line. For instance, you can echo just one side of the block, you can echo all sides of the block, or you can play around with the lines and come up with something different altogether.

In the Patina quilt, I used the echoing to pull several blocks together. It frames the center of the blocks and spotlights the rectangular shapes in the quilt.

I started with the first echo line and then continued echoing inside the previously quilted line until the area was completely filled (**Figure 7**). I quilted my lines ¼" (3mm) apart, but you could space them out farther for less dense quilting.

Black & Gray

Black is stubborn. Black sees things one way and one way only. Black really dominates the room and takes over any conversation that occurs within earshot. A lot of the colors believe that this is largely due to Black never having been included in the rainbow because, well, black isn't really a color at all.

Black's little brother Gray is much more laid back about the whole thing. Gray is pretty cool with being everyone's favorite shadow. The way that Gray sees it, he gets to hang out with all of the colors but doesn't have to line up with them in perfect order. Gray thinks that being the middle kid between Black and White is just about the best place to be, never really having to make a decision about anything.

BLACK & GRAY QUILT TECHNIQUES

Sewing Log Cabins

The log cabin block has endured because it is so striking and offers the piecer so many design possibilities. A simple series of squares and rectangles build on themselves until a striped square emerges; in this case, halfway through the block I ask you to build in the opposite direction to create a block within a block.

On top of that, I will ask you to inject bright pops of colored logs randomly into the block to create what I like to call the "Interrupted Log Cabin," which I have used in the quilt by the same name as well as in the Humble Origins quilt. These interruptions infuse the standard, structured block with a bit of spontaneity and movement.

The sewing is simple and straightforward, each piece building on the last. As always, it all comes down to accurate cutting and consistent seams.

Setting fabric

Binding

inner cabin (dark)

outer cabin (light)

The interruptors!

neon pink

pink sprout

orange dot

red stripe

aqua star

light blue dot

CHOOSING FABRICS

Here, the log cabin block is broken down into two parts, the inner log cabin and the outer log cabin. The inner log cabin is made up of a darker contrasting pair of black and light gray fabrics. The outer log cabin is made of a lighter contrasting pair of white and dark gray fabrics. This pairing causes the inner log cabin to recede deeper into the block, almost like you are walking down a long tunnel.

The neutral nature of black, gray, and white leaves the door of possibilities wide open for adding in color. I chose my setting fabric—gray with bright pops of yellow, pink, and orange—first and pulled my grays and blacks from that piece to match. I used that same setting fabric to pull my interrupter colors from, too. I chose mostly pinks and oranges and added the aqua blue backgrounds that have pink accents. The setting fabric makes all of the other fabrics work together.

HUMBLE ORIGINS

Finished quiltsize: 57" × 57"
(145 × 145 cm)

Finished block size: 10" × 10"
(25.5 × 25.5 cm)

Fabrics
⅙ yd (15 cm) each of 6 bright pink,
orange, red, and aqua prints

½ yd (45.5 cm) of light gray print

½ yd (45.5 cm) of black print

1 yd (91.5 cm) of dark gray print

1¼ yd (114 cm) of white solid

1 yd (91.5 cm) of multi colored print

Backing, Batting & Binding
3⅝ yd (3.3 m) of 40"/42"
(102/107 cm) wide fabric or 1⅞
yd (1.7 m) of 108" (274 cm) wide
backing fabric

½ yd (45.5 cm) of fabric to make
238" (604.5 cm) of 2½" (6.5 cm) bias
binding

65" × 65" (165 × 165 cm) of batting

CUT THE FABRICS

1. From each of the six ⅙ yd (15 cm) bright prints, cut two 1½" (3.8 cm) × WOF (width of fabric) strips.

From each pair of bright print strips, sub cut:
» Five 1½" × 1½" (3.8 × 3.8 cm) squares
» One 1½" × 2½" (3.8 × 6.5 cm) rectangle
» One 1½" × 3½" (3.8 × 9 cm) rectangle
» One 1½" × 4½" (3.8 × 11.5 cm) rectangle
» One 1½" × 5½" (3.8 × 14 cm) rectangle
» One 1½" × 6½" (3.8 × 16.5 cm) rectangle
» One 1½" × 7½" (3.8 × 19 cm) rectangle
» One 1½" × 8½" (3.8 × 21.5 cm) rectangle
» One 1½" × 9½" (3.8 × 24 cm) rectangle
» One 1½" × 10½" (3.8 × 26.5 cm) rectangle

2. From the light gray print, cut seven 1½" (3.8 cm) × WOF strips.

From the 7 strips, sub cut:
» Eighteen 1½" × 1½" (3.8 × 3.8 cm) squares
» Eighteen 1½" × 2½" (3.8 × 6.5 cm) rectangles
» Eighteen 1½" × 3½" (3.8 × 9 cm) rectangles
» Eighteen 1½" × 4½" (3.8 × 11.5 cm) rectangles

3. From the black print, cut eleven 1½" (3.8 cm) × WOF strips.

From the 11 strips, sub cut:
» Twenty-four 1½" × 2½" (3.8 × 6.5 cm) rectangles
» Twenty-four 1½" × 3½" (3.8 × 9 cm) rectangles
» Twenty-four 1½" × 4¼" (3.8 × 11 cm) rectangles
» Twenty-four 1½" × 5½" (3.8 × 14 cm) rectangles

4. From the dark gray print, cut twenty-two 1½" (3.8 cm) × WOF strips.

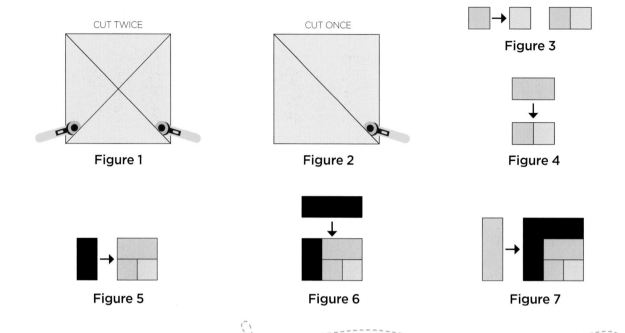

CUT TWICE

Figure 1

CUT ONCE

Figure 2

Figure 3

Figure 4

Figure 5

Figure 6

Figure 7

From the 22 WOF strips, sub cut:
» Twenty-four 1½" × 6½" (3.8 × 16.5 cm) rectangles
» Twenty-four 1½" × 7½" (3.8 × 19 cm) rectangles
» Twenty-four 1½" × 8½" (3.8 × 21.5 cm) rectangles
» Twenty-four 1½" × 9½" (3.8 × 24 cm) rectangles

5. From the white solid, cut twenty-five 1½" (3.8 cm) × WOF strips.

From the 2 WOF strips, sub cut:
» Eighteen 1½" × 5½" (3.8 × 14 cm) rectangles
» Eighteen 1½" × 6½" (3.8 × 16.5 cm) rectangles
» Eighteen 1½" × 7½" (3.8 × 19 cm) rectangles
» Eighteen 1½" × 8½" (3.8 × 21.5 cm) rectangles
» Eighteen 1½" × 9½" (3.8 × 24 cm) rectangles
» Eighteen 1½" × 10½" (3.8 × 26.5 cm) rectangles

6. From the setting fabric, cut four 15½" × 15½" (39.5 × 39.5 cm) squares.

   Cut 2 squares twice diagonally for a total of 8 setting triangles **(Figure 1)**. Cut the remaining 2 squares once diagonally for a total of 4 corner triangles **(Figure 2)**.

MIX THE PIECES

7. Begin each block with a 1½" × 1½" (3.8 × 3.8 cm) colored square. Set 24 of them aside, one for each block.

Mix the remaining 1½" × 1½" (3.8 × 3.8 cm) colored squares randomly with the 1½" × 1½" (3.8 × 3.8 cm) light gray squares.

8. Mix the 2½" × 1½" (6.5 × 3.8 cm), 3½" × 1½" (9 × 3.8 cm), and 4½" × 1½" (11.5 × 3.8 cm) colored randomly with the correspondingly sized light gray rectangles. All of these pieces will be referred to as "light gray."

9. Mix the 5½" × 1½" (14 × 3.8 cm), 6½" × 1½" (16.5 × 3.8 cm)", 7½" × 1½" (19 × 3.8 cm), 8½" × 1½" (21.5 × 3.8 cm), 9½" × 1½" (24 × 3.8 cm), and 10½" × 1½" (26.5 × 3.8 cm) colored randomly with the correspondingly sized white pieces. All of these pieces will be referred to as "white."

TIP!

Randomly mixing pieces can be difficult for an organized mind. Toss the colored pieces into a bag with the corresponding light gray or white pieces and pull them out of the bag as needed without looking to create the random placement of these colored pieces. Some blocks may have several colored interrupter pieces, while other blocks have none at all. This is a good thing, so go with it.

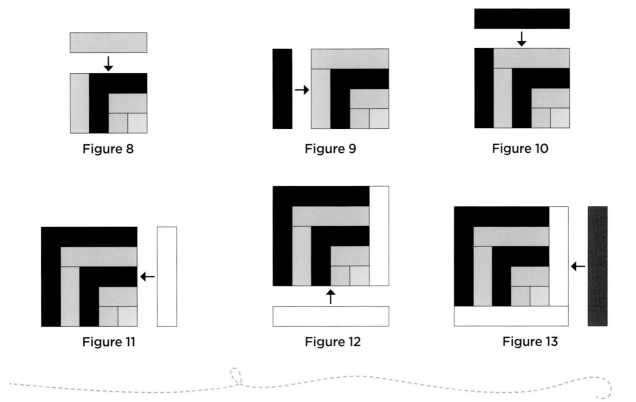

Figure 8

Figure 9

Figure 10

Figure 11

Figure 12

Figure 13

10. Sew one $1\frac{1}{2}$" × $1\frac{1}{2}$" (3.8 × 3.8 cm) light gray square to one of the $1\frac{1}{2}$" × $1\frac{1}{2}$" (3.8 × 3.8 cm) colored squares **(Figure 3)**.

11. Add one $2\frac{1}{2}$" × $1\frac{1}{2}$" (6.5 × 3.8 cm) light gray to the top edge of the unit, keeping the colored square to the right **(Figure 4)**.

12. Add one $2\frac{1}{2}$" × $1\frac{1}{2}$" (6.5 × 3.8 cm) black rectangle to the left edge of the unit **(Figure 5)**.

13. Add one $3\frac{1}{2}$" × $1\frac{1}{2}$" (9 × 3.8 cm) black rectangle to the top edge of the unit **(Figure 6)**.

14. Add one $3\frac{1}{2}$" × $1\frac{1}{2}$" (9 × 3.8 cm) light gray to the left edge of the unit **(Figure 7)**.

15. Add one $4\frac{1}{2}$" × $1\frac{1}{2}$" (11.5 × 3.8 cm) light gray strip to the top edge of the unit **(Figure 8)**.

16. Add one $4\frac{1}{2}$" × $1\frac{1}{2}$" (11.5 × 3.8 cm) black rectangle to the left edge of the unit **(Figure 9)**.

17. Add one $5\frac{1}{2}$" × $1\frac{1}{2}$" (14 × 3.8 cm) black rectangle to the top edge of the unit **(Figure 10)**.

18. Begin building out from the pieced side of the log cabin block. Add one $5\frac{1}{2}$" × $1\frac{1}{2}$" (14 × 3.8 cm) white rectangle to the right edge of the unit **(Figure 11)**.

19. Add one $6\frac{1}{2}$" × $1\frac{1}{2}$" (16.5 × 3.8 cm) white rectangle to the bottom edge of the unit **(Figure 12)**.

20. Add one $6\frac{1}{2}$" × $1\frac{1}{2}$" (16.5 × 3.8 cm) dark gray rectangle to the right edge of the unit **(Figure 13)**.

21. Add one $7\frac{1}{2}$" × $1\frac{1}{2}$" (19 × 3.8 cm) dark gray rectangle to the bottom edge of the unit **(Figure 14, page 132)**.

22. Add one $7\frac{1}{2}$" × $1\frac{1}{2}$" (19 × 3.8 cm) white to the right edge of the unit **(Figure 15, page 132)**.

23. Add one $8\frac{1}{2}$" × $1\frac{1}{2}$" (21.5 × 3.8 cm) white to the bottom edge of the unit **(Figure 16, page 132)**.

24. Add one $8\frac{1}{2}$" × $1\frac{1}{2}$" (21.5 × 3.8 cm) dark gray rectangle to the right edge of the unit **(Figure 17, page 132)**.

25. Add one $9\frac{1}{2}$" × $1\frac{1}{2}$" (24 × 3.8 cm) dark gray rectangle to the bottom edge of the unit **(Figure 18, page 132)**.

26. Add one $9\frac{1}{2}$" × $1\frac{1}{2}$" (24 × 3.8 cm) white rectangle to the right edge of the unit **(Figure 19, page 132)**.

27. Add one $10\frac{1}{2}$" × $1\frac{1}{2}$" (26.5 × 3.8 cm) white rectangle to the bottom edge to complete the unit **(Figure 20, page 132)**.

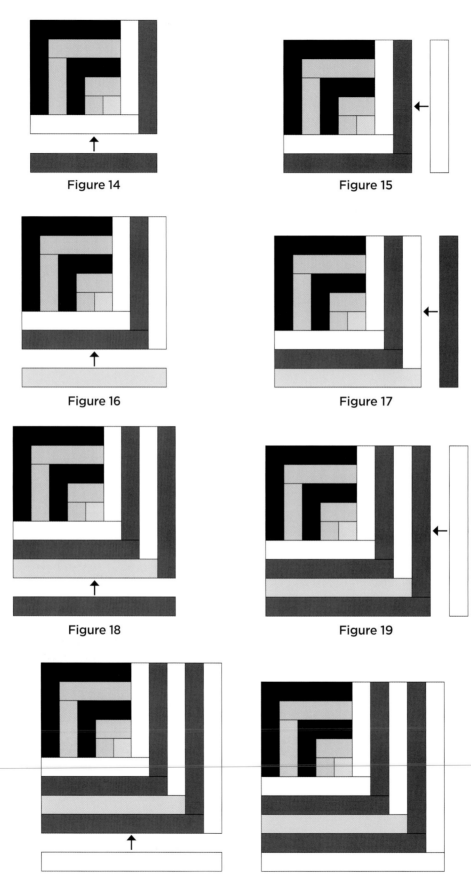

Figure 14

Figure 15

Figure 16

Figure 17

Figure 18

Figure 19

Figure 20

SETTING ON-POINT BLOCKS

The arrangement of the Humble Origins quilt is called "on point," meaning that the blocks are set together in diagonal rows and finished with setting triangles to make the quilt square. Below are a few tips for lining up the setting triangles and corner triangles when completing the diagonal rows.

2 Allow the point of the setting triangle to extend past the top log cabin row ½" (1.3 cm).

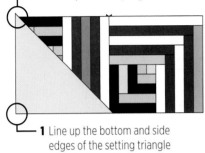

1 Line up the bottom and side edges of the setting triangle with the log cabin row.

3 Find the center of the corner triangle by folding it in half and gently creasing it with your finger. Align the center of the corner triangle with the center seam of the two corner blocks.

4 Allow the points of the corner triangle to extend past the edges of the setting triangles the width of the seam allowance. Sew from intersection to intersection.

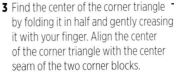

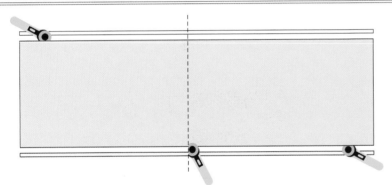

Figure 21

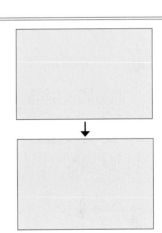

Figure 22

The block should measure approximately 10½" × 10½" (26.5 × 26.5 cm).

28. Repeat Steps 5–22 to create a total of 24 blocks.

ASSEMBLE THE QUILT TOP

29. Assemble the blocks and the setting triangles according to the Humble Origins Assembly Diagram on page 134.

    Add the corner triangles last.

30. To make the backing from 40"/42" (102/107 cm) backing fabric, trim the selvedge. Cut the trimmed backing yardage in half to create two 65" (165 cm) WOF pieces **(Figure 21)**.

31. Place the 2 backing pieces right sides together and sew along the 65" (165 cm) edge **(Figure 22)**.

    Backing should measure about 65" × 82" (165 × 208 cm).

FINISH THE QUILT

32. Follow the instructions for preparing the quilt top for quilting on page 10.

33. Follow the quilting instructions on page 135.

34. To complete the quilt, follow the bias binding instructions on page 183.

HUMBLE ORIGINS ASSEMBLY DIAGRAM

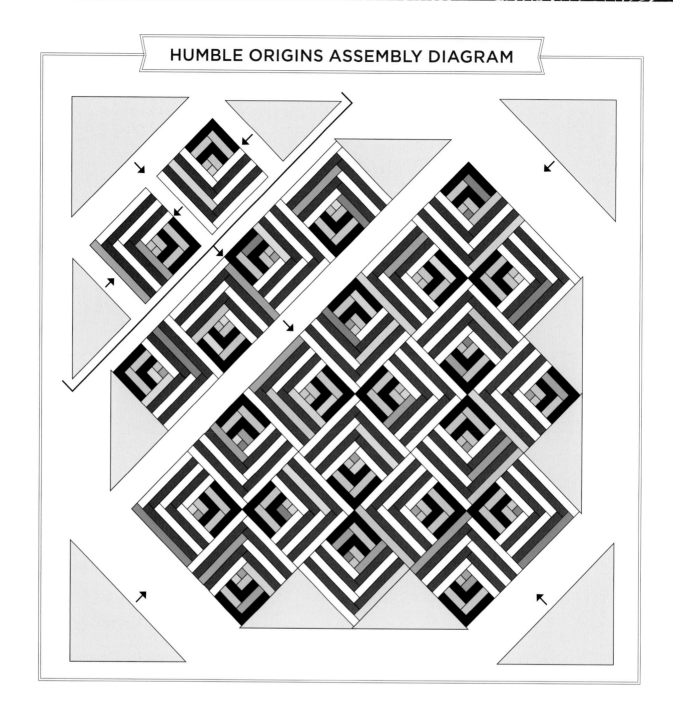

QUILTING BETWEEN THE DOTS

In the solid white strips, I echoed the sides and left the center unquilted. It really makes them pop, especially when compared to the wishbones in the gray stripes and the serpentine lines (see page 29 for instructions) in the prints.

HUMBLE DOT TO DOT

This design is similar to the dot-to-dot design used in the Interrupted Log Cabin quilt (page 136), but it has fewer steps.

1. Starting from the bottom left corner of the small square piece in the block, quilt a continuous line that curves to each corner and returning to the starting point. Move clockwise around the inside of the square **(Figure 1)**.

2. Stitch a single arrow shape diagonally from the bottom right corner of the second small square to the farthest left corner of the next ring of the log cabin, returning to the right corner opposite the starting point **(Figure 2)**.

3. Travel up the edge of the block to the next ring and repeat Step 2, quilting another single arrow shape out to the farthest corner of this ring and then to the right side **(Figure 3)**.

4. Continue traveling along the edge of the block and quilting an arrow in each ring until the block is filled in **(Figure 4)**.

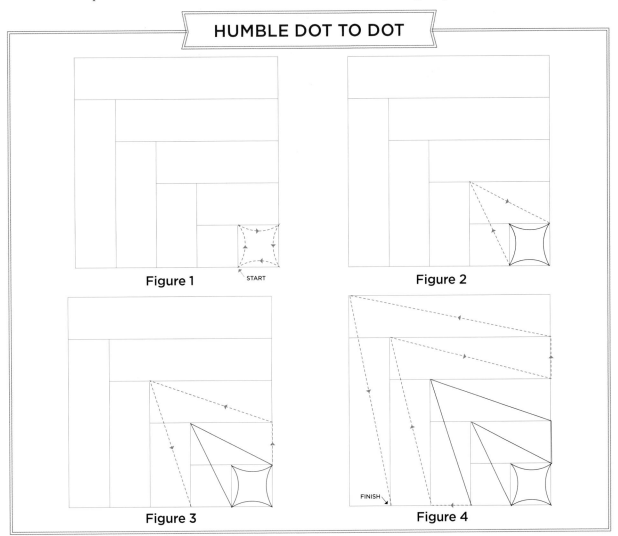

HUMBLE DOT TO DOT

Figure 1   START

Figure 2

Figure 3

Figure 4

INTERRUPTED LOG CABIN

I made the quilt in wide strips of solids and sewed the large blocks together in a straightforward grid, which really opened the space for the quilting to shine.

I chose my backing fabric first—a big, bold, colorful floral print that has a heavy dose of charcoal gray. I matched the individual colors from the print to solid fabrics. These are the interrupters in this log cabin quilt, chosen at random during the piecing process to give this quilt a kick of spontaneity.

Finished quilt size: 80" × 80" (203 × 203 cm)

Finished block size: 20" × 20" (51 × 51 cm)

Fabrics
⅓ yd (30 cm) each of mint, bright peach, hot pink, and red

⅞ yd (80 cm) of light gray solid

1⅛ yd (103 cm) of black solid

2⅛ yd (194 cm) of dark gray solid

2⅝ yd (240 cm) of white solid

Backing, Batting & Binding
8¼ yd (7.5 m) of 40"/42" (102/107 cm) wide fabric or 2½ yd (2.3 m) of 108" (274 cm) wide backing fabric

⅝ yd (57 cm) of fabric to make 330" (838 cm) of 2½" (6.5 cm) bias binding

88" × 88" (223.5 × 223.5 cm) of batting

CUT THE FABRICS

1. From each of the four ⅓ yd bright solids, cut four 2½" (6.5 cm) × WOF (width of fabric) strips.

From each set of WOF strips, sub cut:
» Five 2½" × 2½" (6.5 × 6.5 cm) squares
» One 2½" × 4½" (6.5 × 11.5 cm) rectangle
» One 2½" × 6½" (6.5 × 16.5 cm) rectangle
» One 2½" × 8½" (6.5 × 21.5 cm) rectangle
» One 2½" × 10½" (6.5 × 26.5 cm) rectangle
» One 2½" × 12½" (6.5 × 31.5 cm) rectangle
» One 2½" × 14½" (6.5 × 37 cm) rectangle
» One 2½" × 16½" (6.5 × 42 cm) rectangle
» One 2½" × 18½" (6.5 × 47 cm) rectangle
» One 2½" × 20½" (6.5 × 52 cm) rectangle

2. From the light gray solid, cut nine 2½" (6.5 cm) × WOF strips.

From the WOF strips, sub cut:
» Twelve 2½" × 2½" (6.5 × 6.5 cm) squares
» Twelve 2½" × 4½" (6.5 × 11.5 cm) rectangles
» Twelve 2½" × 6½" (6.5 × 16.5 cm) rectangles
» Twelve 2½" × 8½" (6.5 × 21.5 cm) rectangles

3. From the black solid, cut fourteen 2½" (6.5 cm) × WOF strips.

From the 1 WOF strips, sub cut:
» Sixteen 2½" × 4½" (6.5 × 11.5 cm) rectangles
» Sixteen 2½" × 6½" (6.5 × 16.5 cm) rectangles
» Sixteen 2½" × 8½" (6.5 × 21.5 cm) rectangles
» Sixteen 2½" × 10½" (6.5 × 26.5 cm) rectangles

4. From the dark gray solid, cut thirty 2½" (6.5 cm) × WOF strips.

TIP!

Randomly mixing in pieces can be difficult for an organized mind. Toss the colored pieces into a bag with the corresponding light gray or white pieces. Pull them out of the bag as needed without looking to create the random placement of these colored pieces. Some blocks may have several colored interrupter pieces, while other blocks have none at all. This is a good thing—go with it.

From the 30 WOF strips, sub cut:
- » Sixteen $2\frac{1}{2}$" × $12\frac{1}{2}$" (6.5 × 31.5 cm) rectangles
- » Sixteen $2\frac{1}{2}$" × $14\frac{1}{2}$" (6.5 × 36 cm) rectangles
- » Sixteen $2\frac{1}{2}$" × $16\frac{1}{2}$" (6.5 × 42 cm) rectangles
- » Sixteen $2\frac{1}{2}$" × $18\frac{1}{2}$" (6.5 cm × 47) rectangles

5. From the white solid, cut thirty-six $2\frac{1}{2}$" (6.5 cm) × WOF strips.

From the 36 WOF strips, sub cut:
- » Twelve $2\frac{1}{2}$" × $16\frac{1}{2}$" (42 × 6.5 cm) rectangles
- » Twelve $2\frac{1}{2}$" × $18\frac{1}{2}$" (47 × 6.5 cm) rectangles
- » Twelve $2\frac{1}{2}$" × $20\frac{1}{2}$" (52 × 6.5 cm) rectangles
- » Twelve $2\frac{1}{2}$" × $24\frac{1}{2}$" (52 × 6.5 cm) rectangles

SEW THE BLOCKS

6. Begin all of the blocks with a $2\frac{1}{2}$" × $2\frac{1}{2}$" (6.5 × 6.5 cm) colored square. Pull 16 of them aside, one for each block.

   Mix the remaining $2\frac{1}{2}$" × $2\frac{1}{2}$" (6.5 × 6.5 cm) colored squares in with the $2\frac{1}{2}$" × $2\frac{1}{2}$" (6.5 × 6.5 cm) light gray squares.

7. Mix the $4\frac{1}{2}$" × $2\frac{1}{2}$" (11.5 × 6.5 cm), $6\frac{1}{2}$" × $2\frac{1}{2}$" (16.5 × 6.5 cm), and $8\frac{1}{2}$" × $2\frac{1}{2}$" (21.5 × 6.5 cm) colored rectangles with the correspondingly sized light gray pieces. All of these pieces will be referred to as "light gray."

8. Mix the $10\frac{1}{2}$" × $2\frac{1}{2}$" (26.5 × 6.5 cm), $12\frac{1}{2}$" × $2\frac{1}{2}$" (31.5 × 6.5 cm), $14\frac{1}{2}$" × $2\frac{1}{2}$" (37 × 6.5 cm), $16\frac{1}{2}$" × $2\frac{1}{2}$" (42 × 6.5 cm), $18\frac{1}{2}$" × $2\frac{1}{2}$" (47 × 6.5 cm), and $20\frac{1}{2}$" × $2\frac{1}{2}$" (52 × 6.5 cm) colored rectangles in with the correspondingly sized white pieces. All of these pieces will be referred to as "white."

9. Sew one $2\frac{1}{2}$" × $2\frac{1}{2}$" (6.5 × 6.5 cm) light gray square to a $2\frac{1}{2}$" × $2\frac{1}{2}$" (6.5 × 6.5 cm) colored square **(Figure 1)**.

10. Add one $4\frac{1}{2}$" × $2\frac{1}{2}$" (11.5 × 6.5 cm) light gray rectangle to the top edge of the unit **(Figure 2)**.

11. Add one $4\frac{1}{2}$" × $2\frac{1}{2}$" (11.5 × 6.5 cm) black rectangle to the left edge of the unit **(Figure 3)**.

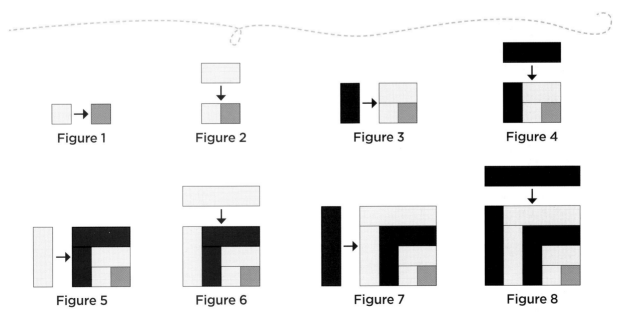

Figure 1   Figure 2   Figure 3   Figure 4

Figure 5   Figure 6   Figure 7   Figure 8

12. Add one 6½" × 2½" (16.5 × 6.5 cm) black rectangle to the top edge of the unit (**Figure 4**, page 137).

13. Add one 6½" × 2½" (16.5 × 6.5 cm) light gray rectangle to the left edge of the unit (**Figure 5**, page 137).

14. Add one 8½" × 2½" (21.5 × 6.5 cm) light gray rectangle to the top edge of the unit (**Figure 6**, page 137).

15. Add one 8½" × 2½" (21.5 × 6.5 cm) black rectangle to the left edge of the unit (**Figure 7**, page 137).

16. Add one 10½" × 2½" (26.5 × 6.5 cm) black rectangle to the top edge of the unit (**Figure 8**, page 137).

17. Add one 10½" × 2½" (26.5 × 6.5 cm) white rectangle to the right edge of the unit (**Figure 9**).

18. Add one 12½" × 2½" (31.5 × 6.5 cm) white rectangle to the bottom edge of the unit (**Figure 10**).

19. Add one 12½" × 2½" (31.5 × 6.5 cm) dark gray rectangle to the right edge of the unit (**Figure 11**).

20. Add one 14½" × 2½" (37 × 6.5 cm) dark gray to the bottom edge of the unit (**Figure 12**).

21. Add one 14½" × 2½" (37 × 6.5 cm) white rectangle to the right edge of the unit (**Figure 13**).

22. Add one white 16½" × 2½" (42 × 6.5 cm) white rectangle to the bottom edge of the unit (**Figure 14**).

23. Add one 16½" × 2½" (42 × 6.5 cm) dark gray rectangle to the right edge of the unit (**Figure 15**).

24. Add one 18½" × 2½" (47 × 6.5 cm) dark gray rectangle to the bottom edge of the unit (**Figure 16**).

25. Add one 18½" × 2½" (47 × 6.5 cm) white rectangle to the right edge of the unit (**Figure 17**).

26. Add one 20½" × 2½" (52 × 6.5 cm) white rectangle to the bottom edge of the unit (Figures 18 and 19).

The log cabin block should measure about 20½" × 20½" (52 × 52 cm).

ASSEMBLE THE QUILT

27. Repeat Steps 6–26 to create a total of 16 blocks.

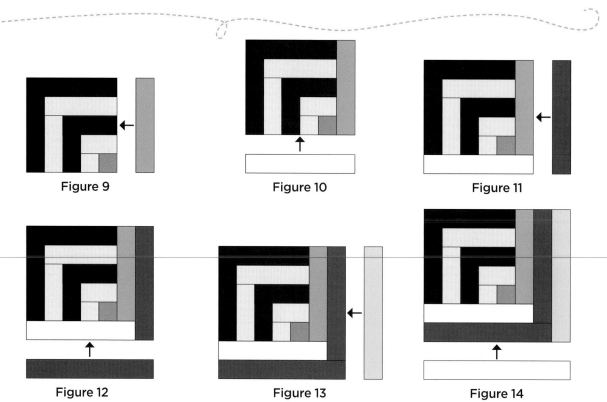

Figure 9

Figure 10

Figure 11

Figure 12

Figure 13

Figure 14

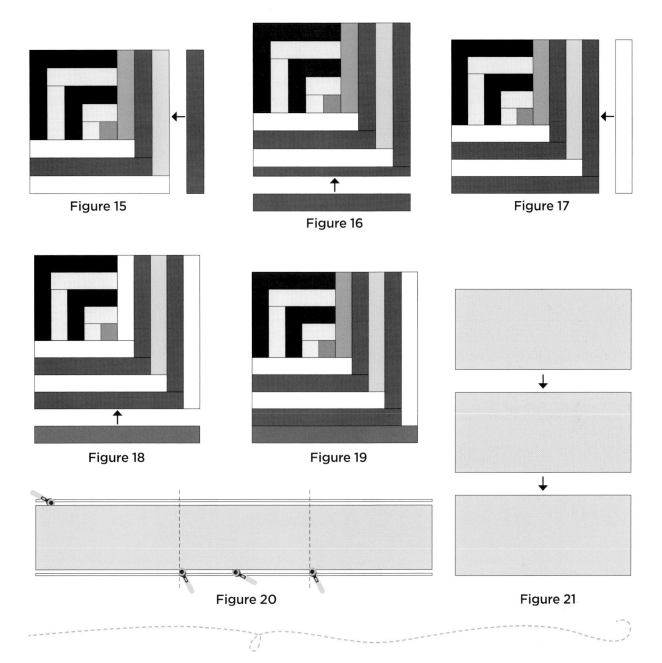

Figure 15

Figure 16

Figure 17

Figure 18

Figure 19

Figure 20

Figure 21

28. Assemble the blocks according to one of the layouts in the Interrupted Log Cabin Assembly Diagram (page 140).

PIECE THE BACKING

29. To make the quilt backing from 0"/42" (112/114.5 cm) backing fabric, trim the selvedge.

    Cut the trimmed backing yardage into 3 equal pieces measuring 99" (251.5 cm) WOF each **(Figure 20)**.

30. Place the 2 backing pieces right sides together and sew along the 99" (251.5 cm) edge. Join the third piece, right sides together, along the bottom edge **(Figure 21)**.

Backing should measure about 99" × 120" (251.5 × 305 cm).

FINISH THE QUILT

31. Follow the instructions for preparing the quilt top for quilting on page 10.

32. Follow the quilting instructions on page 141.

33. To complete the quilt, follow the bias binding instructions on page XX.

INTERRUPTED LOG CABIN ASSEMBLY DIAGRAM

Note: There are so many ways to organize a log cabin block. Turning the blocks can create endless secondary compositions. Try one of these layouts or move the blocks around to create your own! Fun, right? All quilt layouts should be sewn in four rows of four log cabin blocks.

ALTERNATE LAYOUT A

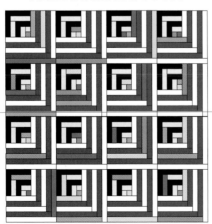

ALTERNATE LAYOUT B

QUILTING GEOMETRICS

Only Tula could take a basic quilt block such as the log cabin and turn it into a stunning new design! When it comes to quilting blocks, this one is my favorite—there are so many different ways it can be quilted. Because the blocks in this quilt are so large, I was able to create really intricate designs.

Why spend time marking quilting designs when you can use the blocks themselves as a guide? It makes the designs fit each block perfectly, and allows you to quickly quilt an area, then move on to the next block. I use this technique often because I am a huge fan of efficient quilting.

DIAMONDS AND ARROWS

By connecting corners within the log cabin blocks, you can create intricate geometric designs. This design is best for larger log cabin blocks. It may look a bit complicated, but it's the same steps repeated over and over.

1. Starting from the bottom right corner of the block and stretching to the top left corner of the first square, quilt a diamond shape that fills in the smallest square **(Figure 1)**.

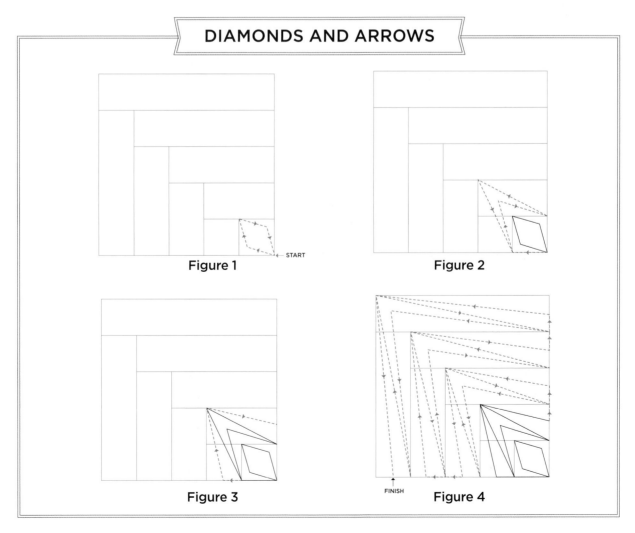

DIAMONDS AND ARROWS

Figure 1

Figure 2

Figure 3

Figure 4

2. Travel along the bottom edge until you reach the second small square. Stitch a double arrow shape that fills the next inner ring of the block, quilting a diagonal line from point to point and returning to the starting point (**Figure 2**, page 141).

The double arrow shape starts at the bottom right corner of the second small square, extends to the top left corner of the first log cabin ring, and ends at the bottom right corner of the ring. The lines of the design should be ½" (1.3 cm) apart at the farthest corner.

3. Travel along the edge of the block, halfway between the two seams. Quilt another diagonal line to the same left outer point as in Step 2. Continue quilting to the other side of the ring of the log cabin, halfway between the two seams (**Figure 3**, page 141).

4. Travel along the edge of the block to the next seam and repeat the quilting done in Step 3, filling in each ring of the log cabin with double arrow shapes until the block is quilted (**Figure 4**, page 141).

CORNER BRACKETS

Want to add something a little curvier? Try corner brackets. The bracket shape adds such an elegant look to the blocks. I like to use it in borders and sashings as well as blocks. Brackets work equally well as a filler with just a few rows or as a design for an entire block. There are also so many variations that you can quilt with it! I liked all of them so much that I used them all in this quilt.

1. Choose an outermost log cabin ring. Quilt a row of brackets (see page 115 for instructions) that touches the edge of the piece, stopping when you reach the inner corner (**Figure 5**). You can make them as long or as short as you like .

2. Change direction and quilt another row of brackets along the horizontal edge until you reach the edge of the block. If you need to make the last bracket smaller to fit it into the space, go ahead! They don't have to all be the exact same size (**Figure 6**).

3. Change direction again and echo outside of the brackets until you reach the starting point (**Figure 7**).

4. Fill in the space between the 2 rows of brackets and the other edge of the block with a different quilting design. I really like how the wishbone design (see page 21 for instructions) fills in the area perfectly (**Figure 8**).

CORNER BRACKETS

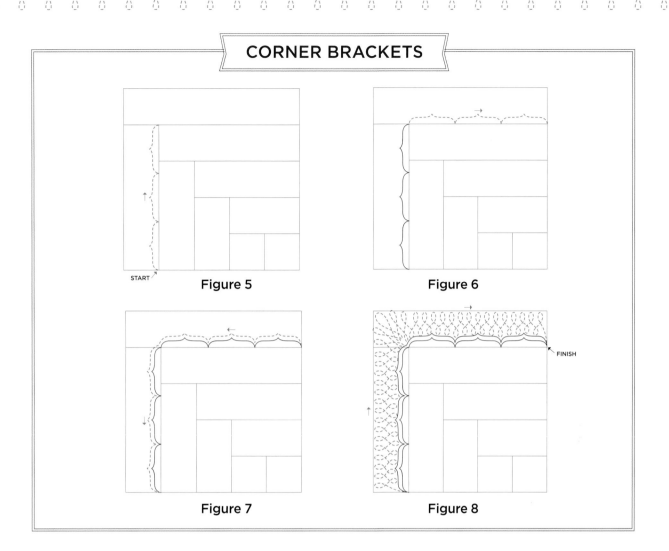

Figure 5

Figure 6

Figure 7

Figure 8

rainbow

When all of the colors get together for a neighborhood BBQ, it's sure to be a fun event. Red tends to pull the most attention, but Orange is never far behind her, reluctantly absorbed in Red's natural charisma. Yellow sits on a lawn chair soaking up the sun, lemonade in hand, nibbling on a salad because she's is a vegetarian. Green, always the peacekeeper, wafts back and forth between the warm and the cool colors, keeping the conversation moving. Blue keeps to the shade, manning the grill and making sure everyone has a cool drink so they don't overheat. Our dear, sweet, brooding Purple sits comfortably on the sidelines, headphones on, making sure everyone knows that she would rather be anywhere but there.

Then there is White, she almost never misses a get-together. White fades to the background, quietly taking in conversations buzzing around her but never directed at her. White makes everyone look good by contrast—next to her general blankness, they all stand out. So they keep her around, the perfect empty backdrop to highlight all of their best qualities.

RAINBOW QUILT TECHNIQUES

Sewing Flying Geese

The Ginger Blossoms block uses a series of flying geese to create its shape. This method creates four flying geese units at a time, which limits the amount of complex cutting. It eliminates the need for templates.

These blocks are very small, finishing at 4" × 4" (10 x 10 cm), and require some careful sewing. This pattern also asks for a scant ¼" (6 mm) seam, which is just a hair under the normal ¼" (6 mm) seam to account for extra bulk when sewing multiple diagonal seams.

Making a House Block

I love a house block. A house block is mostly made up of squares and rectangles with the occasional half -square triangle. The sewing is simple but still dimesional. House blocks come in all shapes and sizes, and some have windows or doors or any number of added details.

In the Hood quilt, I wanted to leave the houses whole without any obstructions. These larger fabric pieces create an excellent opportunity to use bolder, complex prints without losing anything in the seams. This approach creates an opportunity to let the quilting fill in those details. This is the perfect marriage between piecing and quilting, one finishing the other's sentence!

Periwinkle
Serpentine
Macaw
Amazon
Meadow
Okra

Pink
Autumn
Mesa
Mango
Solar
Citrine

Fuchsia
Petunia
Tart
Eggplant
Shadow
Manatee

Mist/white → background and binding

CHOOSING FaBrICS

There is something really beautiful about a tiny hint of color on a huge field of crisp, clean white. It is like when an unexpected flower pops through a soft layer of snow in the middle of winter.

Because this quilt is 80 percent white, the colors, although small, become like little jewels scattered across the quilt top.

The colors that I selected pack a real punch — their presence is limited, so I wanted to make it count. I chose a saturated rainbow of solid fabrics from Free Spirit fabrics to give me as many color combinations as possible for each block. I used solids so that the piecing would be the star and every angle would be clearly defined.

GINGER BLOSSOMS

Finished quilt size: 88" × 96"
(223.5 × 244 cm)

Finished block size: 4" × 4"
(10 × 10 cm)

Fabrics
⅙ yd (15 cm) each of 18 saturated
solids, ranging from red to purple

7½ yd (6.8 m) of solid white

Backing, Binding & Batting
8¼ yd (7.5 m) of 40"/42"
(102/107 cm) wide fabric or 2¾
yd (2.5 m) of 108" (274 cm) wide
backing fabric

¾ yd (68.5 cm) of fabric to make
378" (960 cm) of 2½" (6.5 cm) bias
binding

96" × 104" (244 × 264 cm) of batting

CUT THE FABRICS

1. From each of the ⅙ yd (15 cm) solid pieces, cut:
» Four 3¼" × 3¼" (8.5 × 8.5 cm) squares for a total of 72
» Sixteen 1⅞" × 1⅞" (4.8 × 4.8 cm) squares for a total of 288

2. From the white solid, cut:
» Two 88½" × 6½" (225 × 16.5 cm) strips for the top and bottom borders
» Two 84½" × 6½" (215 × 16.5 cm) strips for the left and right borders
» Ten 76½" × 4½" (194 × 11.5 cm) strips for the sashing
» Sixty-one 8½" × 4½" (21.5 × 11.5 cm) strips for the sashing
» Ten 6½" × 4½" (16.5 × 11.5 cm) strips for the sashing
» Thirty-six 3¼" × 3¼" (8.5 × 8.5 cm) squares for the geese units

» One hundred forty-four 1⅞" × 1⅞" (4.8 × 4.8 cm) squares for the geese units
» Two hundred eighty-eight 1½" × 1½" (3.8 × 3.8 cm) squares for the block corners

SEW THE FLYING GEESE

3. To sew the first set of flying geese units, select two contrasting colors, such as red and aqua. This set will make 4 complete blocks.

From each color, collect two 3¼" × 3¼" (8.5 × 8.5 cm) squares and eight 1⅞" × 1⅞" (4.8 × 4.8 cm) squares.

From the white solid pieces, collect two 3¼" × 3¼" (8.5 × 8.5 cm) squares, eight 1⅞" × 1⅞" (4.8 × 4.8 cm) squares, and sixteen 1½" × 1½" (3.8 × 3.8 cm) squares.

4. Select 1 of the large colored squares and 4 of the contrasting small squares. Draw a diagonal line on the wrong side of the small squares from corner to corner.

5. Place 2 of the 1⅞" × 1⅞" (4.8 × 4.8 cm) squares, right sides together, on opposite corners of the 3¼" × 3¼" (8.5 × 8.5 cm) square. The drawn lines on the wrong side of the small squares should line up **(Figure 1)**. Pin in place.

6. Sew a scant ¼" (6 mm) seam on both sides of the drawn line. Cut on the drawn line **(Figure 2)**.

7. Place another small contrasting square on the top corner of each of the sewn units **(Figure 3)**.

Sew a scant ¼" (6 mm) seam on both sides of the drawn line .

8. Cut on the drawn line to yield 4 matching flying geese units. Each unit should measure about 2½" × 1½" (6.5 × 3.8 cm) **(Figure 4)**.

9. Follow Steps 3–6 to sew another set of flying geeswith the same two colors, but switch the colors of the large square and the small squares; if you used red for the large square in the first set, use aqua in the second set **(Figure 5)**.

10. Follow Steps 3–6 to sew another set of flying geese, but use 1 large colored square, such as red, and 4 small white squares **(Figure 6)**.

11. Follow Steps 3–6 to sew another set of flying geese, but use the other large colored square, such as aqua, and 4 small white squares **(Figure 7)**.

12. Follow Steps 3–6 to sew 2 more sets of flying geese. Use the second large white square, 2 more small colored squares, such as red, and 2 small squares of the third color, such as aqua **(Figure 8)**.

For this set, place 2 matching small squares on opposite corners, then add the contrasting small squares **(Figure 9)**.

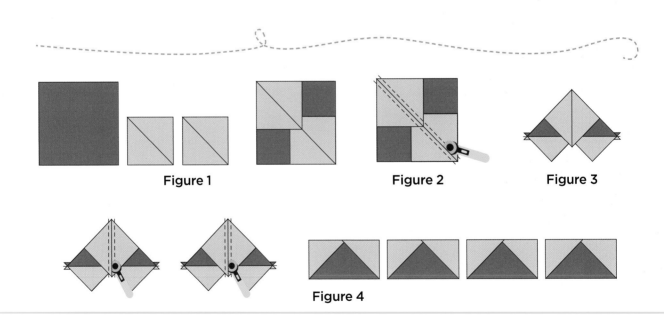

Figure 1

Figure 2

Figure 3

Figure 4

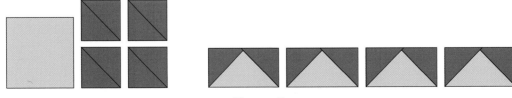

Figure 5

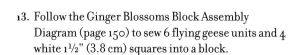

13. Follow the Ginger Blossoms Block Assembly Diagram (page 150) to sew 6 flying geese units and 4 white 1½" (3.8 cm) squares into a block.

The block should measure about 4½" × 4½" (11.5 × 11.5 cm).

14. Use the remaining flying geese and white 1½" (3.8 cm) squares to create 3 more identical blocks.

15. Repeat Steps 1–12 to make a total of 72 blocks or 18 total block sets.

ASSEMBLE THE QUILT

16. Follow the Ginger Blossoms Assembly Diagram on page 151 to join the blocks. First make the odd numbered rows, each consisting of 7 blocks and six 8½" × 4½" (21.5 × 11.5 cm) white sashing strips.

Pay attention to the block placement throughout the quilt top so that the colors are distributed evenly. Press seams toward the sashing pieces.

17. Make the even numbered rows. Each consists of 6 blocks, five 8½" × 4½" (21.5 × 11.5 cm) white sashing strips, and two 6½" × 4½" (16.5 × 11.5 cm) sashing strips. Press seams toward the sashing pieces.

18. Following the assembly diagram, join the odd and even rows by sewing them to the 76½" × 4½" (194 × 11.5 cm) sashing strips. Press seams toward the sashing pieces.

19. Sew the 84½" × 6½" (215 × 16.5 cm) side borders to the left and right sides of the quilt top. Press seams toward the border strips.

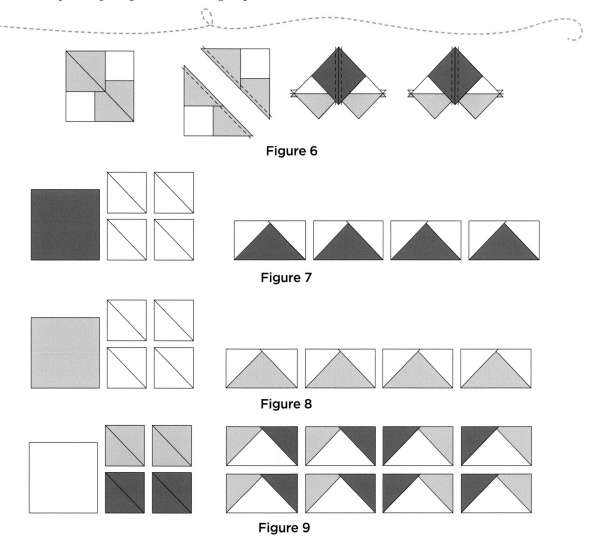

Figure 6

Figure 7

Figure 8

Figure 9

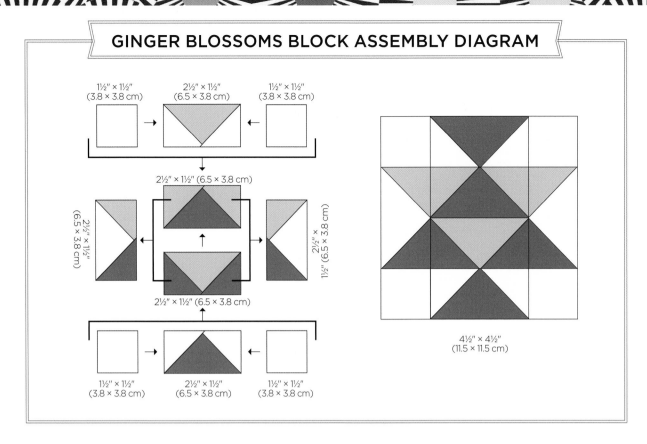

GINGER BLOSSOMS BLOCK ASSEMBLY DIAGRAM

1½" × 1½"
(3.8 × 3.8 cm)

2½" × 1½"
(6.5 × 3.8 cm)

1½" × 1½"
(3.8 × 3.8 cm)

2½" × 1½" (6.5 × 3.8 cm)

2½" × 1½"
(6.5 × 3.8 cm)

2½" ×
1½" (6.5 × 3.8 cm)

2½" × 1½" (6.5 × 3.8 cm)

1½" × 1½"
(3.8 × 3.8 cm)

2½" × 1½"
(6.5 × 3.8 cm)

1½" × 1½"
(3.8 × 3.8 cm)

4½" × 4½"
(11.5 × 11.5 cm)

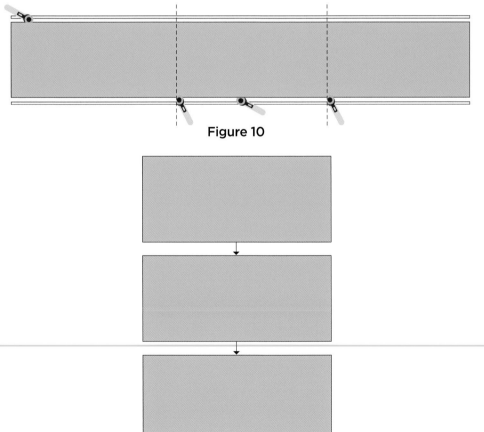

Figure 10

Figure 11

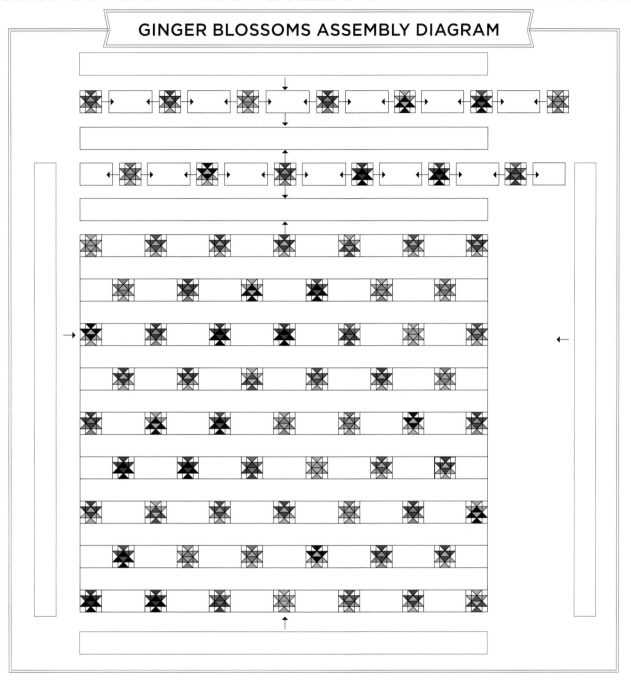

20. Sew the 88½" × 6½" (225 × 16.5 cm) borders to the top and bottom of the quilt top. Press seams toward the border strips.

PIECE THE BACKING

21. To make the quilt backing from 40"/42" (102/107 cm) backing fabric, trim the selvedge. Cut the trimmed backing yardage into 3 equal-pieces each measuring 99" (251.5 cm)×WOF (width of fabric) **(Figure 10)**.

22. Place 2 backing pieces right sides together and sew along the 99" (251.5 cm) edge, then sew the third backing piece, right sides together, along the bottom edge **(Figure 11)**.

Backing should measure about 99" × 124" (251.5 × 315 cm).

FINISH THE QUILT

23. Follow the instructions for preparing the quilt top for quilting on page 10.

24. Follow the quilting instructions on page 152.

25. To complete the, quilt follow the bias binding instructions on page 183.

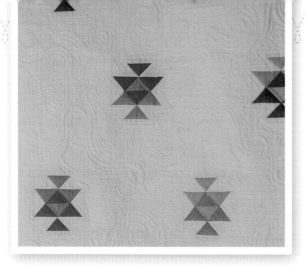

QUILTING FRAMES

From the blocks to the background, the quilting is all about framing. Because the blocks are so cute, I wanted to use the quilting to help separate them from the background filler, especially because Tula did such a great job piecing each of the teeny tiny blocks. I also loved the background quilting framing the quilt by making borders around it.

FRAMING TRIANGLES

Because the blocks are petite, I kept the quilting inside them fairly simple. I traced the lines of the triangles and added a basic continuous curve design in the center of each block.

1. Start at the upper left corner of a block. Stitch along the top seam, then stitch in the ditch in a zig zag down the center of the block, ending at the bottom right corner of the block.

   Continue stitching in the ditch along the bottom seam and back up the center column of the block, creating a mirrored zig zag.

End at the top of the flying geese triangle that points up in the middle of the block (**Figure 1**).

2. Next, curve down and right, then down and left to the bottom point of the center diamond shape. Finish by stitching the curve up and left, then up and to the right, ending at the starting point (**Figure 2**).

3. Continue quilting from the continuous curve, making a straight line to the right edge of the block. Stitch in the ditch to framing the rest of the flying geese triangles, following the outer lines of the colored triangles to the left side of the block, finishing at the top left corner of the upper flying geese unit (**Figure 3**).

CONTINUOUS CURVE

Using different designs to separately frame various blocks. Like on the inside of some blocks, try using continuous curve quilting around the outside of other blocks.

1. Starting ½" (6mm) above the midpoint of the top of the block, quilt a line that curves down to the topmost left corner.

2. Continue quilting a line that curves from corner to corner, working your way down and around the block. At the bottom of the block, quilt a line that curves away from the block, forming a point. Continue quilting until you reach the starting point (**Figure 4**).

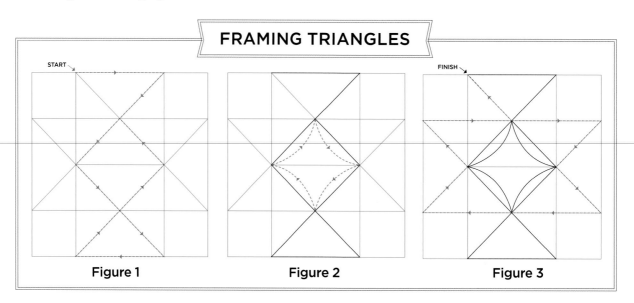

FRAMING TRIANGLES

START

FINISH

Figure 1

Figure 2

Figure 3

CONTINUOUS CURVE

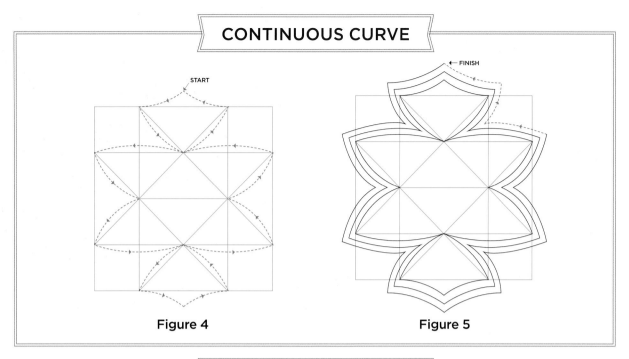

Figure 4

Figure 5

ECHO QUILTING

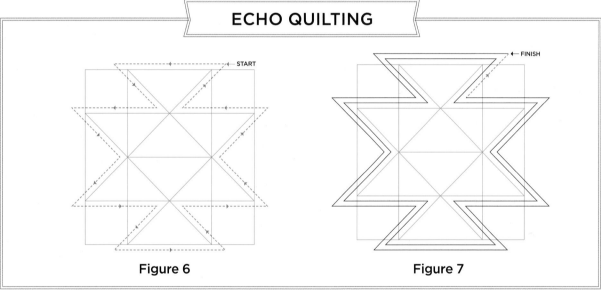

Figure 6

Figure 7

3. To separate the block from the rest of the quilting, echo around the first continuous curved line a few more times. Space the echo lines ¼" (6 mm) apart **(Figure 5)**.

ECHO QUILTING

Show off some favorite blocks by echo quilting around the flying geese triangles.

1. Starting ¼" (6 mm) above the top right corner of the upper triangle, stitch a straight line to the left. Follow the shape of the triangles, stitching all the way around the block until you end up at your starting point **(Figure 6)**.

Contrasting jewel tones pop off a clean white background.

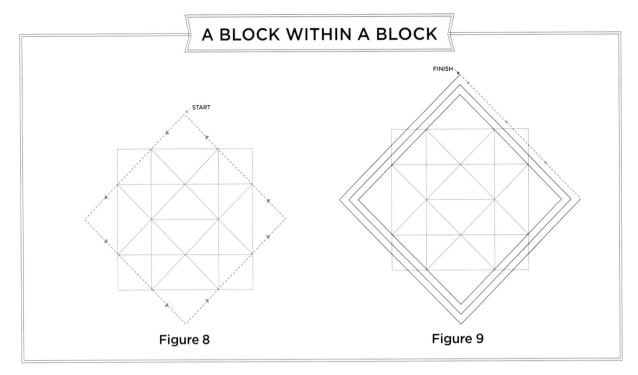

Figure 8

Figure 9

2. Repeat, stitching a second line of echo quilting around the colored triangles. Start and finish at the top right corner of the block (**Figure 7**, page 153).

A BLOCK WITHIN A BLOCK

Frame some of the blocks in an unexpected design. Use the points of the block to create an angular framing effect.

1. Starting 1" (2.5 cm) above the middle of the top of the block, quilt a diagonal line that touches the 2 outer blocks on the left side of the block, stopping 2" (5 cm) from the colored block center.

Swirls and paisley shapes create a border next to straight line quilting.

Repeat, working your way around the block and re-turning to the starting point, stitching an on-point diamond shape around the center of the block (**Figure 8**).

2. Echo stitch twice around the line quilted in Step 1 (**Figure 9**).

PAISLEY FEATHERS

I quilted a paisley feather design so that it went around the outside of the quilt. I love how it appears to add a border to the quilt.

1. Quilt an elongated swirl and echo back to the starting point. Echo the swirl two more times (**Figure 10**). For this design, the more echoing the better!

2. Quilt a skinny paisley by curving out from the swirl and back. Echo the paisley two or three times (**Figure 11**).

3. Continue quilting paisley shapes that work their way around the outside of the swirl until you reach the center of the swirl (**Figure 12**).

4. Add another paisley feather by echoing your way around the outside of the paisley feather. Quilt another elongated swirl that extends away from the first paisley feather.

5. Repeat the steps above to continue quilting paisley feathers and to fill the area (**Figure 13**).

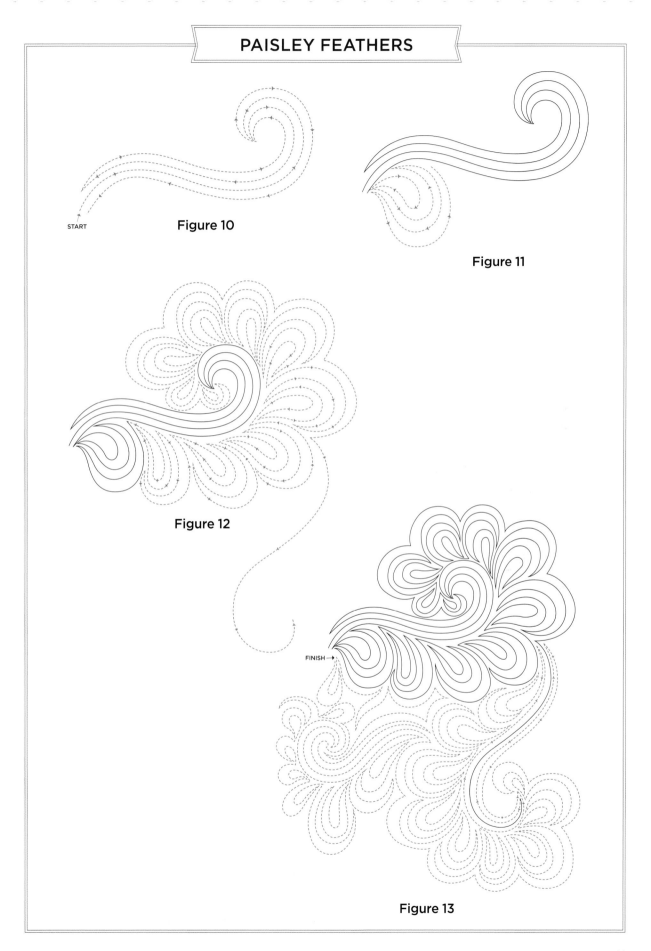

START

Figure 10

Figure 11

Figure 12

FINISH →

Figure 13

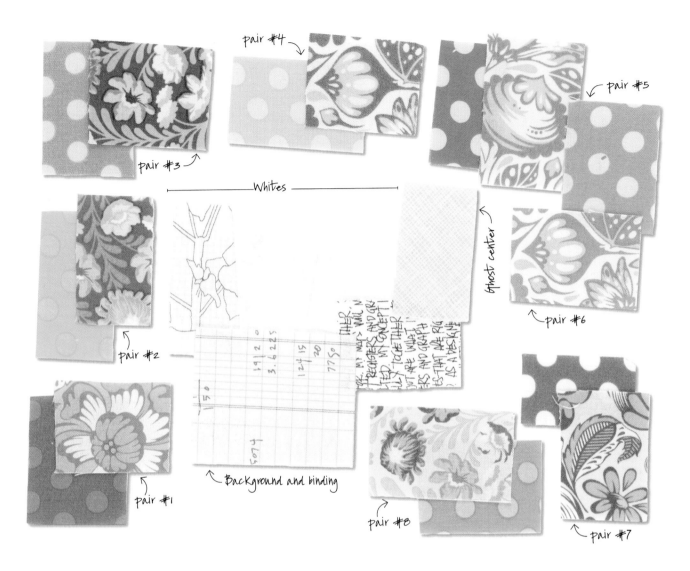

pair #4

pair #5

pair #3

Whites

ghost center

pair #6

pair #2

pair #1

Background and binding

pair #8

pair #7

CHOOSING FABRICS

White does not have to be solid or uniform. What really makes this quilt dance is that the background fabrics are made of a few different prints that are mostly white, but treated as one white fabric throughout.

This quilt is called Ghost Blossoms because when the blocks are sewn together a second identical block is formed in the space between the blocks. The light blue background fabric is just a low-contrast

echo of the blossom center that completes the ghost block.

The colorful prints in each block are made up of eight pairs of contrasting fabrics. I first selected one multicolored floral print, then I chose a polka dot that coordinated with one of the minor colors in the floral print.

In one of the combinations, I chose a small floral print in aqua and green on a navy blue background. This print has a few

scattered flowers that are yellow, but it is definitely the least used color. I chose a lemon yellow and gold polka dot that matches the small barely used flower. This ensured plenty of contrast between the two prints but, on closer inspection, they play with each other quite nicely. I used this strategy throughout the fabric selection process to create surprising but delightful fabric pairs.

GHOST BLOSSOMS

Finished quilt size: 72" × 72"
(183 × 183 cm)

Finished block size: 18" x 18"
(45.5 x 45.5 cm)

Fabrics

⅓ yd (30 cm) each of 16 colorful prints that span the rainbow (8 coordinating pairs)

¾ yd (68.5 cm) of light blue

3¼ yd (3 m) of white or ⅞ yd (80 cm) of 4 prints with white backgrounds

Backing, Binding & Batting

4½ yd (4.1 yd) of 40"/42" (102/107 cm) wide fabric or 2¼ yd (2 m) of 108" (274 cm) wide backing fabric

⅝ yd (57 cm) of fabric to make 298" (757 cm) of 2½" (6.5 cm) bias binding

80" × 80" (203 × 203 cm) of batting

CUT THE FABRICS

1. From each of the sixteen ⅓ yd (30 cm) prints, cut:
   » Eight 3½" × 3½" (9 × 9 cm) squares
   » Four 9½" × 3½" (24 × 9 cm) rectangles
   » Two 12½" × 3½" (31.5 × 9 cm) rectangles

2. From the light blue fabric, cut sixty-four 3½" × 3½" (9 × 9 cm) squares.

3. From the white background fabric, cut :
   » Sixty-four 9½" × 3½" (24 × 9 cm) squares
   » One hundred ninety-two 3½" × 3½" (9 × 9 cm) squares

MAKE ONE BLOCK

4. Choose the first pair of fabrics, such as the pink and orange floral and polka dot prints. From the floral print, select four 3½" × 3½" (9 × 9 cm) squares, four 9½" × 3½" (24 × 9 cm) rectangles, and two 12½" × 3½" (31.5 × 9 cm) rectangles. Draw a diagonal line from one corner to the opposite corner on the wrong side of each square.

5. From the polka dot, select four 3½" × 3½" (9 × 9 cm) squares. Draw a diagonal line from one corner to the opposite corner on the wrong side of each square.

6. From the white fabric, select four 9½" × 3½" (24 × 9 cm) rectangles and twelve 3½" × 3½" (9 × 9 cm) squares. Draw a diagonal line from one corner to the opposite corner on the wrong side of 8 of the squares.

7. From the light blue background fabric, select four 3½" × 3½" (9 × 9 cm) squares. Draw a diagonal line from one corner to the opposite corner on the wrong side of each square.

8. Place 1 floral print square, right sides together, on the right corner of 1 white rectangle. Sew on the drawn line.

Trim away the excess corner, leaving a ¼" (6 mm) seam allowance.

9. Place 1 light blue square, right sides together, on the left corner of the white rectangle. Sew on the drawn line.

    Trim away the excess corner, leaving a ¼" (6 mm) seam allowance.

10. Repeat Steps 8 and 9 to create a second identical unit.

11. Place 1 floral print square, right sides together, on the left corner of 1 white rectangle. Sew on the drawn line.

    Trim away the excess corner, leaving a ¼" (6 mm) seam allowance.

12. Place 1 light blue square, right sides together, on the right corner of the white rectangle. Sew on the drawn line.

    Trim away the excess corner, leaving a ¼" (6 mm) seam allowance.

13. Repeat Steps 11 and 12 to create a second identical unit.

14. Sew together 1 of each of the units, joining the 2 floral print corners **(Figure 1)**. Repeat to make a second identical joined unit.

15. Place 1 white square so that the drawn diagonal line is on the right corner of 1 of the large floral print rectangles . Sew on the drawn line.

    Trim away the excess corner, leaving a ¼" (6 mm) seam allowance.

16. Place another white square so that the drawn diagonal line is on the left corner of the large floral print rectangle . Sew on the drawn line.

    Trim away the excess corner, leaving a ¼" (6 mm) seam allowance.

17. Repeat Steps 15 and 16 to create a second identical unit.

18. Sew the unmarked white squares to both sides of both units **(Figure 2)**.

19. Place 1 contrasting print square, right sides together, on the right corner of one of the small main print rectangles. Sew on the drawn line.

    Trim away the excess corner, leaving a ¼" (6 mm) seam allowance.

20. Place 1 white square so that the drawn diagonal line is on the left corner of the small floral print rectangle. Sew on the drawn line.

    Trim away the excess corner, leaving a ¼" mm) seam allowance.

21. Repeat Steps 19 and 20 to create a second identical unit.

22. Place one polka dot square, right sides together, on the left corner of one small floral print rectangle. Sew on the drawn line.

    Trim away the excess corner, leaving a ¼" (6 mm) seam allowance.

23. Place 1 white square so that the drawn diagonal line is on the right corner of the small floral print rectangle. Sew on the drawn line.

    Trim away the excess corner, leaving a ¼" (6 mm) seam allowance.

24. Repeat Steps 22 and 23 to create a second identical unit.

25. Sew together one each of the completed units, joining the two polka dot corners **(Figure 3)**.

    Repeat to make a second identical joined unit.

26. Follow the Ghost Blossom Block Assembly Diagram (page 160) to complete the block. The block should measure about 18½" × 18½" (47 × 47 cm).

ASSEMBLE THE QUILT

27. Repeat Steps 1–26, using a different pair of floral and polka dot prints each time, to create 15 more Ghost Blossom blocks.

28. Follow the Ghost Blossoms Assembly Diagram on page 160 to join the quilt blocks.

PIECE THE BACKING

29. To make the quilt backing from 40"/42" (102/107 cm) backing fabric, trim the selvedge. Cut the trimmed backing yardage in half so that each piece measures 81" (206 cm) WOF **(Figure 4)**.

30. Place the 2 backing pieces right sides together and sew along the 81" (206 cm) edge **(Figure 5)**.

    Backing should measure about 81" × 82" (206 × 208 cm).

FINISH THE QUILT

31. Follow the instructions for preparing the quilt top for quilting on page 10.

32. Follow the quilting instructions on page 161.

33. To complete the quilt, follow the bias binding instructions on page 183.

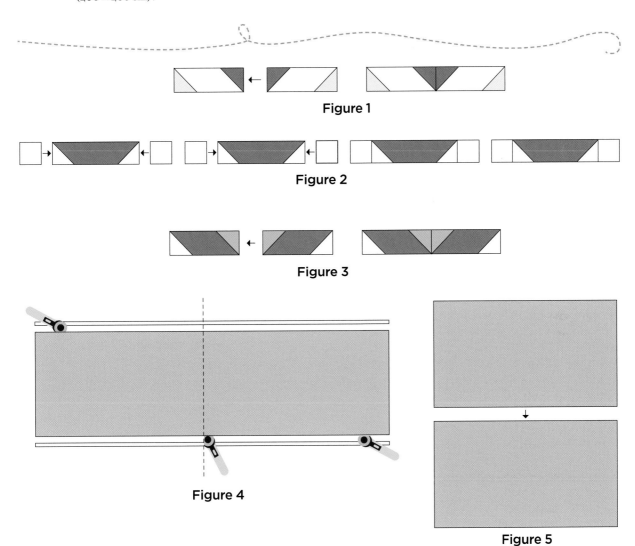

Figure 1

Figure 2

Figure 3

Figure 4

Figure 5

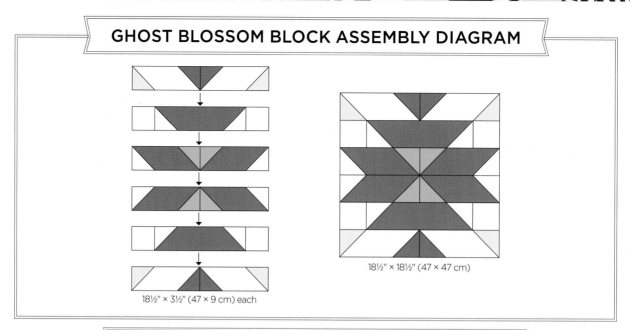

GHOST BLOSSOM BLOCK ASSEMBLY DIAGRAM

18½" × 3½" (47 × 9 cm) each

18½" × 18½" (47 × 47 cm)

GHOST BLOSSOM ASSEMBLY DIAGRAM

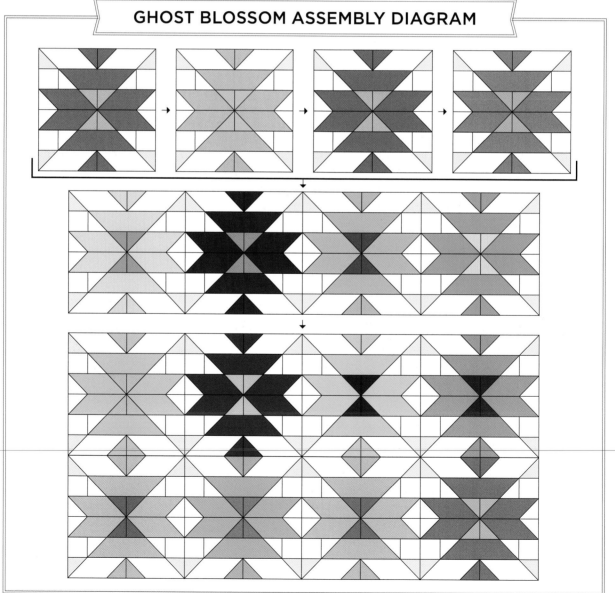

QUILTING OVERSIZED BLOCKS

Unlike the Ginger Blossom blocks, the colorful Ghost Blossoms are larger than life. If you are having trouble deciding what to quilt in these oversized blocks, try breaking them up into smaller shapes. With the blocks in the Ghost Blossom quilt, I opted for simple designs that work well in the individual pieces. The curvy serpentine lines (see page 29 for instructions) contrast nicely with the diagonal lines and are easy to quilt!

COMBINED DESIGNS

1. Starting in the center of the block, quilt a triangle-shaped wedge that fills the top middle triangle, then return to the center. Repeat with the bottom middle triangle, quilting another wedge and returning to the center of the block (**Figure 1**, page 162).

2. Fill the upper left portion of the block with serpentine lines, ending at the middle seam on the left side of the block (**Figure 2**, page 162).

3. Fill in the bottom portion of the block with serpentine lines that mirror the ones above it, working your way from the outside to the middle point of the block. Stop at the middle of the block (**Figure 3**, page 162).

4. Repeat Steps 2 and 3 to fill in the right side of the block. Fill in the upper right section first, ending at the middle seam on the right side of the block (**Figure 4**, page 162).

5. Quilt serpentine lines again in the bottom right section of the block, working your way back to the middle of the block (**Figure 5**, page 162).

6. Quilt Vs (page 83), starting in the center of the block and traveling along the seam in between the middle triangle and the upper left block. Continue quilting until you reach the upper right corner of the next section of the block. Quilt a diagonal line that goes from the corner to the middle of the center triangle and up to the upper left corner of the block (**Figure 6**, page 162).

7. Echo the diagonal V that you just quilted twice more, going from point to point of the block (**Figure 7**, page 162).

8. From the upper right corner of the section, travel along the top edge until you reach the bottom point of the topmost triangle. Quilt a triangle to fill the space (**Figure 8**, page 162).

9. Quilt the bottom portion of the block just as you quilted the top. You either can travel along the edge of the block or use the background quilting to travel to the lower right portion of the block (**Figure 8**, page 162).

10. Quilt the bottom portion of the block just as you did the top.

The background fabrics come together in a clever ghost block.

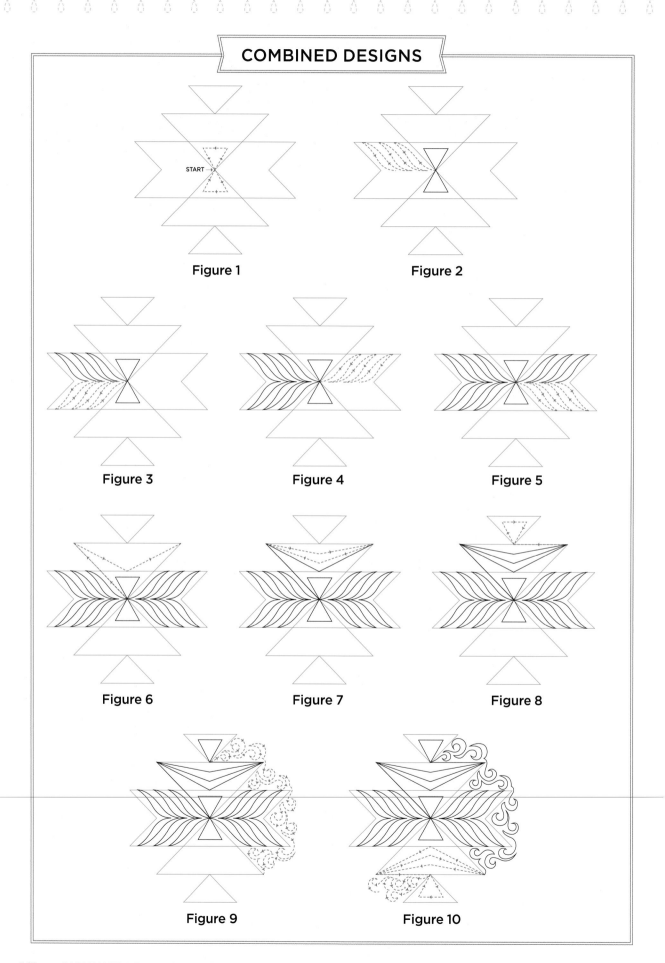

COMBINED DESIGNS

Figure 1

Figure 2

Figure 3

Figure 4

Figure 5

Figure 6

Figure 7

Figure 8

Figure 9

Figure 10

Contrasting colors in the small prints make for a playful rainbow.

Once finished with the block, continue quilting the filler around the rest of the area **(Figures 9 and 10)**. I quilted swirls (page 41), because it's my favorite filler design.

11. Continue quilting the filler design around the rest of the area.

IN THE BACKGROUND

It's obvious from the this quilt that I like to use the background quilting to help me move around the blocks. This is especially helpful for larger blocks like these. Using a meandering design, like my favorite swirl, provides a nice texture while making your quilting more efficient.

In the Ghost Blossom quilt, I love how the different shades of fabric make up the background of the quilt. Since they are all variations of white, using an allover design in all of the blocks helps pull them together. It also helps establish them as the background letting the quilt blocks really shine.

Yellow house — roof, side, front
Teal house — roof, side, front
Purple house — roof, side, front
Binding — backing
Picket fence — fence, grass
Orange house — roof, side, front
Green house — roof, side, front
Navy house — roof, side, front
Backgrounds — Rose, Sunset, Lemon, Citrine, Amazon, Sorbet
Red house — roof, side, front, roof
Light green house — roof, side, front
Blue house — roof, side, front
Violet house — roof

CHOOSING FABRICS

When I use this many fabrics in one quilt and each fabric serves a specific purpose, I create a system to keep the fabric selection process from feeling overwhelming. In this quilt, each neighborhood section contains ten houses. Each house is made of three fabrics: a front, a side, and a roof. I first chose the front of each house by selecting ten bold-print fabrics that represent the entire rainbow, beginning with red/pink and ending in purple.

After I had the start of a house in each color, I matched each front with a darker fabric of a similar color for the side of the house. This gives the house the appearance of dimension.

For the roofs, I used the same polka-dot fabric in ten different colors, which ties all of the houses together. I used Kaffe Spots from Free Spirit Fabrics and matched up a contrasting color spot to each pair of house fabrics.

The Hood contains six neighborhoods, each identified by a different background color. Because this chapter is about all of the colors working together, a single bland background fabric would not suffice. Each house is so intensely colorful, I chose a similar rainbow palette for the backgrounds, but in soft pastel versions. No matter which background color I used, every single house would show up on it.

The border is designed to represent a picket fence framing all of the little houses in their neighborhoods. I used a light cream and gray wood grain texture for the fence and found a mostly green small print to represent the grass between the pickets.

THE HOOD

Finished quilt size: 90" × 104"
(227 × 264 cm)

Finished block size: 8" × 8"
(20.5 × 20.5 cm)

Fabrics

¼ yd (23 cm) each of 10 large prints

¼ yd (23 cm) each of 10 medium prints

⅛ yd (11.5 cm) each of 10 small prints

⅞ yd (80 cm) each of 6 pastel solids

1¼ yd (114 cm) of cream small print

1¼ yd (114 cm) of green small print

Backing, Batting & Binding

8¼ yd (7.5 m) of 40"/42" (102/107 cm) wide fabric or 3¼ yd (3 m) of 108" (274 cm) wide backing fabric

⅞ yd (80 cm) of fabric to make 398" (10 m) of 2½" (6.5 cm) bias binding

98" × 112" (249 × 284.5 cm) of batting

Notions

Erasable fabric-marking tool

CUT THE FABRICS

1. From each of the 10 large print fabrics, cut six 4½" × 6½" (11.5 × 16.5 cm) rectangles for the house fronts.

2. From each of the 10 medium print fabrics, cut six 4½" × 4½" (11.5 × 11.5 cm) squares for the house sides.

3. From each of the 10 small print fabrics, cut for the roofs:
   » Six 4½" × 2½" (11.5 × 6.5 cm) rectangles
   » Six 2½" × 2½" (6.5 × 6.5 cm) squares
   » Six 1½" × 1½" (3.8 × 3.8 cm) squares

4. From each of the 6 solid pastel background fabrics, cut:

   » Twenty 2½" × 2½" (6.5 × 6.5 cm) squares
   » Ten 1½" × 1½" (3.8 × 3.8 cm) squares
   » Ten 3½" × 2½" (9 × 6.5 cm) rectangles
   » Ten 4½" × 2½" (11.5 × 6.5 cm) rectangles
   » Eight 2½" × 8½" (6.5 × 21.5 cm) rectangles
   » Two 2½" × 22½" (6.5 × 57 cm) rectangles
   » Four 2½" (6.5 cm) × WOF (width of fabric) strips

5. From the green fabric, cut for the fences:
   » Two 8½" × 8½" (21.5 × 21.5 cm) squares
   » Seventy-four 2½" × 8½" (6.5 × 21.5 cm) rectangles

6. From the cream fabric, cut seventy-four 2½" × 8½" (6.5 × 21.5 cm) rectangles for the fences.

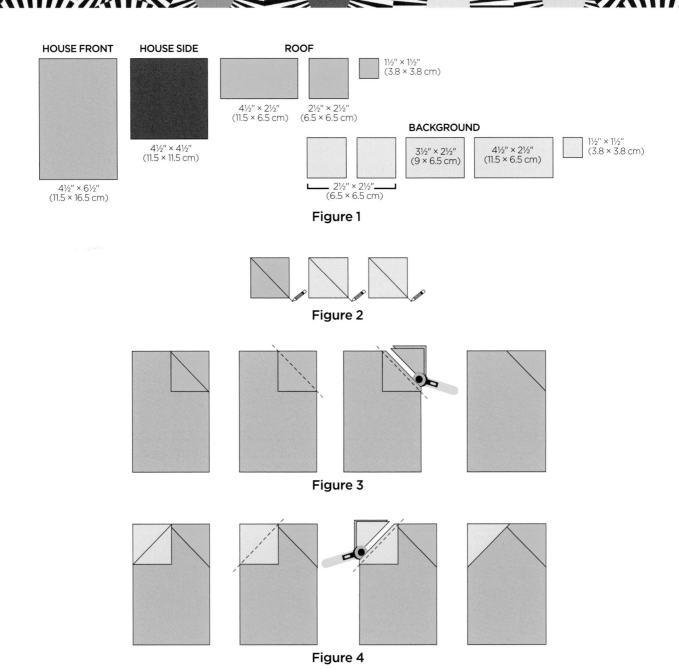

HOUSE FRONT

HOUSE SIDE

ROOF

1½" × 1½"
(3.8 × 3.8 cm)

4½" × 2½"
(11.5 × 6.5 cm)

2½" × 2½"
(6.5 × 6.5 cm)

4½" × 4½"
(11.5 × 11.5 cm)

BACKGROUND

3½" × 2½"
(9 × 6.5 cm)

4½" × 2½"
(11.5 × 6.5 cm)

1½" × 1½"
(3.8 × 3.8 cm)

2½" × 2½"
(6.5 × 6.5 cm)

4½" × 6½"
(11.5 × 16.5 cm)

Figure 1

Figure 2

Figure 3

Figure 4

SEW THE HOUSE BLOCKS

7. Collect all of the coordinating colored pieces for one house, starting with the red house **(Figure 1)**:

»   One 4½" × 6½" (11.5 × 16.5 cm) house front rectangle in the red large print
»   One 4½" × 4½" (11.5 × 11.5 cm) house side square in the red medium print
»   One 4½" × 2½" (11.5 × 6.5 cm) roof rectangle in the red small print
»   One 2½" × 2½" (6.5 c 6.5 cm) roof square in the red small print

»   One 1½" × 1½" (3.8 × 3.8 cm) roof square in the red small print
»   Two 2½" × 2½" (6.5 × 6.5 cm) solid aqua background squares
»   One 3½" × 2½" (9 × 6.5 cm) solid aqua background rectangle
»   One 1½" × 1½" (3.8 × 3.8 cm) solid aqua background rectangle
»   One 4½" × 2½" (11.5 × 6.5 cm) solid aqua background rectangle

8. Draw a diagonal line from one corner to the opposite corner on the wrong sides of the large roof square and the 2 large background squares **(Figure 2)**.

9. Place the red roof square on the upper right corner of the red house front rectangle, right sides together. Sew on the drawn line **(Figure 3)**.

   Trim the excess fabric, leaving a ¼" (6 mm) seam. Press open.

10. Place 1 aqua background square on the upper left corner of the house front rectangle, right sides together. Sew on the drawn line to complete the house front **(Figure 4)**.

   Trim the excess fabric, leaving a ¼" (6 mm) seam. Press open.

11. Place the other aqua background square on the upper right corner of the red roof rectangle. Sew on the drawn line **(Figure 5)**.

   Trim the excess fabric, leaving a ¼" (6 mm) seam. Press open.

12. With right sides together, sew the roof unit to the top edge of the red house side square **(Figure 6)**. Press seam open.

13. With right sides together, sew the longer aqua background rectangle to the top of the house front unit **(Figure 7)**. Press seam open.

14. With right sides together, sew the small aqua background square to the small red roof square to make the chimney **(Figure 8**, page 168). Press seam open.

15. With right sides together, sew the shorter background rectangle to the right side of the chimney unit **(Figure 9**, page 168). Press seam open.

16. With right sides together, join the chimney unit to the top edge of the house side unit **(Figure 10**, page 168). Press seam open.

17. With right sides together, join the house front unit to the house side unit **(Figure 11**, page 169).

   The completed house block should measure 8½" × 8½" (21.5 × 21.5 cm).

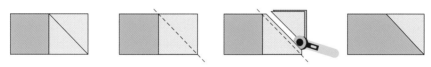

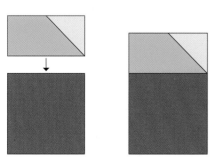

Figure 5

Figure 6

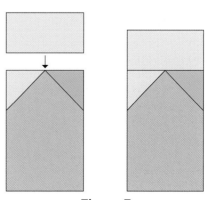

Figure 7

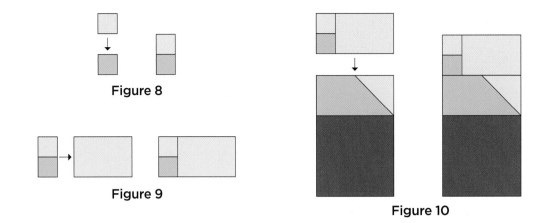

Figure 8

Figure 9

Figure 10

18. Repeat Steps 7–17, using the remaining sets of house front, house side, and roof fabric pieces. Switch out the background fabrics until you have made 6 matching houses with 6 different background fabrics (**Figure 12**).

19. Repeat again to make a total of 10 sets of 6 house blocks each for a total of 60 house blocks.

BUILD THE NEIGHBORHOODS

20. Select the 10 different-colored house blocks with the same background color, such as aqua (**Figure 13**).

21. Sew the four $2\frac{1}{2}$" (6.5 cm) × WOF matching background strips end to end along the $2\frac{1}{2}$" (6.5 cm) edge to create one long strip. Sub cut the strip into three $2\frac{1}{2}$" × $48\frac{1}{2}$" (6.5 × 123 cm) lengths.

22. Following the Neighborhood Block Assembly Diagram (page 170), join the house blocks to the $2\frac{1}{2}$" × $8\frac{1}{2}$" (6.5 × 21.5 cm) matching background rectangles.

    Sew the house blocks and background rectangles together to form 2 rows containing 5 houses each.

23. Sew one $2\frac{1}{2}$" × $48\frac{1}{2}$" (6.5 × 123 cm) background strip to the top of each house row.

24. Join the 2 house rows and add the third $2\frac{1}{2}$" × $48\frac{1}{2}$" (6.5 × 123 cm) background strip to the bottom of the joined house rows.

25. Sew 1 background $2\frac{1}{2}$" × $22\frac{1}{2}$" (6.5 × 57 cm) strip to the left side and 1 strip to the right of the joined house rows.

The completed neighborhood section should measure about $52\frac{1}{2}$" × $22\frac{1}{2}$" (133.5 × 57 cm).

26. Repeat Steps 20–25 to create 5 more neighborhoods, each with a different background color.

MAKE THE FENCES

27. With right sides together, sew 13 green and 13 cream fence rectangles together along the $8\frac{1}{2}$" (21.5 cm) edge, alternating colors to make the top fence border (**Figure 14**).

    Repeat to make the bottom fence border.

    Each border should each measure about $52\frac{1}{2}$" × $8\frac{1}{2}$" (133.5 × 21.5 cm).

28. With right sides together, sew 24 green and 24 cream rectangles together along the $8\frac{1}{2}$" (21.5 cm) edge, alternating colors. Add one green $8\frac{1}{2}$" × $8\frac{1}{2}$" (21.5 cm × 21.5 cm) square to the last cream rectangle, completing one side fence border.

    Repeat to make the second side fence border.

    Each side border should measure about $8\frac{1}{2}$" × $104\frac{1}{2}$" (21.5 × 265 cm).

ASSEMBLE THE QUILT

29. Follow the Hood Assembly Diagram on page 171 to complete the quilt top.

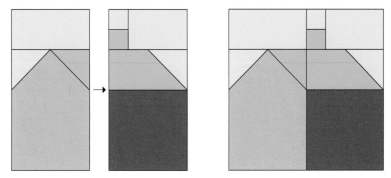

Figure 11

8½″ × 8½″ (21.5 × 21.5 cm)

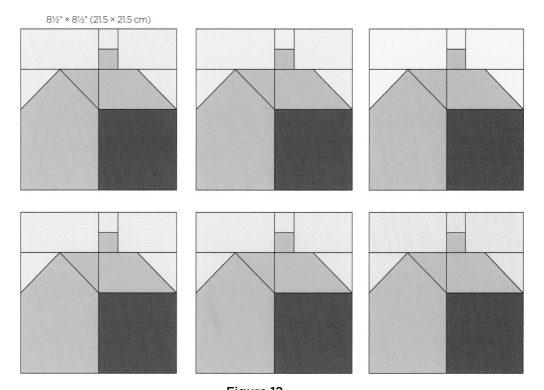

Figure 12

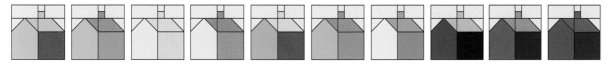

Figure 13

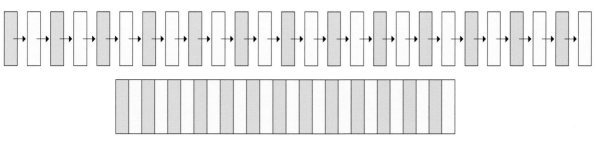

Figure 14

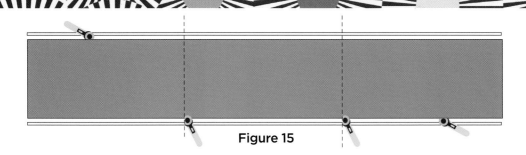

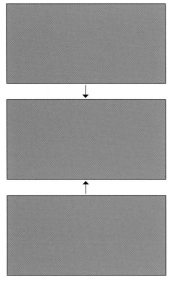

Figure 15

PIECE THE BACKING

30. To make the backing from 40"/42" (102/107 cm) backing fabric, trim the selvedges. Cut the trimmed backing yardage in thirds to create three 99" (251.5 cm) WOF pieces **(Figure 15)**.

31. Place 2 of the 3 backing pieces right sides together and sew along the 99" (251.5 cm) edge. Join the third backing piece **(Figure 16)**.

    Backing should measure about 99" × 123" (251.5 × 312 cm).

FINISH THE QUILT

32. Follow the instructions for preparing the quilt top for quilting on page 10.

33. Follow the quilting instructions on page 172.

34. To complete the quilt, follow the bias binding instructions on page 183.

Figure 16

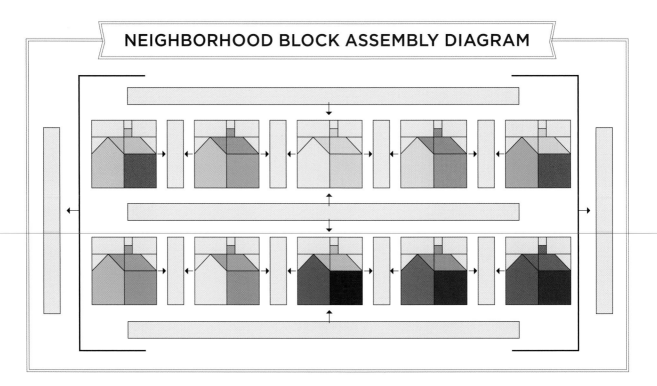

NEIGHBORHOOD BLOCK ASSEMBLY DIAGRAM

NEIGHBORHOOD ASSEMBLY DIAGRAM

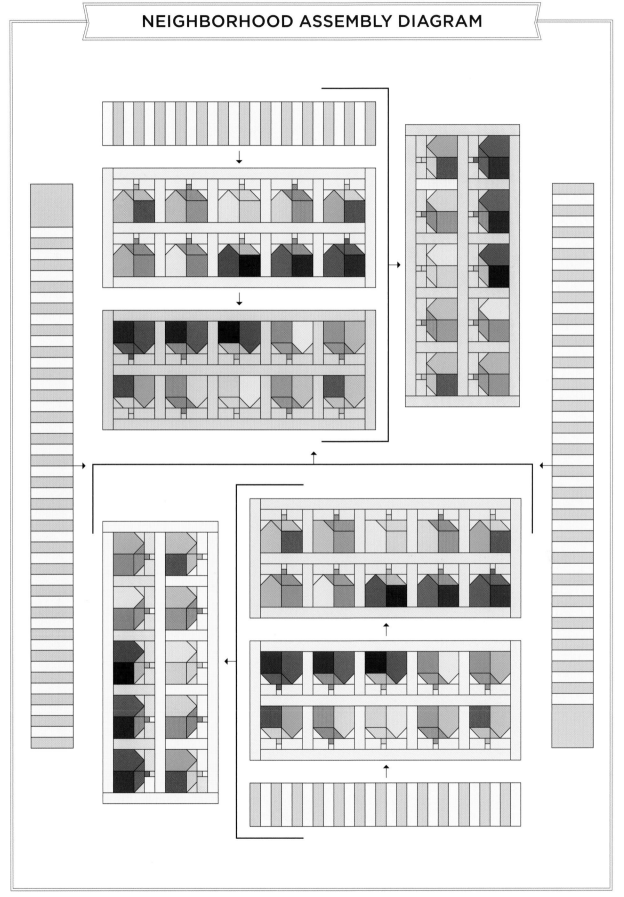

QUILTING
IN THE DETAILS

Using the quilting to add details is such a fun way to go about finishing your quilt. It can show your inspiration behind the quilt pattern, or you can use it to customize your quilt, making it uniquely, whimsically yours. From the houses to the differently colored backgrounds, the Hood quilt provides so many opportunities for fun details such as windows, curtains, pathways, gardens, and more.

DECORATIVE DOORS

Piecing the front of the house with a single piece of fabric means that you can customize your houses with different doors. Try a decorative door that combines straight lines and curves.

1. Starting from the bottom left corner of the front of the house, travel along the bottom seam ¼" (6 mm) from the left side and echo the inside

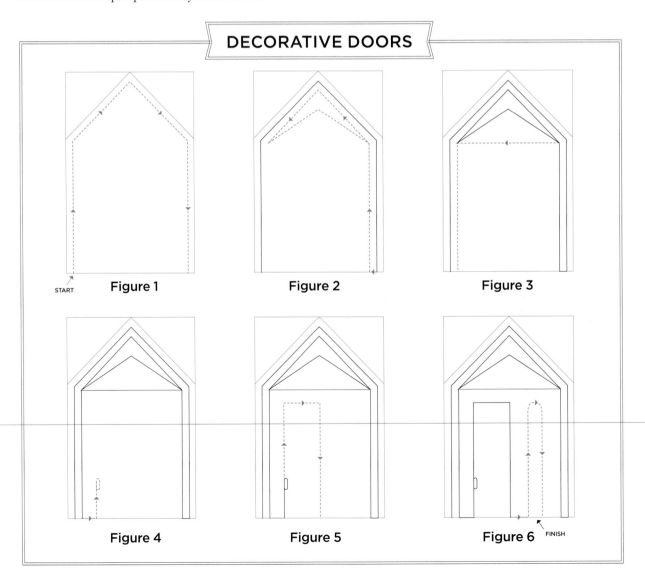

DECORATIVE DOORS

START   Figure 1   Figure 2   Figure 3

Figure 4   Figure 5   Figure 6   FINISH

of the block, ending ¼" (6 mm) away from the bottom right corner **(Figure 1)**.

2. Travel left along the bottom seam ¼" (6 mm), stitch upward and echo the side and roof quilting, stopping ¼" (6 mm) away from the top left corner on the side of the house **(Figure 2)**.

   Moving to the right, stitch a diagonal line up toward the top point, stopping ½" (1.3 cm) away from the quilted peak of the roof. Continue down and to the right, stopping at the upper right corner of the quilted line on the side of the house.

3. Stitch a line directly to the left, stopping at the upper left corner of the quilted line on the left side of the house **(Figure 3)**.

   Continue quilting straight down toward the bottom of the block, stopping at the seam ¼" (6 mm) to the right of the quilted echo lines.

4. Travel right along the bottom edge of the block 1" (2.5 cm), then stitch a straight line up toward the top, looping in an oval shape at the halfway point **(Figure 4)**. Every door has to have a doorknob, right?

5. Continue quilting up toward the top of the block, stopping ½" (1.3 cm) away from the quilted roof line. Echo that line 3" (7.5 cm), then stitch back toward the bottom of the block to complete

Use quilting instead of piecing to add architectural details.

the door. End at the bottom seam of the block **(Figure 5)**.

6. To add a little window to the side of the door, travel ¼" (6 mm) along the bottom seam, then quilt a line that goes up toward the top of the block, curving around and back down to the bottom seam **(Figure 6)**.

A SIMPLE ALTERNATIVE

If all of the door details in the block don't appeal to you, opt for a minimalist design. Try simply echoing the sides of the block. These lines will enhance the shape of the block while still providing interest **(Figure 7)**.

BRICK WALLS

I envisioned houses built with gorgeous brick walls. When quilting bricks on your house, don't worry about making them perfect—you're going for the overall effect. Use this design to cover entire walls or just to add details here and there—like the houses in your own neighborhood.

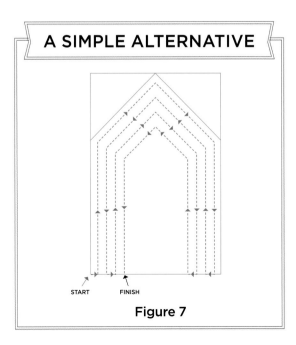

A SIMPLE ALTERNATIVE

START   FINISH

Figure 7

BRICK WALLS

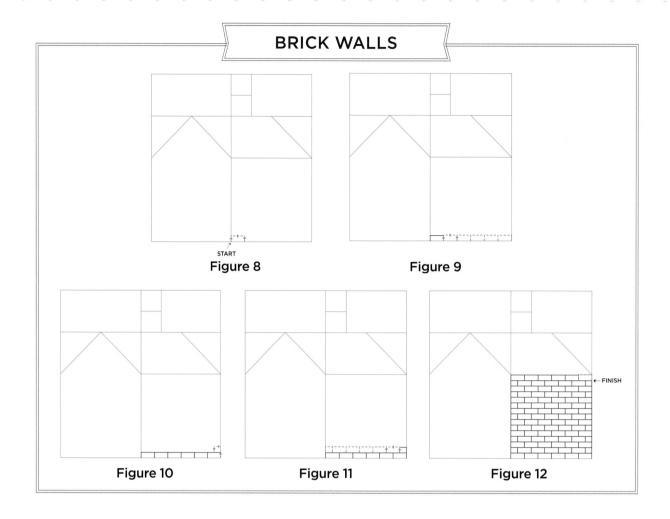

Figure 8

Figure 9

Figure 10

Figure 11

Figure 12

Quilted bricks can single out one house in a neighborhood.

1. Starting from the bottom left corner of a side of a house, travel up along the seam ¼" (6 mm). Stitch a line 1" (2.5 cm) long parallel to the bottom of the block, stitch a line to the bottom of the block, and then travel right back up the left line. This forms one brick **(Figure 8)**.

2. Continue stitching the line parallel to the bottom of the block, pivoting every 1" (2.5) to stitch a vertical line down to the seam and back up to create additional bricks **(Figure 9)**.

3. Travel up the right side of the house ¼" (6 mm), and stitch a line parallel to the straight line quilted in Step 1. Stop in the middle of the first lower brick and quilt a line that goes down and right back up, touching at the midpoint **(Figure 10)**.

4. Continue stitching toward the left side of the house, quilting lines that touch the bricks below. Stop at the left edge of the block **(Figure 11)**.

If the lines don't quite touch the row below or aren't perfectly even, don't worry! It will still look great.

ANGLED BRICKS

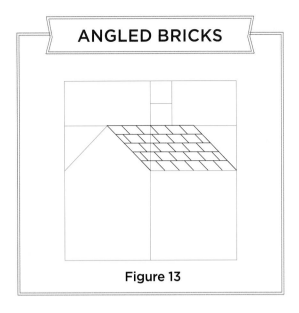

Figure 13

5. Repeat Steps 1–4 until the block is finished. Quilt the last row of bricks by traveling along the top edge of the block **(Figure 12)**.

QUILTED ROOFS

When it came to quilting the roofs of the houses, I felt a little whimsy was in order. Instead of plain shingles or straight lines, I opted for angled or scalloped shingles. They're fast and easy to quilt and very cute.

ANGLED BRICKS

Quilting bricks works for shingles on a roof as well as bricks on a wall **(Figure 13)**. Instead of quilting the lines vertically, quilt them at an angle, following the steps above.

SCALLOPED SHINGLES

1. Starting from the top left corner of the roof, stitch a line of upside-down arcs ½" (1.3 cm) wide until you reach the right side of the roof **(Figure 14)**. Don't worry if you have to make the last arc smaller or bigger to fill the space.

2. Travel down along the right seam of the roof ¼" (6 mm), then quilt half of an upside-down arc that lands at the midway point of the arc above it.

SCALLOPED SHINGLES

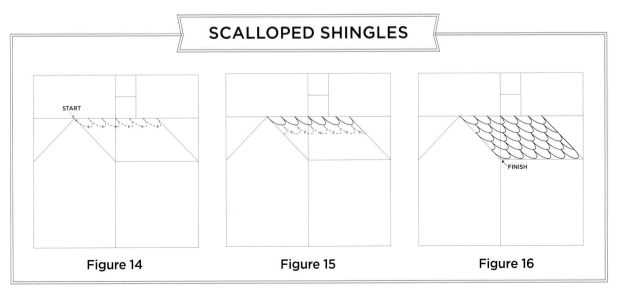

Figure 14   Figure 15   Figure 16

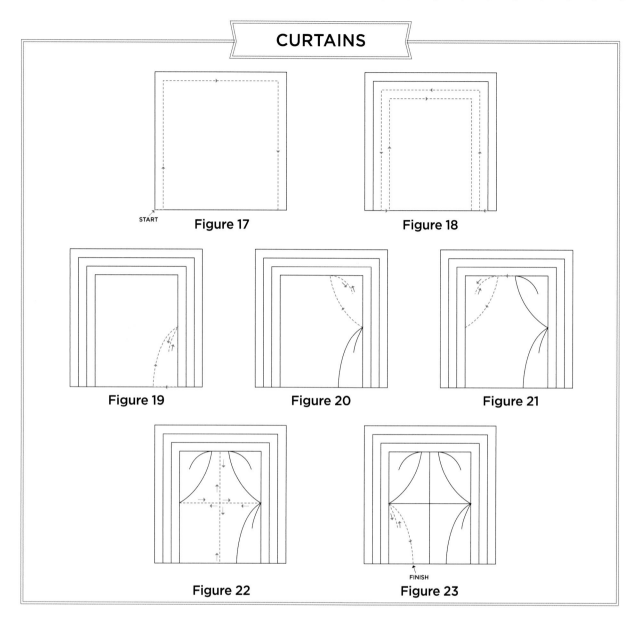

START
Figure 17

Figure 18

Figure 19

Figure 20

Figure 21

Figure 22

FINISH
Figure 23

Continue quilting arcs that touch the midpoint of the previous shingles, working your way back to the left side of the roof. End with a half arc (**Figure 15**, page 175).

3. Repeat Steps 1 and 2 to fill in the roof with scallops (**Figure 16**, page 175).

CURTAINS

What would a window be without a curtain? Give your houses a homey feeling with large windows and curtains pulled back to allow a peek inside.

1. Starting from the bottom left corner of a house block, quilt a line along the bottom seam ¼" (6 mm). Quilt a straight line that echoes the left side, the top, and the right side, ending on the bottom seam ¼" (6 mm) away from the bottom right corner (**Figure 17**).

2. Quilt along the bottom seam ¼" (6 mm), then repeat Step 1 twice, echoing the quilted line and traveling along the bottom seam. End on the right side of the block (**Figure 18**).

3. Travel along the bottom seam 1" (2.5 cm), then quilt a line that curves to the midpoint of the last echo quilted line on the right. Quilt a line that curves down between the two quilted lines ½" (1.3 cm), then travel back to the midpoint (**Figure 19**).

4. Quilt a curved line up to the top echo lines, ending 1" (2.5 cm) away from the top right corner. Quilt a line that curves down and back, returning to the top echo line (**Figure 20**).

5. Travel along the top echo line 1" (2.5 cm) and quilt a line that curves down 1" (2.5 cm) and back. Continue quilting a curved line to the middle of the left echo line **(Figure 21)**.

6. Before finishing the last curtain, quilt the window frame. Quilt a horizontal line across to the midpoint of the left echo line. Travel back along the line until you are in the middle of the window. Quilt a line directly to the top echo line and back, quilt another line directly down to the bottom of the block, and then travel back up to the midpoint. Quilt left along the line until you get to the middle of the left echo line **(Figure 22)**.

7. Quilt a line that curves down about an and back to the midpoint and then quilt a line that curves down

1" (2.5 cm) to the right of the bottom left corner **(Figure 23)**.

BUILDING THE NEIGHBORHOOD

Adding details inside the houses is only half the fun. The background of the quilt is a perfect place to add even gates and pathways.

In between some of the houses, I quilted gates. It not only added a fun detail, but also helped separate the quilting above and below the houses. The easiest option is a straightforward gate made of straight lines.

PLAIN GATE

1. Starting at the bottom right corner of the first house, quilt a line up along the seam 3" (7.5 cm),

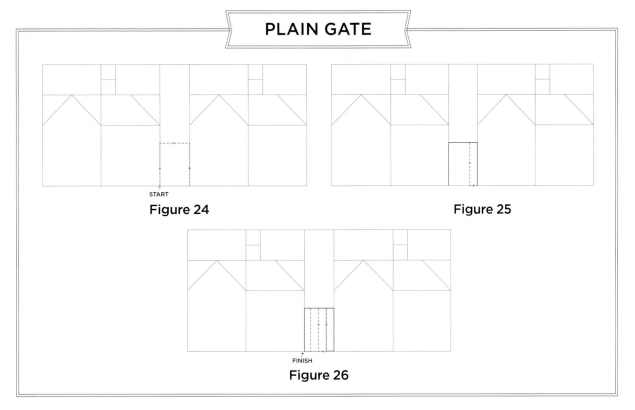

PLAIN GATE

START

Figure 24

Figure 25

FINISH

Figure 26

A gate connects the house and separates the sky quilting from the yard quilting.

2. Starting at the bottom left corner of the second house, stitch a ½" (1.3 cm) line toward the house on the left. Stitch a vertical line up to the first quilting line (**Figure 25**, page 177).

3. Continue stitching vertical straight lines that mimic a gate, filling in the space between the two houses. End at the bottom right-hand corner of the second house (**Figure 26**, page 177).

CURVED GATE

1. Starting at the bottom right-hand corner of the house on the left, travel up along the edge to the upper right-hand corner. Quilt a line that curves up, then down to the upper left-hand corner of the house on the right. Travel along the seam to the bottom left-hand corner of the right house (**Figure 27**).

2. Quilt a ½" (1.3 cm) horizontal line back to the first house on the left. Echo the curved top and straight sides quilted in Step 1, ending ½" (1.3 cm) away from the bottom right-hand corner of the first house (**Figure 28**).

3. Travel and echo stitch the shape one more time (**Figure 29**).

then stitch a horizontal line across to the second house to the left, stopping at the seam. Travel along the seam until you reach the bottom left side of the second house (**Figure 24**, page 177).

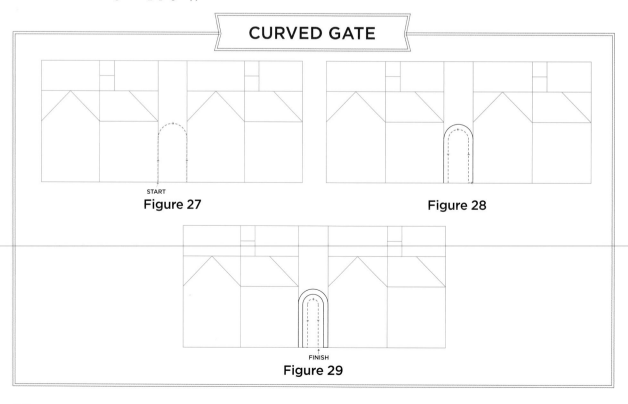

CURVED GATE

START
Figure 27

Figure 28

FINISH
Figure 29

PAVED PATHWAYS

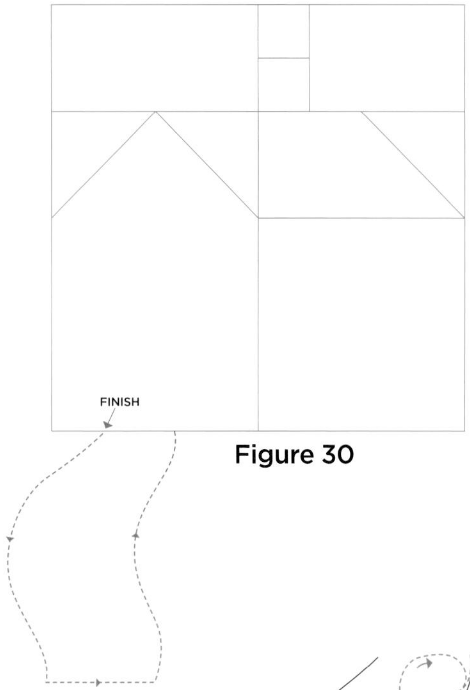

Figure 30

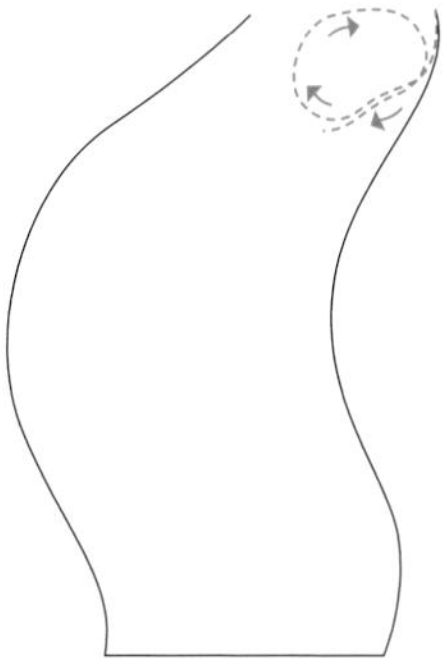

FINISH

Figure 31

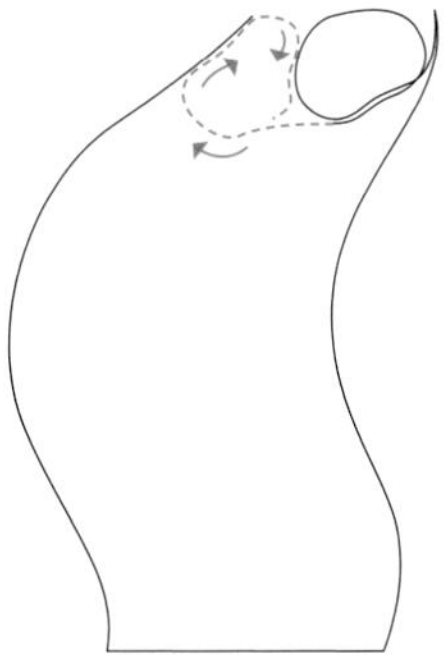

Figure 32

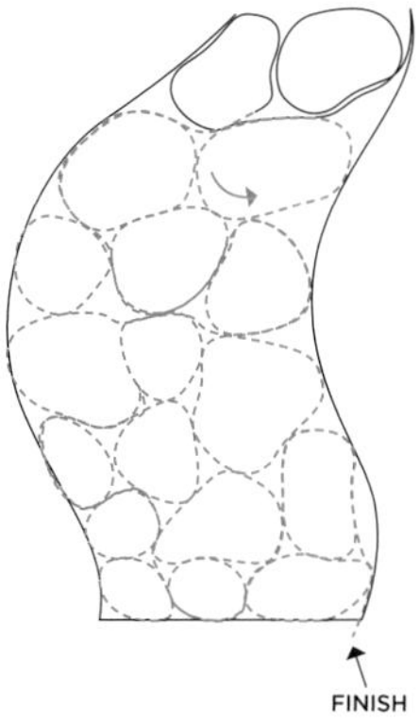

Figure 33

FINISH

PAVED PATHWAYS

What is more quaint than a cobblestone path that leads up to a charming house? This design is fun and fast, and the less perfect it is, the better it looks.

1. Starting from the lower left corner of a quilted door (or 3" [7.5 cm] away from the edge of the block), quilt a gently curving line until it runs into another house block. Travel along the edge of the block 2" (5 cm) and echo the line back to the house **(Figure 30)**.

2. Fill in the pathway with cobblestones. Stitch a wavy circle—the more organic, the better **(Figure 31)**.

3. Travel around the wavy circle until you get to the left side. Quilt another wavy circle that touches the first one **(Figure 32)**.

4. Continue quilting wavy circles, traveling around them if needed, until you fill in the pathway **(Figure 33)**.

LANDSCAPING

Imagine what a little landscape can do for your quilted houses! I quilted little trees to spruce things up.

1. Quilt a vertical line 5" (12.5 cm) (or as large as you'd like the tree to be). Travel back along the line about one-third of the way **(Figure 34**, page 180).

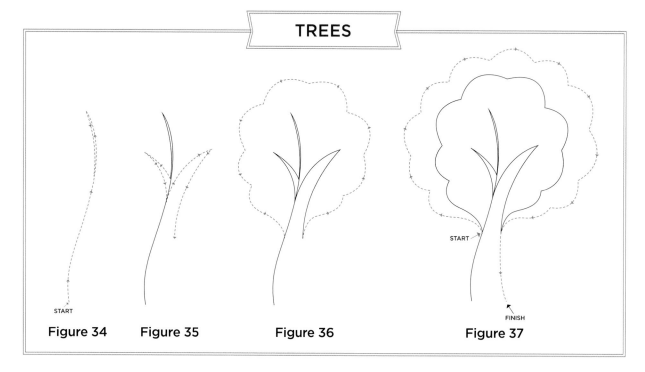

Figure 34   Figure 35   Figure 36   Figure 37

2. Quilt a line that curves out toward the left 1"–2" (2.5–5 cm) and travel back to the vertical line. Quilt a line that curves out toward the right 1"–2" (2.5–5 cm) and echo the line ending 1" (2.5 cm) to the right of the vertical line **(Figure 35)**.

3. Quilt a bumpy line that curves up and around the previously quilted lines, ending about halfway down the vertical line **(Figure 36)**. There is no wrong way to do this, so don't stress out about making it perfect.

4. Quilt another bumpy line that goes around the previously quilted line, ending on the right side

of the tree where the first bumpy line started. Quilt a line down that echoes the first vertical line **(Figure 37)**. Add more bumpy lines to make your tree even bigger.

BACK-AND-FORTH BACKGROUND

Using a basic filler design between the elements of your quilt will help provide some continuity. For this quilt, I used a back-and-forth line design.

This design is a great option if you prefer a minimal approach to quilting. It's easy to quilt, and you can stitch these lines as dense or as far apart as you'd like.

Note: Although the illustrations show the lines being quilted horizontally, they also can be quilted vertically. Use the direction that feels the most comfortable to you.

1. Starting from one side of the quilting area (between 2 blocks, other quilted lines, or even the whole quilt), quilt a line across to the next side. As you approach the edge of the quilting area, curve down and around so that the curve is close to, but not touching, the edge **(Figure 38)**.

2. Echo the line just quilted, keeping the spacing as consistent as possible. As you approach the other edge of the quilting area, loop down and begin quilting your next line **(Figure 39)**.

3. Continue quilting your lines until you fill in the area completely **(Figure 40)**.

Quilting a tree behind the houses adds depth.

BACK-AND-FORTH BACKGROUND

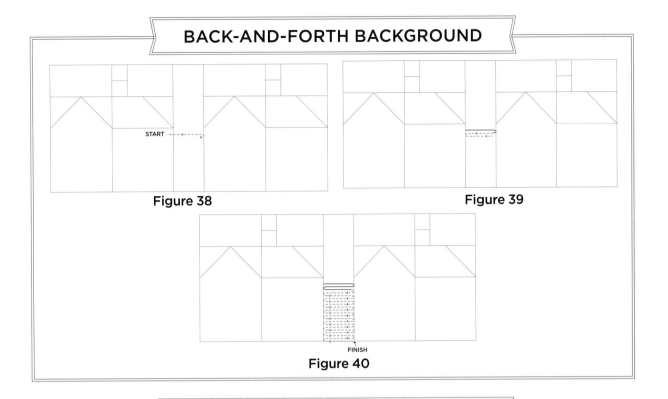

Figure 38

Figure 39

Figure 40

3 TIPS FOR ADDING DETAILS

It's pretty obvious that I love to have fun with quilting. From bricks on the front of the houses to mountains in the background, I packed into The Hood as many realistic elements as I could think of. I hope that these other details will inspire you to think of even more possibilities for your quilt.

Here are three tips to help ensure you are thrilled with the results.

1. It doesn't have to be realistic or overly detailed.

The details you add with the quilting don't have to be realistic. You aren't necessarily trying to thread-paint artistic scenes over the quilt. Adding just a hint of detail is more than enough to get your point across. For instance, instead of quilting trees behind some of the houses, I quilted a leafy meander. The overall effect is the same, but with less work!

2. You don't have to have a plan.

It may be tempting to sketch out details or plan them out beforehand. Instead, just get started. If you don't like how one particular area turns out, try something different in another area. The trick is to have fun with it!

3. Use a matching thread color.

Using many details on a quilt is fun, but it could overwhelm the pattern. To prevent that from happening, try using a thread color that blends into the quilt. It allows the details to be subtle, but impactful.

Glossary

Bias: To cut on the bias or to have bias edges on a fabric piece means that the fabric has been cut at a diagonal angle to the grain of the fabric. Usually, it is found in curved and triangle pieces. This bias edge leaves loosely woven threads at the cut edge. Therefore, it can stretch much more easily than a straight grain cut. These edges should be handled more carefully.

Contrasting Quilting Designs: Two designs that have a different shape, density, or direction. Using contrasting designs highlights important areas of your quilt.

Density: Refers to the amount of quilting in an area. Quilting designs with more density have less space between the quilting lines. Less dense designs have more space between the lines.

Dot-to-Dot Quilting: A technique that allows you to use reference points on a quilt to create intricate looking designs with little or no marking.

Echoing: Quilting a line that is the same as a previously quilted line with consistent spacing in between.

Free-Motion Quilting Foot: Also known as a hopping foot or a darning foot, this foot allows the quilt sandwich to move in any direction while the machine is quilting. It is necessary for quilting multi-directional designs such as swirls, pebbles, or feathers.

Grain: The grain of the fabric refers to the woven threads that make up the fabric. The grain runs parallel and perpendicular to the selvedge of the fabric. The most stable cuts are those cut on the grain. These cuts will have a limited amount of stretch and are ideal for piecing.

Pressing the Seams Open: Most of the instructions in this book ask you to press the seams open instead of to one side. Open the seam allowance and press each fabric away from the seam. This will keep the seems from getting bulky and greatly reduce frustration during the quilting process. While this is not essential, it will improve accuracy and create a smoother finished quilt top.

Right and Wrong Sides of the Fabric: The right side of the fabric is the side that you want showing when the quilt top is completed. The wrong side of the fabric is the back of the fabric. This is easy to determine in most printed fabrics, but solids, wovens, and batiks can be tricky because they often look the same on both sides. I gave up trying to determine the right and wrong sides of solid fabrics years ago.

Selvedge: The finished edges of the fabric. Most people only see this as being the printed edge, usually containing the name of the fabric, designer, and manufacturer. The selvedges are actually both finished edges of the fabric. You can identify the selvedges by the difference in texture as well as the tiny pinholes that sometimes run along the edges. Stitch in the Ditch: Stitching along a seam of the quilt to stabilize the top or as a way to move onto the next quilting area. It's not as tough as it sounds and is a great skill to have because it lets you quilt more efficiently with less starts and stops.

Sub Cut: Term always follows an initial cutting instruction. To sub cut is to cut again that same piece that was cut in the previous instruction. For example, the instructions may read "cut a 2½" (6.5 cm) × WOF (width of fabric) strip; sub cut ten 2½" × 2½" (6.5 × 6.5 cm) squares." This means that from the 2½" (6.5 cm) strip, you cut across that strip in 2½" (6.5 cm) intervals to create ten 2½" × 2½" (6.5 × 6.5 cm) squares.

Traveling: Stitching along a previously quilted line to get to the next quilting area, allowing you to quilt without starting and stopping.

Walking Foot: A sewing machine foot perfect for machine quilting straight lines on a quilt. It's used with the feed dogs up.

WOF: "WOF" means "width of fabric." The width of the fabric is the distance between the two selvedges, 40" to 42" (102 to 107 cm) on a standard cotton quilting fabric.

resources

Tula's favorite materials and supplies are found exclusively at independent fabric and quilt shops both locally and online:

FABRICS

Free Spirit Fabrics
www. freespiritfabrics.com
Most of the fabrics, including the solids, found in this book are manufactured by Free Spirit Fabrics.

THREADS

Aurifil
www.aurifil.com
All of the quilts in this book were pieced using *Aurifil 50 wt Cotton* thread.

SEWING MACHINES

BERNINA
www.bernina.com

SCISSORS

Brewer
www.brewersewing.com
Brewer is the exclusive manufacturer and distributor of Tula Pink Hardware, including scissors, snippers, seam rippers, and more!

making bias binding

Binding a quilt with bias-cut strips allows the edge of the quilt to move freely without stiffness. The binding of a quilt gets the most wear, and bias binding can be stronger than straight-grain binding, perfect for a quilt that will be handled and washed frequently.

1. Trim off the selvedges of the binding fabric.

2. Fold the top left corner down to align with the bottom edge of the binding fabric. Fold the bottom right corner up to align with the top edge of the binding fabric **(Figure 1)**.

3. Rotate the folded binding fabric so that the folded edges are facing you. Line up a ruler with the folded edge and cut along the edge to create a clean, straight starting point .

4. Rotate the binding fabric so the cut edge is on your left. Line up your ruler to the 2½" (6.5 cm) cut edge of the fabric and cut **(Figure 2)**.

5. Continue cutting 2½" (6.5 cm) strips until you have enough to equal the required length for the binding.

6. Starting with the longest strips and using a ¼" (6 mm) seam allowance, sew the bias cut strips end to end to make one long binding strip. Press seams open.

7. Fold the strip in half lengthwise, wrong sides together, and press.

JOIN THE BINDING

8. Beginning with the angled end of the binding strip, align the raw edges with the edge of the finished quilt between corners.

   Using a walking foot and a ¼" (6 mm) seam allowance, stitch the binding strip to the quilt at least 6" (15 cm) down from the angled binding edge .

   Stop ¼" (6 mm) from the corner and backstitch in the seam allowance.

9. Remove the quilt from the sewing machine. Fold the binding up and away from the quilt so that it forms a 45-degree angle **(Figure 3)**.

   Fold the binding back down over itself so that the new fold is aligned with the edge of the quilt **(Figure 4)**.

10. Backstitch, then begin sewing along the next edge, starting ¼" (6 mm) from the folded corner. Miter each corner as you come to it as in Step 9.

11. Continue stitching the binding down around the quilt. Stop about 8" (20.5 cm) from where you began **(Figure 5)**.

12. Open the ending tail of the binding and pin it to the quilt with one raw edge aligned to the edge of the beginning tail. Lay it over the ending tail. Trace the 45-degree line along the cut edge of the beginning tail onto the ending tail **(Figure 6)**.

13. Draw a second line, adding ½" (1.3 cm) to the tail and cut the tail only on the second line **(Figure 7)**.

14. Place the cut edges of the binding with right sides together, offsetting the points, and sew together using a ¼" (6 mm) seam **(Figure 8)**.

   Press the seam open, refold, and line up the raw edges with the raw edge of the quilt.

15. Finish stitching the binding to the quilt. Overlap the beginning stitches by at least 1" (2.5 cm) .

16. Pin the binding to the back of the quilt and handstitch in place using a basic whipstitch .

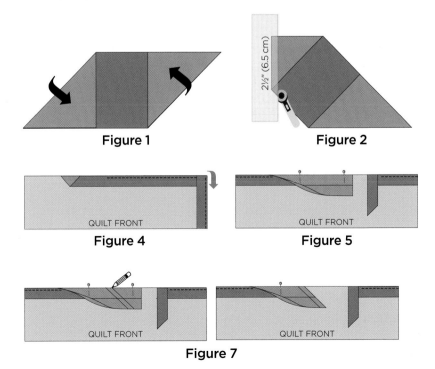

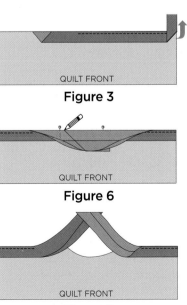

Figure 1   Figure 2   Figure 3

Figure 4   Figure 5   Figure 6

Figure 7   Figure 8

templates

To make the Eclipse E template, trace the two E shapes and join them together. When the happy face is complete, the template is aligned. Trace the complete shape onto the template plastic.

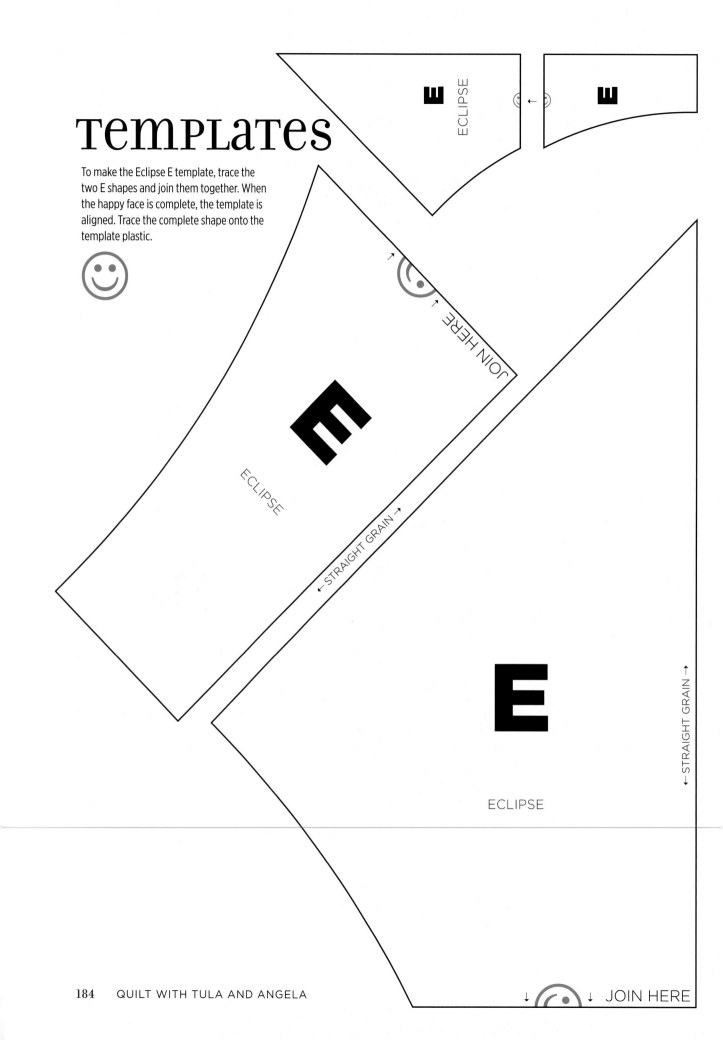

ECLIPSE

ECLIPSE

JOIN HERE

← STRAIGHT GRAIN →

ECLIPSE

ECLIPSE

← STRAIGHT GRAIN →

JOIN HERE

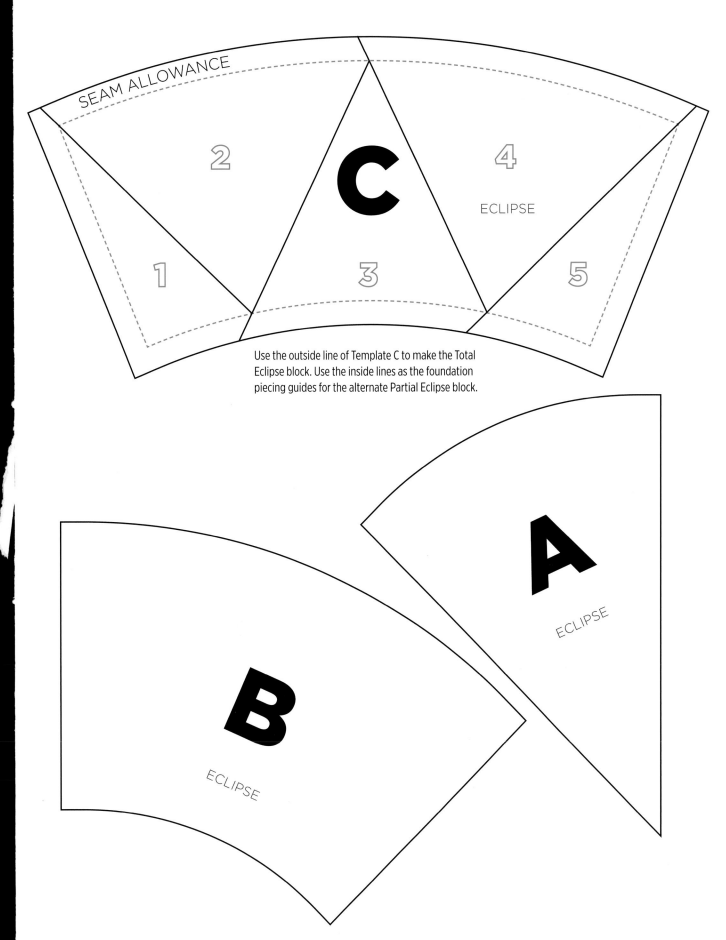

SEAM ALLOWANCE

2

C

4

ECLIPSE

1

3

5

Use the outside line of Template C to make the Total Eclipse block. Use the inside lines as the foundation piecing guides for the alternate Partial Eclipse block.

A

ECLIPSE

B

ECLIPSE

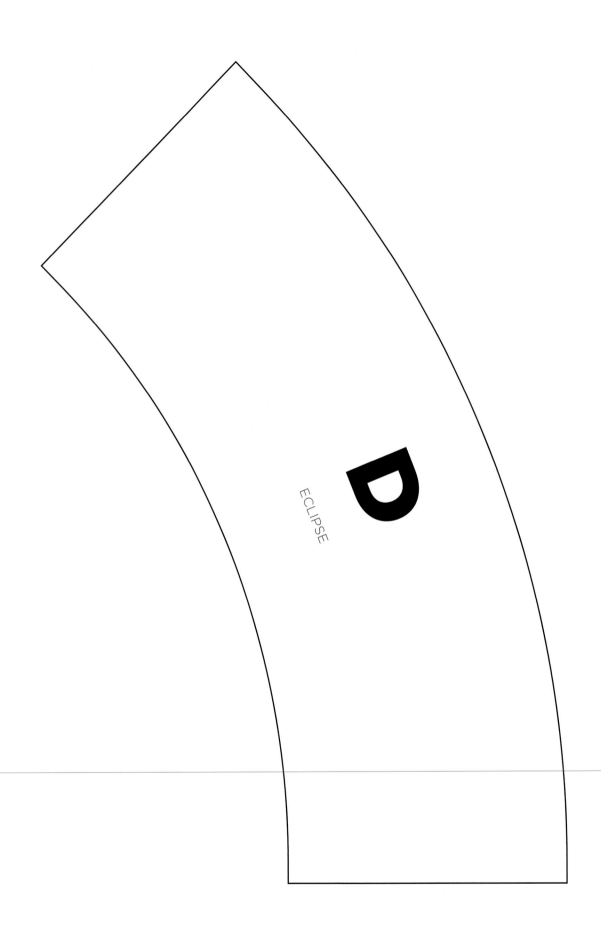

ECLIPSE

D

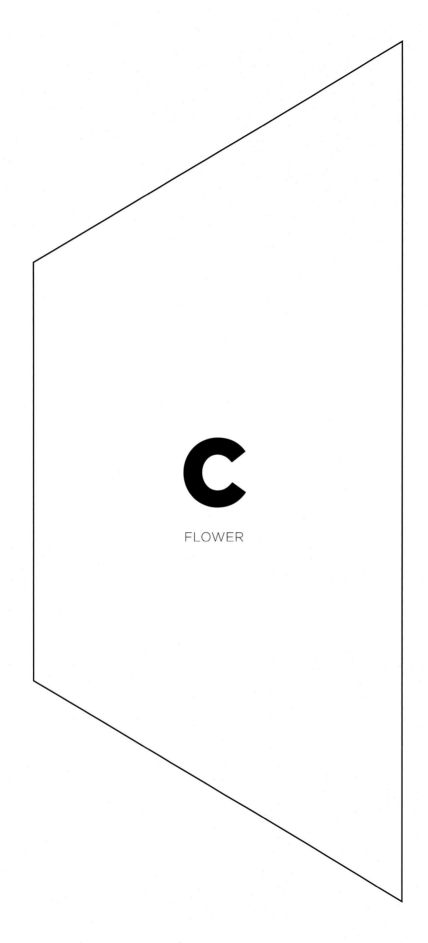

C

FLOWER

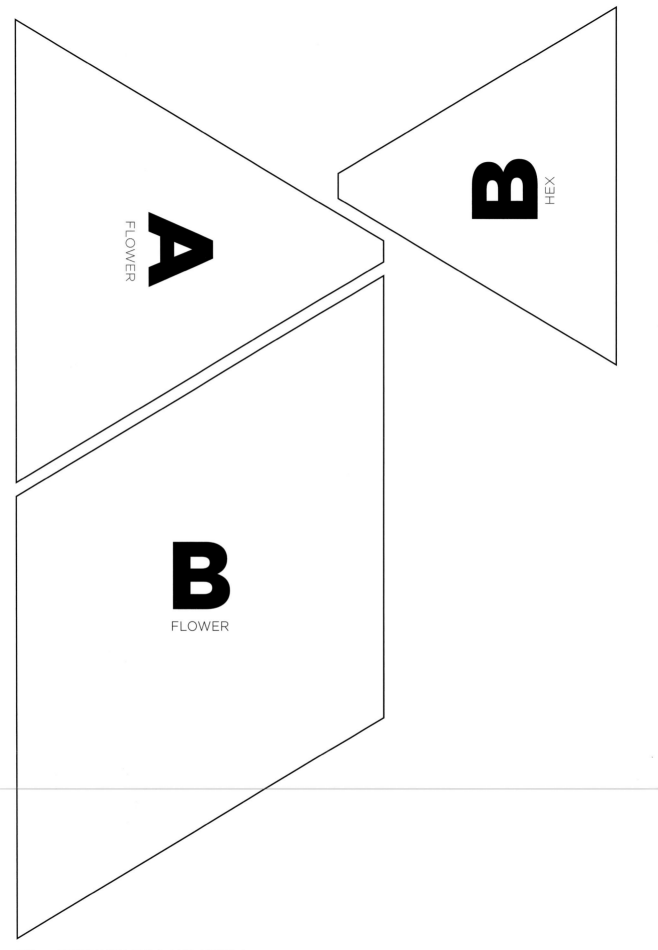

A
FLOWER

B
HEX

B
FLOWER

To make the Hex A template trace the two A shapes and join them together. When the happy face is complete, the template is aligned. Trace the complete shape onto the template plastic.

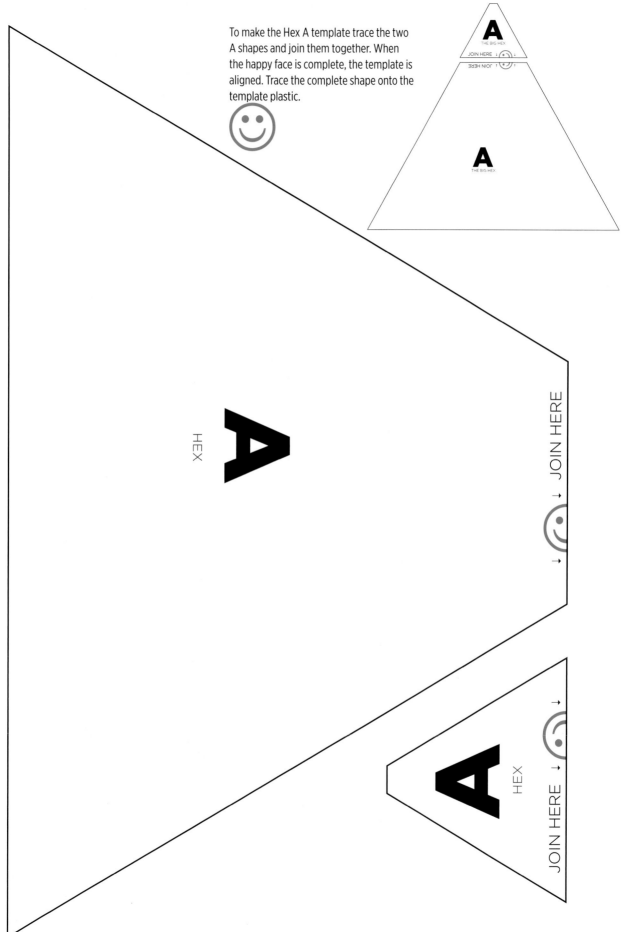

A
THE BIG HEX

JOIN HERE

JOIN HERE

A
THE BIG HEX

HEX

A

JOIN HERE

JOIN HERE

HEX

A

JOIN HERE

acknowledgments

I believe very strongly that a quilt belongs to the maker, not the designer. I dedicate this book to anyone who makes one of the quilts in these pages. A quilt pattern is just the framework of an idea, the choices that a person makes from fabric, to color to quilting is what animates the idea and makes it real. There is so much more to a quilt than cotton, and the person behind the quilt is the magic ingredient.

On a personal note, I have to dedicate at least some part of these pages to the people who keep everything from falling apart while I am lost in drawing and sewing. To Cameron, the guardian of my brand and the only person that can tell me I am wrong without making me angry; he is my brother and my right hand in this crazy world of sewing and fabric. Second, to my mom, Kat, the gatekeeper and master planner who meticulously accounts for every minute of my day, keeps things running smoothly, and can parallel park a trailer better than anyone I have ever seen.

This book would never have existed without Angela. To our enduring friendship that transcends quilting! Over many years and too many quilts to count, you continue to impress me with your skill and creativity.

It's crazy to think that a single quilt can lead to an amazing, fun career. I owe a huge debt of gratitude to everyone who has helped me on the way. Especially to my patient husband, Jeremy, who knows that "10 more quilting minutes" actually means an hour, and to my kids who have grown up listening to the hum of my quilting machine.

And, of course, huge love and thanks to Tula who has pushed me creatively from Day 1. From quilting feathers with spiderwebs to alien spaceships, I never know what we'll do next. Thanks for cheering me on along the way, for all the coffee dates, and, most importantly, for "doing life" with me.

about the authors

TULA PINK is an American textile designer and quiltmaker with a dark sense of humor buried in a sea of print and pattern. She plays with images the way a poet plays with words, turning innocuous traditional designs into mischievous little critters. Her love affair with textiles began early, and an obsession with sewing soon followed. Several years and more than 20 fabric collections later, design is her true passion. Tula began quilting in an effort to use up her ever-growing stash of fabric so she could justify buying more. Twenty years later, she has a lot of quilts and more fabric than when she started. Visit Tula online at tulapink.com.

ANGELA WALTER began her quilting career alongside her husband's grandfather. Together they made her first quilt, a nine-patch that is still on her bed today. Thousands of swirls, feathers, and parallel lines later, Angela has turned her love of stitches and fabric into a thriving business focused on modern machine quilting. Visit Angela online at quiltingismytherapy.com.

INDEX

METRIC CONVERSION CHART

To Convert	To	Multiply By
Inches	Centimeters	2.54
Centimeters	Inches	0.4
Feet	Centimeters	30.5
Centimeters	Feet	0.03
Yards	Meters	0.9
Meters	Yards	1.1

QUILT
—and color—
WITH TULA!

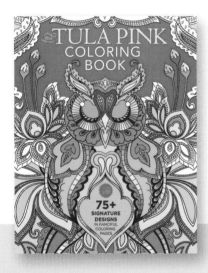

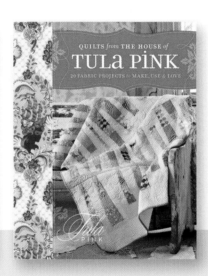

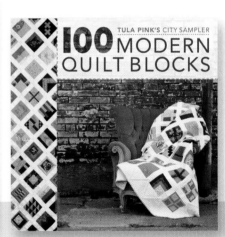

The Tula Pink Coloring Book
75+ Signature Designs in
Fanciful Coloring Pages

Tula Pink

ISBN: 9781440245428 | Price: $15.99

**Quilts from the
House of Tula Pink**
20 Fabric Projects to Make, Use and Love

Tula Pink

ISBN: 9781440218187 | Price: $24.99

Tula Pink's City Sampler
100 Modern Quilt Bocks

Tula Pink

ISBN: 9781440232145 | Price: $27.99

Available at your favorite retailer or shopfonsandporter.com.